Berlin

WHAT'S NEW | WHAT'S ON | WHAT'S BEST

www.timeout.com/berlin

Contents

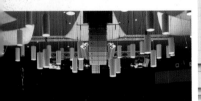

RIE EIGEN +A

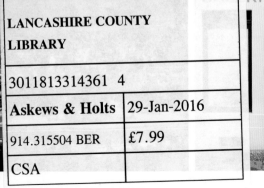

Berlin by Area

Essentials

Time Out Digital Ltd
4th Floor
125 Shaftesbury Avenue
London WC2H 8AD
Tel: + 44 (0)20 7813 3000
Email: guides@timeout.com
www.timeout.com

Published by Time Out Digital Ltd, a wholly owned subsidiary of Time Out Group Ltd.
Time Out and the Time Out logo are trademarks of Time Out Group Ltd.

© **Time Out Group Ltd 2015**
Previous editions 2007, 2010.

Chairman & Founder Tony Elliott
Chief Executive Officer Tim Arthur
Chief Financial Officer Matt White
Managing Director Europe Noel Penzer
Publisher Alex Batho

Editorial Director Sarah Guy
Group Finance Controller Margaret Wright

10 9 8 7 6 5 4 3 2 1

This edition first published in Great Britain in 2015 by Ebury Publishing
20 Vauxhall Bridge Road, London SW1V 2SA

Ebury Publishing is part of the Penguin Random House group of companies whose addresses
can be found at global.penguinrandomhouse.com

Distributed in the US and Latin America by Publishers Group West (1-510-809-3700)

For further distribution details, see www.timeout.com

ISBN: 978-1-90504-297-5

A CIP catalogue record for this book is available from the British Library.

Printed and bound in China by Leo Paper Products Ltd.

Berlin Shortlist

The **Time Out Berlin Shortlist** is one of a series of pocket-sized guides that draws on Time Out's background as a magazine publisher to keep you current with everything that's going on in town. As well as Berlin's key sights and the best of its eating, drinking and leisure options, it picks out the most exciting venues to have opened in the last year and gives a full calendar of annual events. It also includes features on the important news, trends and openings, all compiled by locally based editors and writers. Whether you're visiting for the first time in your life or the first time this year, you'll find the *Time Out Berlin Shortlist* contains all you need to know, in a portable and easy-to-use format.

The guide divides Berlin into seven main areas, each containing listings for Sights & Museums, Eating & Drinking, Shopping, Nightlife and Arts & Leisure, and maps pinpointing their locations; a further chapter rounds up the best of the rest. At the front of the book are chapters rounding up these scenes city-wide, and giving a shortlist of our overall picks. We also include itineraries for days out, plus essentials such as transport information and hotels.

Our listings give phone numbers as dialled within Germany. From abroad, use your country's exit code followed by 49 (the country code for Germany) and the number given.

We have noted price categories by using one to four euro signs (€-€€€€), representing budget, moderate, expensive and luxury. Major credit cards are accepted unless otherwise stated.

All our listings are double-checked, but places do sometimes close or change their hours or prices, so it's a good idea to call a venue before visiting. While every effort has been made to ensure accuracy, the publishers cannot accept responsibility for any errors that this guide may contain.

Venues are marked on the maps using symbols numbered according to their order within the chapter and colour-coded as follows:

1 Sights & Museums
1 Eating & Drinking
1 Shopping
1 Nightlife
1 Arts & Leisure

Time Out **Berlin** Shortlist

EDITORIAL
Consultant Editor Arsalan Mohammad
Copy Editors Edoardo Albert,
  Keith Davidson, Cath Phillips
Proofreader Marion Moisy

DESIGN & PICTURE DESK
Art Editor Christie Webster
Group Commercial Senior Designer
  Jason Tansley
Picture Editor Jael Marschner
Deputy Picture Editor Ben Rowe
Picture Researcher Lizzy Owen

ADVERTISING
Managing Director St John Betteridge

MARKETING
Senior Publishing Brand Manager
  Luthfa Begum
Head of Circulation Dan Collins

PRODUCTION
Production Controller
  Katie Mulhern-Bhudia

CONTRIBUTORS
This guide was written and researched by the writers of *Time Out Berlin*, with additional
material by Arsalan Mohammad.

PHOTOGRAPHY
pages 2 (top left), 12 Giovanni Dominice; 2 (top right), 3 (bottom left), 36, 82, 90, 103,
107, 108, 134, 136, 155 Elan Fleisher; 2 (bottom left), 24 Monika Rittershaus; 2 (bottom
right), 43 Uwe Walter; 5 Ppictures/Shutterstock.com; 7 Eddy Galeotti/Shutterstock.com;
19 Linus Lintner Fotografie; 20, 122 Camille Blake; 21, 22, 38, 85, 100, 106, 111, 114
Britta Jaschinski; 26, 146 360b/Shutterstock.com; 27 WorldWide/Shutterstock.com; 28
Lienhard Schulz/Wikimedia Commons; 29 De Visu/Shutterstock.com; 30 Bocman1973/
Shutterstock.com; 31 martinkay/Shutterstock.com; 33, 47 mkrberlin/Shutterstock.com;
39 Jean-Pierre Dalbéra/Wikimedia Commons; 40 Theo Cook; 41 Anders Sune Berg; 42
Courtesy Katharina Grosse and KÖNIG GALERIE/© VG Bild-Kunst, Bonn/Roman März;
44/45, 46, 78, 95, 120, 128/129, 152 Jael Marschner; 48 Morenovel/Shutterstock.com;
53 Claudio Divizia/Shutterstock.com; 55 © Staatliche Museen zu Berlin/Achim Kleuker;
58 (top) ken schluchtmann/dirk daehmlow; 58 (bottom) © Galeries Lafayette (Deutschland)
GmbH; 64 (top) Steve Herud; 64 (bottom) Ailine Liefeld; 70 Uwe Walter/Berlin Biennale für
zeitgenössische Kunst; 71 Timo Ohler; 73 Till Bortels for OONA; 76 Frank-Michael Arndt;
86 iiolab/Shutterstock.com; 96 Ana del Castillo/Shutterstock.com; 104 Kerstin Ehmer,
Katja Hiendlmayer; 123 carol.anne/Shutterstock.com; 138/139 Clovis Bouhier; 140
-jkb-/Wikimedia Commons; 148 (top) Mangan2002/Wikimedia Commons; 148 (bottom)
BenBuschfeld/Wikimedia Commons; 149 Frank Hensel; 156 © Wolfgang Scholvien/
visitBerlin; 161, 170 James Pfaff

The following images were supplied by the featured establishments: 3 (top left, top right
and bottom right), 13, 15, 16, 18, 35, 63, 81, 92, 93, 118, 126, 145, 162, 166, 167, 172,
173, 174/175, 176

Cover photograph: Matthias Haker Photography/Getty Images/Flickr RF

MAPS JS Graphics (john@jsgraphics.co.uk).

About **Time Out**

Founded in 1968, Time Out has expanded from humble London beginnings into the leading
resource for those wanting to know what's happening in the world's greatest cities. As well
as our influential what's-on weeklies in London and New York, we publish nearly 30 other
listings magazines in cities as varied as Beijing and Tel Aviv. The magazines established
Time Out's trademark style: sharp writing, informed reviewing and bang up-to-date inside
knowledge of every scene.

Time Out made the natural leap into travel guides in the 1980s with the City Guide
series, which now extends to over 50 destinations around the world. Written and
researched by expert local writers and generously illustrated with original photography,
the full-size guides cover a larger area than our Shortlist guides and include many
more venue reviews, along with additional background features and a full set of maps.

Throughout this rapid growth, the company has remained proudly independent. This
independence extends to the editorial content of all our publications, this Shortlist
included. No establishment has been featured because it has advertised, and no
payment has influenced any of our reviews.

Don't Miss

Altes Museum

WHAT'S BEST
Sights & Museums

In 2015, Berlin celebrated the 25th anniversary of German reunification while the complicated process of uniting the city into a smoothly functioning, cohesive-21st century capital continued. (Don't mention the scandalously delayed new airport, unless you want to get some very dirty looks.) Berlin has been undergoing an infrastructural overhaul of massive proportions at every level, from public transport to the consolidation of its major public art collections. Old landmarks have been renovated, a whole bunch of new ones commissioned and constructed, while others have been wiped out altogether, including most of what was once the most notorious of them all – the Berlin Wall.

The **Brandenburger Tor** (p52) is Berlin's key landmark, though it literally faces Brutalist competition from the **Fernsehturm** (p61), the television tower on Alexanderplatz. To the north and south of the Brandenburger Tor, various monuments catch the eye: the postmodern towers of Potsdamer Platz; the undulating field of tilting concrete blocks that is the **Denkmal für die ermordeten Jüden Europas** (Memorial to the Murdered Jews of Europe, p52); the Bundeskanzleramt (Federal Chancellery) and the government quarter. There's also Norman Foster's revamped **Reichstag** (p97), complete with a glass cupola, open to visitors. A walk to the top is a must.

These new landmarks mainly lie along the line of the former Wall and, in one way or another, are intended to heal and bind the city back together. On what is now the border of Mitte and Tiergarten (the city's central park stretches away on the western side), the iconic Brandenburger Tor, once the ceremonial entrance to Berlin, stands at the top of Unter den Linden, the grand avenue leading east. It's full of mighty, neoclassical paeans to the imperial era. Some are genuine; others are like the imminent Humboldtforum which, as part of the Berlin City Palace (Stadtschloss, due for completion in 2019), replicates the grand, Baroque architectural styles of pre-Weimar Berlin. Local opinion is divided about the City Palace, with some warning of a whitewashing of recent history by developers. The demolition of the nearby iconic East German parliament, the Palast der Republik, in 2009 was mourned by many who felt the imposing, bronze-clad imperialist structure should remain in its prominent place.

Nearby is **Museumsinsel** (p48), an island in the River Spree, designated a World Heritage Site by UNESCO in 1999 and comprising five world-class institutions, each of which offers a stunning repository of cultural artefacts and heritage from around the world: the **Altes Museum** (p49), **Neues Museum** (p54), **Alte Nationalgalerie** (p48), **Bode-Museum** (p49) and **Pergamonmuseum** (p56).

While Museumsinsel is the biggest agglomeration of traditional landmarks – apart from its big five, it is also home to the **Berliner Dom** (p49), while the **Staatsoper** (p59) and the reunified **Deutsches Historisches Museum** (p53) are nearby on Unter den Linden – there are further cathedrals and concert halls to the south, around the Gendarmenmarkt area.

Elsewhere in the city, other post-Wall additions to the landscape include the **Jüdisches Museum** (p132) in Kreuzberg, housed in a remarkable building by Daniel

SHORTLIST

City icons
- Berliner Dom (p49)
- Brandenburger Tor (p52)
- Fernsehturm (p61)
- Olympiastadion (p115)
- Reichstag (p97)
- Siegessäule (p97)
- Tiergarten (p96)

World War II
- Denkmal für die ermordeten Juden Europas (p52)
- Kaiser-Wilhelm-Gedächtnis-Kirche (p108)
- Sowjetisches Ehrenmal (p138)
- Topographie des Terrors (p134)

Cold War
- Checkpoint Charlie (p132)
- DDR Museum (p60)
- East Side Gallery (p87)
- Gedenkstätte Berlin-Hohenschönhausen (p94)
- Gedenkstätte Berliner Mauer (p150)
- Stasi Museum (p94)

City classics
- Altes Museum (p49)
- Bode-Museum (p49)
- Deutsches Historisches Museum (p53)
- Neues Museum (p54)
- Philharmonie (p106)
- Schloss Charlottenburg (p116)

Art museums
- Alte Nationalgalerie (p48)
- Brücke Museum (p155)
- Gemäldegalerie (p102)
- Hamburger Bahnhof (p61)
- Martin-Gropius-Bau (p132)
- Museum für Fotografie (p110)
- Sammlung Boros (p71)

DON'T MISS

Libeskind; a whole slew of embassies, mostly clustered south of the Tiergarten; the renovated **Olympiastadion** (p115) in the west of Charlottenburg; and the huge steel and glass edifice of the Berlin Hauptbahnhof, Europe's biggest railway station.

Neighbourhoods

This guide is organised according to area. Mitte is the city's historic centre. In the days of division it lay on the eastern side, but today it is once again the centre in every respect – historically, culturally, politically and commercially. Its southern reaches are full of sights and grand avenues, major hotels and new department stores. Things get more bohemian at its northern end, particularly around the Scheunenviertel, Berlin's historic Jewish quarter.

Kastanienallee leads north into Prenzlauer Berg, east Berlin's most picturesque residential neighbourhood and Mitte's fashionable adjunct in terms of nightlife and gastronomy; it's popular with affluent young families. The streets around Kollwitzplatz are inviting, and there's lots of activity in the 'LSD' neighbourhood – Lychener Strasse, Stargarder Strasse and Dunckerstrasse – while east Berlin's gay district focuses on the northern reaches of Schönhauser Allee.

Moving clockwise, we next come to Friedrichshain, the most 'Eastern' in feel of the inner-city districts. Its spine is the broad, DDR-era Karl-Marx-Allee, while the lively area around Simon-Dach-Strasse, once the neighbourhood of choice for bohos and young radicals, is today increasingly populated by students and young tourists.

South over the river, we cross the former border into the west and come to Kreuzberg, once the city's main alternative-lifestyle nexus and

the capital of Turkish Berlin. Today, the grimy eastern area around Schlesisches Tor is smartening up, while to the west, Bergmannstrasse remains the district's focus. The northern part of the borough, bordering Mitte, contains some important museums, such as the **Deutsches Technikmuseum** (p131) as well as Friedrichstrasse's Cold War landmark, **Checkpoint Charlie** (p132).

West of Kreuzberg lies Schöneberg, a residential district centred around Winterfeldtplatz, with its popular twice-weekly market, and the historic gay district that stretches along and around Motzstrasse and Fuggerstrasse. Wittenbergplatz, at Schöneberg's north-western corner, is the location of **KaDeWe** (p118), continental Europe's biggest department store, and marks the beginning of Berlin's West End.

North of Schöneberg, Tiergarten is centred around the huge wooded park of the same name. The district contains the diplomatic quarter, as well as the entertainment and commercial district of Potsdamer Platz, and the neighbouring Kulturforum zone, home to institutions such as the temporarily shut **Neue Nationalgalerie** (p102) and the **Philharmonie** (p106).

Finally, there is the well-heeled district of Charlottenburg, Berlin's West End, whose main arteries are the Kurfürstendamm, a typical high-end shopping drag, and the parallel Kantstrasse. Most of the area's main sights, such as the **Museum für Fotografie** (p110) and **Kaiser-Wilhelm-Gedächtnis-Kirche** (p108), damaged by war, are in the borough's eastern end.

Getting over the Wall

'Is there anything left of the Wall?' That's the first question asked by many visitors. The answer is, 'Not very much.' A short section has been preserved on the border between Mitte and Wedding at the **Gedenkstätte Berliner Mauer** (p150). It's kept in pristine condition – any graffiti is removed straight away – but is the only place where you can see what the various layers of defence looked like. A section of the inner Wall, the side that faced East Berlin, stands on the Friedrichshain bank of the Spree along Mühlenstrasse. Now known as the **East Side Gallery** (p87), it was covered with paintings by international artists in the 1990s and is currently fighting off demolition by degrees thanks to the efforts of property developers. And on Niederkirchnerstrasse, along the border between Kreuzberg and Mitte, there's a stretch preserved with graffiti and pockmarks inflicted by the hammers and chisels of souvenir-chipping 'Wall tourists' in the winter of 1989-90.

The area directly south of Niederkirchnerstrasse features the chilling **Topographie des Terrors** (p134), once the site of the subterranean Gestapo headquarters. Only a few Nazi structures are left standing, but the tragedy of the Holocaust is memorialised across the city in a variety of ways (p36 **The Memory Trail**). The site of Hitler's bunker is now concealed under a mundane car park, while the Olympiastadion is the biggest single example of Nazi-era architecture still extant.

Making the most of it

If you're planning to visit a lot of museums, then you may want to invest in a discount card. Most of the major museums and galleries are administered by the Staatliche Museen zu Berlin (SMPK), including the Altes Museum,

the Pergamonmuseum, the **Gemäldegalerie** (p102) and the **Ethnologisches Museum** (p153). SMPK offers a three-day card (€24; €12 reductions), available from any of its museums. It doesn't cover temporary exhibitions, however. Most museums are closed on Mondays but open until 10pm on Thursdays, when they are free after 6pm. For more information, see www.smb.spk-berlin.de.

Another deal is the WelcomeCard, which combines free travel on public transport with discounted tours, boat trips and entry to museums, theatres and other attractions in both Berlin and Potsdam. They are available from **tourist information** (p187), S-Bahn offices and many hotels. For central fare zones A and B it costs €19.50 for 48 hours, €26.70 for 72 hours (€40.50 including 72 hours Museumsinsel access) and €34.50 for five days; for a card including travel to and within Potsdam, it's €21.50 for 48 hours, €28.70 for 72 hours and €39.50 for five days. For more information, visit www.visitberlin.de/welcomecard.

Berliner Dom p9

Bite Club

WHAT'S BEST
Eating & Drinking

Dining out in Berlin has undergone a sea change in the past few years, taking the city from an austere cabbage-and-pork swamp to something approaching a thriving gastronomic landscape with everything from *bibimbap* to *udon* now on the menu. This is down to various factors, from the influx of young incomers to the ambition of the city's chefs, diners and entrepreneurs. New highs in diversity and quality are driving standards up; formerly drab districts such as Mitte and Kreuzberg are emerging as foodie havens, while Neukölln's vast hipster population is fuelling an underground experience of pop-ups and street food. The only aspect of eating out that has remained wonderfully and reassuringly the same is Berlin's legendarily brusque service.

Restaurants often have bars, which you're usually welcome to use even if you have no intention of eating, and bars, in their turn, often serve food. Cafés by day are popular for a long breakfast, light lunch or afternoon *Kaffee und Kuchen* ('coffee and cake') and then often turn into bars by night.

At the upper reaches of the market, there are still a few trusty warhorses serving the great and good their allocation of upmarket meat and veg. Much-revered venues such as **Borchardt** (p56), **Grill Royal** (p64), **Lutter und Wegner** (Charlottenstrasse 56, 2029 5415, www.l-w-berlin.de), **Weinbar Rutz** (p68), **Malatesta** (Charlottenstrasse 59, 2094 5071, www.ristorante-malatesta.de) and **Pauly Saal** (Auguststrasse 11-13, 3300 6070, paulysaal.com) are

SHORTLIST

Austrian-German food
- Austria (p134)
- Café Einstein (p103)
- Café Sybille (p87)
- Florian (p111)
- Gugelhof (p80)
- Henne (p126)
- Marjellchen (p112)
- Prater (p14)
- Schwarzwaldstuben (p67)

Fine dining
- Borchardt (p56)
- Grill Royal (p64)
- Hugos (p104)
- Katz Orange (p65)
- Pauly Saal (p12)
- Solistes by Pierre Gagnaire, Les (p112)
- Weinbar Rutz (p68)

Cocktail kings
- Beckett's Knopf (p79)
- Buck & Breck (p15)
- Green Door (p117)
- Newton Bar (p57)
- Schwarze Traube (p128)

Dive bars
- Bar 3 (p63)
- Barbie Deinhoff's (p124)
- Chelsea Bar (p64)
- Lebensstern (p105)
- Luzia (p127)
- Neues Odessa Bar (p81)

Historic haunts
- Café Einstein (p103)
- Diener Tattersall (p111)
- Galerie Bremer (p111)
- Green Door (p117)

Snacktime superstars
- Burgermeister (p124)
- Konnopke's Imbiss (p80)
- Markthalle IX (p129)
- Mustafa's Gemüse Kebap (p134)

sprinkled with Michelin stars and attract a plutocratic clientele.

Meanwhile, at the other end of the scale, there has been something of a mini-revolution with new experiences proliferating within the current vogue for eclectic pop-ups and street food. Events such as **Bite Club** (biteclub.de), and **Markthalle IX** (p129) with its **Street Food Thursday** (www.facebook.com/StreetFoodThursday) are demonstrating the dynamic new DIY ethic reinvigorating the city's eating-out scene; intrepid young cooks are creating anything from tapioca dumplings to ceviche, Nigerian *fufu* to Korean buns. Local hipsters now tend to rate dining experiences with the zeal and fervour hitherto only merited by rare import vinyl and Japanese sneakers.

If you want a taste of old Berlin, there are a few places such as Prenzlauer Berg's **Café Entweder Oder** (Oderberger Strasse 15, 448 1382, cafe-entwederoder.de), **Kellerrestaurant im Brecht-Haus** (Chausseestrasse 125, 282

3843, www.brechtkeller.de) and **Prater** (Kastanienallee 7-9, 448 5688, www.pratergarten.de) that bear some resemblance to their historic form. Berlin's traditional cooking has always been of the meat-and-two-veg variety. *Eisbein* is the signature local dish, a leathery skinned and extremely fatty pig's trotter, sometimes marinated, usually served with puréed peas. You won't find it on the menu, however, in anything but the most doggedly old-school establishments. Other regional cuisines from Germanic Europe are superior and probably better represented such as south German (**Schwarzwaldstuben**, p67; **Florian**, p111), Austrian (**Schneeweiss**, p88; **Austria**, p134; **Café Einstein**, p103), Swiss (**Nola's am Weinberg**, p66) or Alsatian (**Renger-Patzsch**, p117; **Gugelhof**, p80). In the decidedly traditional atmosphere of **Marjellchen** (Mommsenstrasse 9, 883 2676, www.marjellchen-berlin. de) you can even sample the cuisines of formerly German regions such as East Prussia, Pomerania and Silesia, while European Jewish dishes are served at **Bleibergs** (Nürnberger Strasse 45A, 2191 3624, www. bleibergs.de). And for a taste of DDR-era dining (you are really sure about this?) **Osseria** (Langhansstrasse 103, 9606 8525, www.osseria.de) is catering for tourists and nostalgic locals yearning for the stodge and blandness of the communist days.

Meanwhile, café life has been thriving in Berlin since time immemorial and its reputation as an excellent drinking city is well-deserved. Cafés serve breakfast all day, bars stay open deep into the night, and restaurants tend to be relaxed, roomy and delightfully cheap compared to other western European capitals. Seek out cosy corners such as **Anna Blume** (p79),

Lois (Linienstrasse 60, 0179 704 9041), **House of Small Wonder** (p65), **Melbourne Canteen** (p142) and **Spindler** (Paul-Lincke-Ufer 43, 6959 8880, www.spindler-berlin.net).

The world is not enough

The brevity of Germany's colonial experience has meant no deep-rooted link with a foreign cuisine. Turkish food, however, which arrived with post-war *gastarbeiter* ('guest workers'), is now deeply embedded in the western side of town. Kreuzberg can claim to be the place where the doner kebab was invented, in the early 1970s, forever associated with **Hasir** (Adalbertstrasse 10, 614 2373, www. hasir.de). Berlin's other post-war culinary innovation is also a snack at street level: *Currywurst*, a pork sausage sliced and drenched in warm ketchup and curry powder. Try the traditional version under the railway arches at Prenzlauer Berg's venerable **Konnopke's Imbiss** (p80), or the upmarket organic version – and the city's best chips – at **Witty's** (p118).

Reunification has meant a more well-travelled population, and, in the beginning at least, lots of relatively cheap real estate where young restaurateurs could try out their ideas. With an increasingly cosmopolitan clientele to encourage ethnic variety at street level, Berlin dining has been getting steadily more international.

Italian cuisine has long been well represented (**Osteria No.1**, p135; **Sale e Tabbachi**, p135) and good-quality Japanese food is now common, along with other east Asian cuisines such as Vietnamese (**Si An**, p83), Thai (**Edd's**, p104), Chinese (**Asia Deli**, p150) and Indonesian (**Mabuhay**, Köthener Strasse 28, 265 1867).

Indian food presents something of a problem. There are places all over town, but standards are mediocre.

DON'T MISS

Those in the know attest to the best south Asian food being in west Berlin, around Kantstrasse. While it's unlikely that curry connoisseurs will be beating a path to the city, locals have made attempts at east-west fusion cuisine; fast food shack **W-Der Imbiss** (Kastanienallee 49, 4435 2206, www.w-derimbiss.de) does 'international dressings', 'naan pizzas' and 'rice shells' for example.

The latest immigrants have also brought their own culinary traditions. An influx of Russians may not have had much to do with the fashionable borscht and vodka on offer at places such as **Gorki Park** (Weinbergsweg 25, 448 7286, gorki-park.de), **Pasternak** (p82) and **Café Oberwasser** (Zionskirchstrasse 6, 448 3719, www.oberwasser-berlin.de), but the ever-growing community of young Americans in east Berlin has certainly made its gastronomic mark with a wave of fancy burger joints such as the **Bird** (p79). Thanks to this, perhaps, gourmet burgers are now big news; there's even the sporadic **Burgers & Hip Hop** open-air party which combines

handmade burgers with DJs (www.facebook.com/burgersandhiphop).

Berliners do like a drink. The capital's changing demographics mean that tiny, elite cocktail bars are on the increase. Places such as **Buck & Breck** (Brunnenstrasse 177, 3231 5507, www.buckandbreck.com), **Becketts Kopf** (p79) and the previously mentioned Pauly Saal are setting the benchmark for avant-garde mixology, but cultured snorts can be found in every part of town at venues such as **Victoria Bar** (p105), **Galerie Bremer** (p111), **Tier** (p144) and **Cordobar** (p64), the latter being the cognoscenti's current wine bar of choice. There are also still plenty of characterful dives and unpretentious watering holes – almost one on every corner in some parts of town.

In summer, café tables spread out on to the pavements, beer gardens bustle and beach bars spring to life in waterside locations. Beer is the main tipple, although local brews such as Berliner Kindl, a party staple, are poor compared to the best of Bavaria or Bohemia.

Tipping & etiquette

In restaurants, it's customary to tip around ten per cent. Tips are handed directly to the server – or you tell staff how much to take – rather than left on the table. At the moment of handing over the cash, don't say *danke* ('thank you') unless you want them to keep the change. In bars, people tend to pay their own way and drink at their own pace – partly because in many places bills are only totted up as you leave – but ceremonial rounds of Jägermeister, tequila or vodka are a local nightlife feature. Even though the general tendency is for bars to close earlier than they used to, hardly anywhere shuts before 1am and most stay open much later – some until the last customers leave.

Anna Blume

DON'T MISS

WHAT'S BEST
Shopping

The shopping landscape in Berlin is, like almost everything else here, a jumble of disparate elements unified not by geography but accident, experiment, individualism and innovation.

In a city that prides itself on its spirit of creativity, the lowbrow and highbrow, mainstream and avant-garde, designer chic and street style coexist and interconnect, coming together in striking juxtapositions. A quirky independent art bookshop might thrive next to a global mega-chainstore, a cheeky sex shop can nestle comfortably among some of the city's most expensive boutiques. Even the influx of big-name global brands over the past two decades hasn't dampened the impulse of Berlin's progressives to keep things interesting. They'll just move to one side and start up a pop-up kiosk in a former cat sanctuary selling home-made *bimibap*. Or something.

Berlin has never had one single downtown or retail focus and, these days, things are more mixed up than ever. Malls and international franchises are more in evidence, a nod to the broader smartening-up of the city – or soul-destroying commercialism, depending on your point of view. Still, there is plenty of colourful, home-grown talent and entrepreneurial spirit to discover, with fashion, food and 'lifestyle' leading the way.

Perhaps the best example of the contrasts in the city's shopping scene is the vast **Bikini Berlin** (Budapesterstrasse 38-50, 5549 6454, www.bikiniberlin.de), which could be described as a mega-mall for affluent, arty hipsters. A minimal, stylish 'experience' featuring more esoteric brands than one would expect to find in the average identikit shopping centre – as well as major international labels – Bikini Berlin bills itself as a 'concept mall' aimed at the 'urban customer'. For a similar vibe, but in smaller premises, head across town to beneath Mitte's **Soho House** (p168) where **The Store** (thestore-berlin.com) has recently opened, a gorgeous, imaginative space selling luxury items ranging from fashion, books, plants and cult cosmetics to cold-pressed juices. There's even a retro-style hair and beauty salon at the rear.

The west end has remained the upmarket showpiece it always was. Major department stores and the flagship outlets of familiar international names march westwards from **KaDeWe** (p118) on Wittenbergplatz and along the Kurfürstendamm, west Berlin's major shopping avenue. Luxury brands cluster on Fasanenstrasse while more discreet boutiques, interior design outlets and tasteful bookshops are scattered around the streets between the Ku-damm and Kantstrasse, in the area around Savignyplatz. Department stores and yet more international brands line Friedrichstrasse, including high-designer outlet **Departmentstore Quartier 206** (p57) as well as an elegant branch of **Galeries Lafayette** (p58).

Meanwhile, in between east and west, there's the big **Arkaden** mall (Alte Potsdamer Strasse 7, 255 9270, www.potsdamer-platz-arkaden.de). Nearby in Potsdamerstrasse, Andreas Murkudis's high-end 'concept' store **Murkudis** (p105), in the Tagesspiegel building, showcases a tasteful spectrum of luxury goods, from Dries van Noten to beautifully crafted, insanely expensive trinkets, baubles and fripperies from home and abroad.

SHORTLIST

Fashion
- Murkudis (p105)
- Baerck (p18)
- DSTM (p69)
- C'est Tout (p18)
- Lala Berlin (p70)
- Das Neue Schwarz (p71)
- Starstyling (p18)
- Worlds End (p18)

Oddities, knick-knacks and Berliner design style
- Ampelmann Galerie Shop (p68)
- RSVP (p71)
- Stil Raum Berlin (p91)
- The Store (left)

Department stores and malls
- Bikini Berlin (p16)
- Galeries Lafayette (p58)
- KaDeWe (p118)

Books
- Another Country (p135)
- Bücherbogen (p112)
- Ebert und Weber (p18)
- Motto (p129)
- Marga Schoeller Bucherstube (p113)
- Saint George's (p84)
- Taschen (p113)

Outdoor markets
- Kunst und Trödel Markt (p100)
- Mauerpark Flohmarkt (p84)
- Türkischer Markt (p145)
- Winterfeldtplatz Market (p120)

Food emporia
- Dong Xuan Center (p95)
- Kado (p129)
- Olivia (p91)
- Weichardt Brot (p122)

Devoted entirely to buttons
- Paul Knopf (p135)

Over on the other side of Mitte, the area between Alexanderplatz and Rosenthalerplatz fizzles with adventurous and eccentric shops and nearby, the shady side street Mulackstrasse is where the fashion pack list their favourite stores. **Das Neue Schwarz** (p71) for second-hand threads is well worth visiting, as are boutiques such as **Baerck** (Mulackstrasse 12, 2404 8994, baerck.net), **Worlds End** (Mulackstrasse 26, 8561 0073, www.facebook.com/WorldsEndBerlin) and **C'Est Tout** (Linienstrasse 65A, 0172 860 1809, cesttout.de) all offering up quirky and quality fashion. Local brands, such as **Starstyling** (Mulackstrasse 4, 9700 5182, www.starstyling.net) and **Lala Berlin** (p70) design and produce their own gear, much loved by locals in the know. Also in the neighbourhood, the graffitied, eastern end of Torstrasse is now also becoming something of a Berlin Madison Avenue, with concept stores and big brands selling everything from high-end sneakers to covetable antiques, jewellery, and more minimal and tasteful fashion.

This gentrification of Mitte has been driving less affluent shoppers mostly in the direction of Friedrichshain and Kreuzberg, where a more student (and 'perennial student') population dominates. The Bergmannstrasse neighbourhood in Kreuzberg is where you find second-hand shops, small designer outlets, music stores, bookshops and delis.

In Charlottenburg, Knesebeckstrasse, on either side of Savignyplatz, is good for bookshops. **Marga Schoeller Bucherstube** (p113) has an excellent English department, it sold anti-Nazi pamphlets in the 1930s and is still going strong; for art and architecture try **Bücherbogen** (p112). One of the best bookshops in the city, **Another Country** (p135) has been catering to Kreuzbergers in German and English for decades, as has the charming, little **Ebert and Weber** nearby (Falckensteinstrasse 44, 6956 5193, www.ebertundweber.de).

There are several interesting flea markets. Sunday's **Mauerpark Flohmarkt** (p84) has an eclectic selection, but is regarded as somewhat touristy by locals and gets rammed quickly. The **Kunst und Trödel Markt** (p100) is the best place for collectors while the **Flohmarkt am Boxhagener Platz** (p91) mixes old furniture and bric-a-brac work by local artists and T-shirt designers.

Prenzlauer Berg has its own recent addition to the pack, courtesy of Street Food auf Achse at **KulturBrauerei** (p85), a weekly Sunday market where hipsters snack on Indian *vada pav* and wild game burgers. Over in

Galeries Lafayette p17

KaDeWe p17

graffiti-bedecked Revaler Strasse, **Neue Heimat** (Revaler Strasse 99/ Dirschauer Strasse, www.neue heimat.com), which burst onto the scene recently, continues to add new attractions to its repertoire. Swing by Thursday, Friday or Saturday night for live jazz, DJs and munchies, or on Sunday afternoons for the Village Market.

For something more traditional, farmers' markets can be a wonderful way to spend a sunny morning or afternoon. At the biweekly **Türkischer Markt** (p145) on Maybachufer, you can find everything from fresh baked bread or organic cheese to Greek olives, while the **Kollwitzplatz Farmers' Market** (p84) which runs on Saturdays, and a smaller version on Thursdays, carries a wide range of local artisan products. Although you won't find fruit or veg for sale at

Wilmersdorf's **Preussenpark** (p121), during weekends in the summer you will find a delicious Thai food market run by Berlin's Asian community.

Opening hours

Shops generally open at around 9am or 10am. More traditional and smaller stores tend to close around 6pm, but a relatively recent relaxation of laws means that places can now stay open until 10pm – most bigger stores and more adventurous smaller retailers stick it out at least until 8pm. It's also now possible to go shopping on Saturday afternoons. All but a few shops are closed on Sunday. Plastic in all its aspects (credit and debit cards, PINs, PIN machines, contactless payment) is less widely used than in London, with most transactions in cash.

WHAT'S BEST
Nightlife

Berlin's reputation for decadence and nocturnal high jinks stretches all the way back to the 1920s when – apart from the cabaret scene of legend – it was the first city to have anything one might recognise as a gay community, in the modern sense. Nazism and war might have dampened its party spirit for a time, but even in the years of division, East Berlin had more liberal licensing laws than London, while the western side of town teemed with draft-dodging youth and nihilistic artists, few of whom had anything important to get up for in the morning.

In reunified Berlin you can stay out until dawn pretty much any night of the week, there are late-night bars all over town, and bands and DJs will appear in just about any space large enough to accommodate a bar and stage. Music is everywhere. Concert audiences are among the most enthusiastic in the world, every second person you meet seems to be some kind of DJ, while in any half-decent, late-night bar, staff will have been recruited as much for their taste in tunes as their cocktail abilities.

From division to DIY

As in most other aspects of city life, Berlin's history has an effect still felt today. In the Cold War years, West Berlin was an island, remote from the musical mainstream; East Berlin was remoter still. The feeling that nothing that came out of here would be commercial led to an attitude of confrontation and experiment across the arts. This was epitomised by Einstürzende Neubauten, making music with hammers and drills,

Berghain

SHORTLIST

Cabaret cool
- Café Theatre Schalotte (p23)
- Chamäleon (p74)
- Kleine Nachtrevue (p120)
- Scheinbar (p23)

Techno caves
- Berghain/Panorama Bar (p92)
- Tresor (p58)
- Watergate (p131)

Edge of the underground
- ://about blank (p91)
- Chalet (p130)
- Salon zur Wilden Renate (p93)
- Sisyphos (p95)

Bars with beats
- Café Futuro (p22)
- CCCP (p23)
- Sameheads (p145)

Live venues
- Duncker (p85)
- Fritzclub im Postbahnhof (p93)
- Lido (p130)
- Olympiastadion (p115)
- Waldbühne (p23)

Genre music
- Bassy Cowboy Club (p85)
- Clärchens Ballhaus (p73)
- K17 (p92)
- Roadrunner's Paradise (p85)

reflecting the city's post-war experience of rebuilding itself from rubble. They are still regarded as Berlin's signature band, long after their heyday.

Things really kicked off after the fall of the Wall, as the West Berlin avant-garde collided with a party-starved East Berlin generation on makeshift dancefloors in spaces left accessible by the abandonment of border defences and the collapse of East German industry. The techno scene of the no-man's-land years is long gone, but some of the DIY spirit of those days lives on in a variety of forms. While the bigger clubs still play formulaic tech-house – like **Watergate** (p131) and **Panorama** at Berghain (p92) where the line-ups are generally average in quality – there are other, smaller scenes to be found around the city.

Moveable parties – accessed via social media groups and tip-offs, flyers or word-of-mouth – exploit spaces that haven't yet been brought into the commercial mainstream. Meanwhile, small underground

Tresor p22

Bohannon

places like **Prince Charles** (p130), **Wilde Renate** (Alt-Stralau 70, 2504 1426, www.renate.cc) which is keeping the spirit of the city's late, lamented Bar 25 alive, **Chalet** (p130) and **://about blank** (p91) are currently among the in-crowd's destinations of choice. If you want the coolest new underground music, Neukölln is where to go; for starters try **Café Futuro** (Pannierstrasse 12, 2432 5901, cafefuturo.com) or **Sameheads** (p145).

Then there is the continuing tradition of landmark clubs taking over obsolete power stations. **Berghain** (p92) has long been occupying one such venue in Friedrichshain, its original fittings polished for added post-industrial detail. Across the river, **Tresor** (p58), the post-Wall era's very first club, is installed in one corner of what used to be a gigantic heating plant.

It makes sense not to show up at any Berlin club as part of a pack of braying, English blokes – or in a posse of overexcited tourists sporting anoraks. Nor is it clever to appear deranged, dull, drugged or drunk. The strict door policy at Berghain for instance is the stuff of legend. But in general the approach to clubbing here is incredibly laid-back: be cool, be quiet, speak German if possible and you should be fine.

Sounds of the city

Ricardo Villalobos and Richie Hawtin remain the best local exponents of the minimal techno that used to be Berlin's signature sound, but that gave way to electro late in the last decade – look out for Kaos or Ellen Allien. Once a trend has started here however, it tends to stick around.

Kreuzberg will forever be characterised by an anarcho-punk aesthetic, buskers in Friedrichshain strum Beatles or Nirvana tunes, disco is always popular in Mitte clubs such as **Bohannon** (p73), while you'll still find a few clones in Schöneberg's gay quarter. And various scenes retain some kind of niche, such as goth at **K17** (p92) or **Duncker** (p85), blues 'n' rockabilly at **Roadrunner's Paradise** (p85) or even ballroom dancing at **Clärchens Ballhaus** (p73). Some boundaries remain blurred, however. A place like **CCCP** (Tor Strasse 58, www.facebook.com/cccpbar, formerly Kaffee Burger) might be a literary salon one minute, a live venue the next, and end the night as a debauched disco that could keep going until morning rush hour.

Not many live venues in Berlin consistently book top acts, but quite a few are capable of hosting a great live show. Even so, it's impossible to recommend a single location; booking policies vary wildly and venue loyalty is unknown. **Fritzclub im Postbahnhof** (p93) is where the likes of Arcade Fire, Mercury Rev or John Grant might stop off, while stadium acts tend to appear at arenas such as the **Olympiastadion** (p115) or the **Waldbühne** (Am Glockenturm, 7473 7500, www.waldbuehne-berlin.de), great for summer open-air gigs.

Cabaret, meanwhile, is still alive and well, though don't go looking for the reincarnation of Liza Minnelli. The political satire sprinkled with songs and sketches that Berliners call *Kabarett* is largely impenetrable to outsiders. Acrobats, dancing girls and magicians are the staple of the form called *Varieté* and **Chamäleon** (p74) in the Hackesche Höfe is the best place to check this out. Drag cabaret, known as *Travestie*, isn't as common as many expect it to be, but you can still find a show in the old Berlin tradition at the friendly **Kleine Nachtrevue** (Kurfürstenstrasse 116, 218 8950, www.kleine-nachtrevue.de). A more daring kind of cabaret thrives in smaller, out-of-the-way places such as **Scheinbar** (Monumentenstrasse 9, 784 5539, www.scheinbar.de) in

Schöneberg or **Café Theater Schalotte** (Behaimstrasse 22, 341 1485, www.schalott.de) in Charlottenburg.

Also look out for acts such as Die O-Ton Piraten (clever drag musical theatre that montages famous film dialogues into irrelevant story lines), Gayle Tufts (charming American entertainer who mixes pop music with stand-up in a jumble of German and English) or Bridge Markland (gender-bending dance and poetry).

Finding the party

Though we've listed the best venues, much of what goes on here is beyond the scope of a travel guide: once-a-week clubs in crumbling locations for example, or temporary collectives throwing multi-act parties. Much of the scene remains constantly on the move – even more so since the police began harassing improperly licensed venues. Many clubs don't bother updating their websites, or only post events for the next week, while party promoters move from venue to venue.

Berlin's two fortnightly listings magazines, *tip* (www.tip-berlin.de) and *Zitty* (www.zitty.de), do a good job of covering the basics, but there's always something underground or last-minute going on. Look for flyers in shops, bars and cafés, where copies of the city's two free gay magazines, *Siegessäule* (www.siegessaeule.de) and *Blu* (www.blu.fm) can be found. It might also be worth consulting *Exberliner* (www.exberliner.com), Berlin's English-language monthly. Website www.dorfdisco.de covers the local scene in both German and English, while there's plenty of information, in German only, at www.berlinonline.de. Just remember that although our listings were correct at the time of writing, in Berlin nothing ever stays the same for very long.

Philharmonie

WHAT'S BEST
Arts & Leisure

Berlin is a major performing arts capital with enough classical music and opera for any two normal cities, one of the world's most important film events, a rich and experimental theatre culture, a growing reputation for dance, and a calendar full of festivals.

Orchestral manoeuvres

The Berliner Philharmoniker (www. berliner-philharmoniker.de), based at the **Philharmonie** (p106) and currently going from strength to strength under the perennially popular Sir Simon Rattle (who has announced he will be ending his tenure in 2018), has long been one of the world's leading orchestras. But the 'Phil' is only the tip of an iceberg that features six other major orchestras, a number of smaller

ensembles and no fewer than three opera houses. The Deutsches Symphonie Orchester (www.dso-berlin.de) enjoyed an avant-garde programme under previous principal conductor, Ingo Metzmacher, who ceded leadership to Russian Tugan Sokhiev in 2010. Groundbreaking contemporary work is also the staple of the Rundfunk-Sinfonieorchester Berlin under Marek Janowski (www.rso-online.de), the former radio orchestra of East Germany. Meanwhile, the old masters are well served by the Konzerthausorchester Berlin (www.konzerthausorchester. de), which plays at the **Konzerthaus** (p59), under the chief conductor Iván Fischer.

Of the smaller ensembles, the Deutsches Kammerorchester Berlin (www.dko-berlin.de), under manager Stefan Fragner, has an excellent reputation for working with rising-star conductors and soloists, while the Ensemble Oriol (www.ensemble-oriol.de) is a fine group that emphasises contemporary work.

The **Staatsoper Unter den Linden** (p59) is the grandest of the opera houses, and leaps from one success to another thanks to the popularity of general music director Daniel Barenboim. High quality performances are sometimes marred by overly spectacular staging however. Much-needed renovations began in 2010 and may continue until 2017, during which time the Staatsoper is decamping to the Schiller Theater on Bismarckstrasse. The **Komische Oper** (p59) has carved out its own niche with controversial and topical productions, while over in Charlottenburg, the **Deutsche Oper** (p114) remains one of the city's most eminent musical forces under Scottish-born musical director Donald Runnicles. Among smaller ensembles, look out for the edgy **Novoflot** (www.novoflot.de).

There are top-quality festivals throughout the year, including **MaerzMusik** (p28) in March, for esoteric contemporary music, **UltraSchall** (p34) for more new music, and the **Classic Open Air** concert series (p30) in the Gendarmenmarkt each July. September sees the vast **Musikfest Berlin** (p31) bringing some of the world's finest orchestras to the city. For something different, look out for monthly **Yellow Lounge** events (www.yellowlounge.de), which drags classical music into a contemporary context with DJs, top-notch VJs and intimate club performances.

Theatre meets dance

Berlin has long enjoyed a reputation for cutting-edge theatre, which dates back to the days of Brecht and Piscator. Dance and theatre cohabit

SHORTLIST

Classical classics
- Deutsches Kammerorchester Berlin (p24)
- Deutsche Oper (p114)
- Konzerthaus (p59)
- Staatsoper (p59)

Best experimental theatre & dance
- HAU (p137)
- Radialsystem V (p94)
- Schaubühne am LehninerPlatz (p114)
- Sophiensaele (p74)
- Volksbühne (p74)

Modern classics
- Berliner Ensemble (p74)
- Deutsches Theater (p74)
- Maxim Gorki Theater (p59)
- Philharmonie (p106)

English entertainment
- Babylon Kreuzberg (p131)
- CineStar IMAX Sony Center (p106)
- English Theatre Berlin (p137)
- Odeon (p120)

Essential cinema
- Arsenal (p106)
- Berlin International Film Festival (p34)
- Hackesche Höfe Kino (p74)

Contemporary art galleries
- Contemporary Fine Arts (p57)
- Kwadrat (p41)
- König Gallery (p41)
- Kunst-Werke Institute for Contemporary Art (p43)
- ME Collector's Room (p43)
- Michael Fuchs (p43)
- Neugerriemschneider (p43)

under one roof at houses such as **Hebbel am Ufer** (HAU) (p137), the **Sophiensaele** (p74), and the **Schaubühne am Lehniner Platz** (p114). At the latter, Thomas Ostermeier, who has successfully combined dance with theatre for many years, now collaborates with choreographer Constanza Macras on productions such as a recent radical reinterpretation of *A Midsummer Night's Dream*. Radical interpretations, avant-garde experimentation and socially aware productions find themselves at the HAU which has proved a great success. Elsewhere, Mitte's **Volksbühne** (p74), soon to be under the aegis of Tate Modern's Chris Dercon, continues its bloody-minded, somewhat didactic approach to contemporary and experimental theatre, while the **Berliner Ensemble** (p74) mixes modern productions of Brecht with the work of modern German-language writers and directors such as Robert Wilson. Traditionalists seek refuge at the **Deutsches Theatre** (p74), renowned for its high-class productions of the classics. English-language theatre, meanwhile, thrives at the **English Theatre Berlin** (p137) in the F40 Künstlerhöfe in Kreuzberg. For dance, your best bet at present is to check out the programme at the **Radialsystem V** (p94) arts space, where contemporary dance rubs shoulders with classical, singing and performance of all kinds.

Cinema city

As befits a city so associated with the early days of cinema, Berlin's commitment to the moving image remains central to its artistic identity. The legendary **Berlin International Film Festival** (p34) or 'Berlinale' takes over Potsdamerplatz each February with star-studded

Berlin International Film Festival

premières and a colossal programme of new cinema from around the world. But it's not the only film festival on the calendar. Summer's **Fantasy Film Fest** (p30) premières the latest in international fantasy, sci-fi and horror. And since 2006, the **XPOSED International Queer Film Festival** (p28), held annually in May, shows a programme of left-field LGBT shorts and features, as well as running the Lolly Awards and offering funding and advice to filmmakers.

Mainstream Hollywood movies are mostly dubbed into German, but the CineStar Original – in the same Sony Center building as the **CineStar IMAX** (p106) – is devoted to showing films in their original language. Movies in English can also be found at Schöneberg's **Odeon** (p120), Mitte's **Hackesche Höfe Kino** (p74) and the **Babylon** in Kreuzberg (p131). Also in the Sony Center, the two-screen **Arsenal**

Olympiastadion

(p106) has an eclectic programme of non-mainstream cinematic fare from every corner of the globe.

Sporting events

The city that hosted the 2015 UEFA Champions League final, won by Barcelona, has less top class football per capita than just about any comparable metropolis.

It's difficult for an outsider to love Hertha BSC (www.herthabsc.de) but it's not hard to get tickets for their games at the **Olympiastadion** (p115). The club has been relegated a couple of times in its recent history but currently plays in the Bundesliga. The Olympiastadion also hosts the annual final of the DFB-Pokal (www.dfb.de), Germany's equivalent of the English FA Cup. FC Union Berlin (www.fc-union-berlin.de) is the city's smaller team, playing second tier football at their stadium in Köpenick where fans are noisy and passionate.

Alba (www.albaberlin.de), the city's basketball team, is one of Germany's most successful, while Eisbären Berlin (www.eisbaeren.de) compete creditably in the German ice hockey league. Both Alba and Eisbären play their home games at the Mercedes-Benz Arena, formerly known as the O2 World arena. Berlin's handball team, Füchse Berlin (www.fuechse.berlin), based at Max-Schmeling-Halle in Prenzlauer Berg, compete in the Handball-Bundesliga while the Berliner 6-Tage-Rennen (www.sechstagerennen-berlin.de), a major indoor cycling race, takes place at the Velodrom cycling arena in Prenzlauer Berg, which also doubles up as a major concert venue.

Possibly the best-known event internationally is the **Berlin Marathon** (p31) each September. One of the World Marathon Majors, the event boasts the highest number of world records at this distance.

Calendar

Gallery Weekend

Spring

late Mar **MaerzMusik – Festival für aktuelle Musik**
Various venues
www.berlinerfestspiele.de
A holdover from the more culture-conscious days of the former East Germany, this ten-day contemporary music festival invites international avant-garde composers and musicians to present new works.

late Apr **Gallery Weekend**
Various venues
www.gallery-weekend-berlin.de
Around 40 galleries time their openings for the last weekend in April, making for an arty extravaganza attended by leading dealers as well as art lovers.

1 May **May Day Riots**
Around Kottbusser Tor, Kreuzberg
An annual event since 1987, when Autonomen clashed violently with the police, recent years have been quieter – but Kreuzberg is still lively on May Day with street parties, music and protests.

May **Theatertreffen Berlin**
Various venues
www.berlinerfestspiele.de
A jury picks ten of the most innovative and controversial new theatre productions from companies across Austria, Germany and Switzerland. The winners perform their pieces over two weeks.

May **XPOSED Queer Film Festival**
Moviemento Kino, Kottbusser Damm, Kreuzberg

www.xposedfilmfestival.com
Four days of LGBT cinema, awards and advice sessions for film-makers.

late May **DFB-Pokalfinale**
Olympiastadion
www.dfb.de
Germany's domestic cup final has been taking place at the Olympiastadion annually since 1985. It regularly attracts a capacity crowd; tickets are very hard to come by.

May/June **Karneval der Kulturen**
Kreuzberg
www.karneval-berlin.de
Inspired by London's Notting Hill Carnival and intended as a celebration of ethnic and cultural diversity, this festival, held on the Pentecost holiday weekend, centres on Sunday's 'multi-kulti' parade: dozens of floats, hundreds of musicians, thousands of spectators.

late May/early June **ILA Berlin Air Show**
Berlin ExpoCenter Airport
www.ila-berlin.de
This popular biennial event – the next is in 2016 – is held over six days at Schönefeld airport. It features around 1,000 exhibitors from 40 countries, with aircraft of all kinds, and a serious focus on space travel.

ILA Berlin Air Show

Summer

June/July **Berlin Philharmonie at the Waldbühne**
Waldbühne, Am Glockenturm, Charlottenburg
www.berliner-philharmoniker.de
The Philharmonie ends its season with an open-air concert that sells out months in advance. After dark, over 20,000 Berliners light up the atmospheric 'forest theatre' with candles.

mid June-mid July **Deutsch-Französisches Volksfest**
Zentraler Festplatz, Kurt-Schumacher-Damm, Reinickendorf
www.deutsch-franzoesisches-volksfest.de
A survivor from the days when this area was the French Sector, the month-long German-French Festival offers fairground rides, French music and cuisine, and Bastille Day fireworks.

21 June **Fête de la Musique**
Various venues
www.fetedelamusique.de
A regular summer solstice happening since 1995, this music extravaganza of bands and DJs takes place across the city. The selection is mixed, ranging from the heaviest of metal to the schmaltziest of *schlager*.

late June **Lesbisch-Schwules Stadtfest**
Nollendorfplatz & Motzstrasse, Schöneberg
www.regenbogenfonds.de
The Lesbian & Gay Street Fair takes over Schöneberg every year, filling several blocks. Participating bars, clubs, food stands and musical acts make this a dizzying, non-stop event that also serves as a kickstarter for the following week's Christopher Street Day Parade.

Sat in late June **Christopher Street Day Parade**
www.csd-berlin.de
Originally organised to commemorate the 1969 riots outside the Stonewall Bar

on Christopher Street in New York, this fun and flamboyant parade has become one of the summer's most enjoyable and inclusive street parties, attracting straights as well as gays. Check the website for details of the route.

early July & late Jan
Berlin Fashion Week
Various venues
www.fashion-week-berlin.com
OK, so it's not quite Paris. But Berlin's twice-yearly style shindig is slowly being taken a little more seriously. Bread & Butter, an international trade fair for streetwear and urbanwear, takes place at the same time in the former Tempelhof airport. There's a late-night shopping night and plenty of parties too.

early July Classic Open Air
Gendarmenmarkt, Mitte
www.classicopenair.de
Big names usually open this concert series held over five days in one of Berlin's most beautiful squares.

July/Aug Deutsch-Amerikanisches Volksfest
Heidestrasse 30, Tiergarten
www.deutsch-amerikanisches-volksfest.de
Established by the US forces stationed in West Berlin, the German-American

Festival lasts about three weeks and offers a tacky but popular mix of carnival rides, cowboys doing lasso tricks, candy floss, hot dogs and beer.

Aug Tanz im August
Various venues
www.tanzimaugust.de
This three-week event is Germany's leading modern-dance festival, with big-name participants.

Aug Fantasy Film Fest
CineStar, Sony Center, Tiergarten
www.fantasyfilmfest.com
Running over 12 days, this is the Berlin segment of a festival that happens in a number of German cities in August and early September. If you like fantasy, horror or sci-fi flicks, you'll love it.

Aug Internationales Berliner Bierfestival
Karl-Marx-Allee, from Strausberger Platz to Frankfurter Tor, Friedrichshain
www.bierfestival-berlin.de
Describing itself as 'the world's longest beer garden', and now nearly 20 years old, this two-day shindig showcases hundreds of beers from over 80 countries, bringing conviviality to the city's premier Stalinist boulevard.

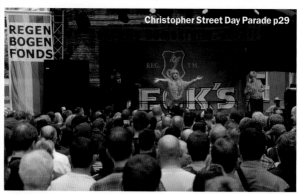
Christopher Street Day Parade p29

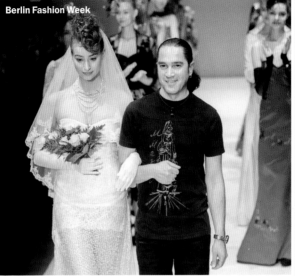

Berlin Fashion Week

Aug **Young.euro.classic**
Konzerthaus, Gendarmenmarkt 2, Mitte
www.young-euro-classic.de
This summer concert programme brings together youth orchestras from around Europe for two weeks.

last Sat in Aug **Lange Nacht der Museen**
Various venues
www.lange-nacht-der-museen.de
Around 100 museums, collections, archives and exhibition halls stay open into the early hours of the morning, with special events, concerts, readings, lectures and performances. A ticket gets you free travel on special shuttle buses and regular public transport.

Autumn

Sept **Musikfest Berlin**
Various venues
www.berlinerfestspiele.de

This major classical music festival, held over three weeks, presents more than 70 works by 25 composers. Orchestras, instrumental and vocal ensembles, and numerous soloists take part, with many from abroad. In recent years this has meant Denmark, Israel, Sweden, the UK and the USA.

Sept **Internationales Literaturfestival Berlin**
Various venues
www.literaturfestival.com
A major literary event, with readings, symposiums and discussions over ten days, the Internationales Literaturfestival attracts well-known authors and rising stars from around the world.

last Sun in Sept **Berlin Marathon**
City-wide
www.bmw-berlin-marathon.com
Fewer than 300 people took part in the inaugural Berlin Marathon in 1974;

WHEREVER CRIMES AGAINST HUMANITY ARE PERPETRATED.

Across borders and above politics.
Against the most heinous abuses
and the most dangerous oppressors.
From conduct in wartime
to economic, social, and cultural rights.
Everywhere we go,
we build an unimpeachable case
for change and advocate action
at the highest levels.

HUMAN RIGHTS WATCH TYRANNY HAS A WITNESS

WWW.HRW.ORG

HUMAN
RIGHTS
WATCH

now, it's one of the biggest and most popular road races in the world with more than 40,000 runners, plus a million spectators lining the route.

3 Oct Tag der deutschen Einheit
No official venue

The Day of German Unity is a public holiday commemorating the day the two Germanies became one, back in 1990. Head to Brandenburger Tor to join the party.

mid Oct Festival of Lights
Various venues

www.festival-of-lights.de/en

Berlin's world-famous sights and monuments (most situated in the city centre) become the canvas for spectacular light and video projections. The illuminations are switched on at 7pm nightly.

1st weekend in Nov JazzFest Berlin
Various venues

www.berlinerfestspiele.de

Offering a wide range of jazz from an array of internationally renowned artists, the festival has been a fixture since 1964. The concurrent Fringe Jazz Festival, organised by JazzRadio, showcases less established acts.

Nov Berliner Märchentage
Various venues

www.berliner-maerchentage.de

The fortnight-long Berlin Fairytale Festival celebrates tales from around the world with some 400 storytelling and musical events in a carnival atmosphere. The theme changes each year: in 2014, the 25th anniversary, it was stories from the UK; in 2015, stories from North Africa to Arabia.

Winter

Dec Christmas Markets
Kaiser-Wilhelm-Gedächtniskirche, Breitscheidplatz, Charlottenburg

www.weihnachtsmarkt-deutschland.de

Traditional markets spring up across Berlin during the Christmas season, offering toys, mulled wine and gingerbread. This is one of the biggest.

Berlin Marathon p31

Silvester

31 Dec **Berliner Silvesterlauf**
Grunewald
www.berliner-silvesterlauf.de
The New Year's Eve Run starts off
in Grunewald at the intersection of
Waldschulallee and Harbigstrasse.

31 Dec **Silvester**
No official venue
Thousands celebrate New Year's Eve
at the Brandenburger Tor, or trek up
to the Teufelsberg at the northern tip
of Grunewald or the Viktoriapark in
Kreuzberg to watch the fireworks.

Jan **Grüne Woche**
Messegelände am Funkturm,
Messedamm 22, Charlottenburg
www.gruenewoche.de
Dedicated to food, agriculture and hor-
ticulture, this ten-day show is an oppor-
tunity to enjoy food and drink from the
far corners of Germany and beyond.

mid Jan **Ultraschall Berlin
– Festival für Neue Musik**
Various venues
ultraschallberlin.de
New music played in high-profile venues by some of the world's leading specialist ensembles.

late Jan/early Feb **Berliner
6-Tage-Rennen**
Velodrom, Prenzlauer Berg
www.sechstagerennen-berlin.de
Six days of amateur and professional
cycle racing at the Velodrom, with gigs
and other entertainments.

late Jan/early Feb **Transmediale**
Haus der Kulturen der Welt, John-
Foster-Dulles-Allee 10, Tiergarten
www.transmediale.de
One of the world's largest festivals for
media art and digital culture.

mid Feb **Berlin International
Film Festival**
Various venues
www.berlinale.de
The city's biggest cultural event and
one of the world's most prominent film
festivals (after Cannes and Venice).

Itineraries

Denkmal für die ermordeten Juden Europas

The Memory Trail

Berlin's tumultuous 20th-century history has proven a fertile ground for the thriving culture of remembrance, and its present position as a node of global creativity has given rise to a memorial landscape as challenging as it is diverse. It ranges from impromptu, low-budget projects by avant-garde artists to expansive, government-funded affairs built by world-renowned architects. Some are conceptual, others concrete; some experimental, others traditional. They commemorate a wide range of people, victims and events, and have sparked political controversy and public debate.

Allow a day for this itinerary, which focuses on World War II-era memorials in the city centre. You will pass through areas heavily frequented by both locals and tourists, so there will be no shortage of refreshment stops along the way.

It begins at the **Denkmal für die ermordeten Juden Europas** (Memorial to the Murdered Jews of Europe, p52); if you need a rendezvous point, there is a row of cafés along Cora-Berliner-Strasse on its eastern side. Berlin's most central and arguably most ambitious monument, this undulating grid of tilting stelae spreads across 19,000 square metres of prime real estate just south of the Brandenburger Tor. Designed by Peter Eisenman and inaugurated in 2005, the €25 million construction serves as the city's principal Holocaust memorial, complete with a subterranean information centre housing a sombre and powerful exhibition.

Cross the street towards the Tiergarten at the south-west corner of the memorial, where Ebertstrasse meets Hannah-Arendt-Strasse. Follow a short sand path into the park to find Michael Elmgreen and

Ingar Dragset's **Denkmal für die im Nationalsozialismus verfolgten Homosexuellen** (Memorial to the Homosexual Victims of National Socialism), a concrete slab erected among the trees. Take a moment to watch the video loop inside the unadorned cuboid before heading back on to Ebertstrasse and walking north towards the Brandenburger Tor.

Turn left on to the broad unnamed path leading back into Tiergarten, just past the Strasse des 17 Juni. The double line of cobblestones that cuts through the intersection marks the route of the Wall that once stood here. Walking into Tiergarten, follow the Simsonweg path to reach the **Memorial to the Sinti and Roma Victims of National Socialism.** Designed by Israeli artist Dani Karavan, it is a small, meditative pool ringed with stones inscribed with a poem by Roma poet Santo Spinelli.

Detour briefly down the path, to the left, and you'll find the 1945 **Sowjetisches Ehrenmal** (Soviet War Memorial) – or just keep heading straight until you reach the Reichstag. Out front, you'll see an arrangement of stone tablets. This is the **Memorial to the Murdered Members of the Reichstag** – 96 opposition party politicians killed by the Nazis. Walk clockwise around the building and notice the bullet holes and graffiti scrawled by Soviet soldiers, left as reminders of a violent past. At the north-east corner of the building, you'll find **two small memorials**: a plaque thanking Hungary for opening its western border to East Germans in 1989, and a slab of the wall of Gdansk shipyard, birthplace of the Polish trade union Solidarity. Both made crucial contributions to the end of the Cold War and to reunification.

Look down towards the water, and you'll see the **Weisse Kreuze** memorial, seven white crosses dedicated to all those killed trying to escape from East to West Berlin.

Coming around the building, you'll find yourself back at Ebertstrasse. Follow it to the Brandenburger Tor, walk through, and continue on to Unter den Linden. Here you can walk a few blocks – which means you can stop for refreshment at Café Einstein on the corner of Neustädtische Kirchstrasse – or take a bus two stops (to Staatsoper, and then walk back a few yards in the direction you have just come) to arrive at **Bebelplatz** on the south side of Unter den Linden. At its centre, you'll find a glass plate set into the ground, through which you can view an underground room of empty white bookcases. This is Israeli artist Micha Ullman's **Bibliotek**, a memorial to the notorious Nazi book-burning that took place here in 1933. A line from Heinrich Heine is engraved several times around the perimeter of the square: 'Where they burn books, they ultimately burn people.'

Across the street, you'll find the **Neue Wache**. A neoclassical building by Schinkel dating from 1816, it was rededicated in 1993 as the **Central Memorial of the Federal Republic of Germany to the Victims of War and Tyranny**. The single room houses a moving enlarged replica of a Käthe Kollwitz sculpture called *Mother with Dead Son*, under which the remains of an unknown German soldier and unknown concentration camp victim are enshrined.

Keep heading east along Unter den Linden, which soon becomes Karl-Liebknecht-Strasse. Take a left on to Rosenstrasse, and enter the park on your left. There, you'll find Ingeborg Hunzinger's **Block der Frauen** (Block of Women), a memorial to the thousands of non-Jewish women in mixed marriages who gathered at this site in February

Missing House

1943 to demand the release of their husbands; the men were being detained by the Nazis in a Jewish community building. After five days of protest, they were miraculously released back to their loved ones.

Cutting diagonally across the park, you come to the **site of Berlin's oldest synagogue** where a commemorative plaque tells the history of the building that stood on this spot between 1714 and 1945. Take a right out of the park on to Heidereutergasse and walk back towards Rosenstrasse, where you'll see a **rose-coloured advertising column** bearing information (in German only) about the events that took place here.

Next stop is the **Gedenkstätte Stille Helden** (Silent Heroes Memorial) near the Hackescher Höfe. To get there, walk north down Rosenstrasse away from the park and take a right on An der Spandauer Brücke. Follow this street until you reach Rosenthaler Strasse, on to which you'll take a right. On the left side, just past Starbucks, you'll see something called a courtyard entrance, with a sign for the **Anne Frank Zentrum** (p59). As you walk into the courtyard, notice the *Stolpersteine* ('stumbling stones'), set into the pavement at your feet. These small brass plaques, found all over Berlin, mark the homes of people persecuted by the Nazis and are engraved with the name, birth date and death date (if known) of the person who lived there. The project was conceived by sculptor Gunter Demnig in 1996.

In the courtyard, you'll also see a small door on your left. Take this up to the Silent Heroes Memorial, which commemorates those who hid and otherwise helped Jews persecuted by the Nazi regime. Free of charge, the two-storey centre is full of compelling documentation of heroism and resistance.

Deeper into the courtyard, you'll find **Museum Blindenwerkstatt Otto Weidt** (Museum of Otto Weidt's Workshop for the Blind), where a free exhibition documents the story of one such silent hero and the Jewish employees he risked his life to protect. With five small rooms and a short film, the museum is informative and manageable. You can stop for beer or tea at the cosy Café Cinema on your way out.

Der Verlassene Raum

When you re-emerge on to Rosenthaler Strasse, turn right and walk to the corner, then right again on to Oranienburger Strasse. Take the first right on to Grosse Hamburger Strasse and on the right you'll find the remains of **Berlin's oldest Jewish Cemetery**, first dedicated in 1672 and the last resting place of German-Jewish philosopher Moses Mendelssohn. There's a plaque commemorating the Jewish old people's home that once stood here, an information board detailing the history of the cemetery, and a memorial to the 55,000 Jews who were held here by the Gestapo before deportation to Auschwitz and Theresienstadt. The ground on which the memorial stands pays homage to the fallen building: red bricks follow the lines of the original foundation, and rubble from the demolished old people's home was deliberately left in the spaces between the lines.

Further down Grosse Hamburger Strasse, you'll find the **Missing House** on the left. The empty space was once home to an apartment building destroyed during World War II. When French artist Christian Boltanski came across the site in 1990, he learned that many of the building's former residents had been Jews; in their honour, he dedicated this memorial to 'absence'. The signs on the adjacent buildings show the names of the former residents along with their dates of birth and death, their occupations and the approximate locations of their apartments within the building.

Follow Grosse Hamburger Strasse even further north, and you'll wind up at Koppenplatz, a green space among the apartment blocks and the last stop on this itinerary. At the north end of these gardens is **Der Verlassene Raum** (Deserted Room), a simple but effective bronze sculpture by Karl Biedermann erected in commemoration of Kristallnacht. Across the park at Koppenplatz 6, a plaque hanging in the building's courtyard offers lines from the Baal Shem Tov: 'To forget is banishment. To remember is salvation.' A family tree is painted on the wall behind the plaque, a memorial to the building's former Jewish owners, most of whom lost their lives in the Holocaust.

Art Tour

In a city that pulsates with art and culture, trying to navigate the wealth of galleries, museums and foundations can be a daunting proposition. There are dozens of new and established galleries to be found across the city, and a profusion of museums with art from the Middle Ages to the present. And, of course, Berlin's annual art calendar is packed with events and happenings on an almost daily basis.

This tour is not comprehensive, nor is it intended to be a complete and exhaustive guide to every part of Berlin, focusing instead within the most vibrant parts of the city's art scene, Mitte and Kreuzberg.

Kreuzberg is the once-gritty, anarchic district, home to immigrants, artists, punks, squatters, anarchists and dissidents since the DDR era. Today, it's home to some of Berlin's most intriguing galleries and institutions: typically, those reflecting the district's rough and ready, politically engaged character. And it's here in Kreuzberg that every September, the city's **ABC** art fair (www.artberlincontemporary.com) takes place at Station-Berlin in Luckenwalderstrasse.

Begin at the **Berlinische Galerie** (Alte Jakobstrasse 124-128, www.berlinischegalerie.de, p131), which recently reopened after a thorough restoration. It's a state-funded museum, focusing on modern art, photography and architecture in Berlin, from 1870 to the present day. The city's cultural history is comprehensively documented via permanent and temporary exhibitions, which touch on anything from painting, graphics, sculpture and multimedia to photography, architecture and artists' archives. Local art-histories are represented in collections covering Dada in

Kunst-Werke Institute for Contemporary Art p43

Not far away is **Gitte Bohr – Club für Kunst und politisches Denken** (Skalitzerstrasse 133, www.gittebohr.de). Founded by Diego Castro and Eva May in Neukölln in 2010, this multimedia space presents politically charged art within an energetic programme of exhibitions, presentations and talks reflecting on myriad social and political issues dominating discourse in Berlin's underground. Gitte Bohr's premise is to 'wrestle' viewers out of passivity and invite them to participate in the various modes of art on display.

It's a short walk from Gitte Bohr to **Kwadrat** (Manteuffelstrasse 92, www.kwadrat-berlin.com), one of the city's more esoteric smaller spaces, run by the ebullient dealer Martin Kwade. If Kwade is in the building, he's always glad to give guests a guided tour of the exhibition and explain the story behind the art. (Until recently, Kwade was the instigator of the legendary 'Artists Night' all-night parties at the now sadly defunct Kingsize bar in Mitte.) A diverse programme takes in installation, sculpture, painting and drawing.

It's time to head to **Mitte**. Take the U-Bahn from Görlitzer Bahnhof westwards to Hallesches Tor, where you'll take the U6 northbound. Exit at Friedrichstrasse and walk along Georgenstrasse until you reach Am Kupfergraben, where **Contemporary Fine Arts** (Am Kupfergraben 10, www.cfa-berlin.de, p57) is located. A bright, airy, two-floor gallery run by veteran dealers Nicole Hackert and Bruno Brunett, the gallery has a reputation for working with notable names such as the late Norbert Schwontowski, Berliner Jonathan Meese and Georg Baselitz.

Walk over the Monbijoubrücke bridge to reach the Bode-Museum, one of the five large museums within

ITINERARIES

Berlin, the anti-Expressionist Neue Sachlichkeit (New Objectivity) movement and art from the DDR era and beyond.

Next, head over to **König Gallery** (Alexandrinenstrasse 118-121, www.johannkoenig.de), where prominent Berlin dealer Johann Koenig runs one half of his mini-empire, in the former St Agnes church. It's worth visiting for the architecture as much as the art within – Koening's project space is a harsh, Brutalist-style church, built in the mid 1960s. The space has seen installations and performances by some of the most exciting artists at work in Berlin today, including Alicia Kwade, Jeppe Hein and Katharina Grosse.

From here, take a 15-minute wander down Ritterstrasse towards the grimy heart of Kreuzberg, Kottbusser Tor. Just to the south is the **Künstlerhaus Bethanien** (Kottbusserstrasse 10, www.bethanien.de), a long-running residency/project space where local artists regularly show work.

the city's cultural heart of Museum Island (Museumsinsel) – it's well worth setting a full day aside so that you can explore it properly. This is where you'll find the **Altes Museum** (specialising in classical antiquities, p49); the **Neues Museum** (prehistoric and early historic collections, ethnography and the Egyptian museum, p54); the **Alte Nationalgalerie** (Neoclassical, Romantic, Biedermeier, Impressionist and early Modernist artworks, p48); the **Bode-Museum** (Byzantine and Gothic art of northern and southern Europe, Renaissance and Baroque-era artworks, p49); and the **Pergamon Museum** (containing Islamic and Middle Eastern museums, including the legendary Ishtar Gate, p56).

From here, cross back over Monbijoubrücke and turn left on to Friedrichstrasse, before taking a right on to Reinhardtstrasse. Here, you'll easily spot a large, squat building that looks somewhat brutal and forbidding. This is the **Sammlung Boros** (p71), a former World War II bunker now housing the collection of Berlin art patron Dr Christian Boros. One of the most esoteric and wide-ranging collections of international contemporary art in the city, this historic and starkly impressive building makes for a striking context in which to find some seriously good work. Artists in the collection include luminaries ranging from Ai Weiwei to local husband-and-wife team Awst & Walther, by way of Cosima von Bonin, Olafur Eliasson, Alicja Kwade, Roman Ondák, Michael Sailstorfer, Tomás Saraceno, Thomas Scheibitz, Danh Vo, Cerith Wyn Evans and Thomas Zipp. Booking ahead is essential.

Walk back up Friedrichstrasse towards Oranienburger Tor, cross over into Johannistrasse and it's a short walk to Auguststrasse, which, since the early 1990s, has been one of the unofficial hubs of Mitte's sprawling art world. On the corner of Tucholskystrasse and Auguststrasse, you'll find **Dittrich & Schlechtriem** (Tucholskystrasse 38, www.dittrich-schlechtriem.com), with an esoteric roster of predominantly local artists of a more experimental bent.

Around the corner on Auguststrasse is a red-brick former girls' school, the **Jüdische Mädchenschule** (Auguststrasse 11-13, www.maedchenschule.org). Head upstairs to find the **CWC Gallery** (www.camerawork.de), which specialises in contemporary

König Gallery p41

photography, and the **Michael Fuchs** gallery (www.michael fuchsgalerie.com), on the floor above. Here, the former assembly hall and two classrooms house a lively programme of solo and group exhibitions, mainly of contemporary art.

Head down Auguststrasse and you'll see the white façade of **Kunst-Werke Institute for Contemporary Art** (Auguststrasse 69, www.kw-berlin. de, p69), commonly known as KW. This is a Berlin art institution in every sense, with a penchant for edgy, confrontational programming. It's where you'll find some of the best in avant-garde art from Germany and beyond, with regular interactions with global outfits such as MoMA PS1, Documenta and the Venice Biennale. There's a handy, counter-cultural coffee shop in which you can relax over an espresso and ponder the sheaf of pamphlets, flyers and assorted bumf a visit to KW invariably generates.

Next door is the **ME Collector's Room** (Auguststrasse 68, www. me-berlin.com), the two-storey building housing work from Berlin doctor Thomas Olbricht's personal collection. A hugely enjoyable, intriguing assortment of painting, sculpture, photography, installation and new media from the 16th century to the present day, the collection features work by Thomas Schütte, Eric Fischl, Cindy Sherman, Marlene Dumas and Gerhard Richter, Wolfe von Lenkiewicz, Simmons & Burke, Grayson Perry, Julie Heffernan, Elmgreen & Dragset, Kate McGwire and many more.

Further along, you arrive at one of the city's most progressive galleries, **Eigen + Art** (Auguststrasse 26, www.eigen-art.com, p69), run by Gerd Harry Lybke, a key figure in shaping post-DDR art in Germany. The founder of the famous Leipzig

Eigen + Art

School, Lybke is something of a legend in the city for his discovery of such major figures as Neo Rausch, Stella Hamberg, Uwe Kowski and Matthias Wiescher. Today, he's still pushing boundaries with an eclectic roster of quality artists.

Also on Auguststrasse is one of Berlin's best art bookshops: **Do You Read Me** (no.28, www. doyoureadme.de, p69). A browser's paradise, it features books and magazines covering fashion, art, design, lifestyle, architecture and literature from around the world.

If energy levels permit, cross over to Linienstrasse (it runs parallel to Auguststrasse) for more. Recommendations include **Neugerriemschneider** (Linienstrasse 155, www. neugerriemschneider.de), **Kicken Berlin** (Linienstrasse 161A, www. kicken-gallery.com) and **Galerie Neu** (Linienstrasse 119, www. galerieneu.net). One final heave takes you to nearby Oranienburgerstrasse, and one of Berlin's best-known galleries, **Sprüth Magers** (Oranienburgerstrasse 18, www.spruethmagers.com, p72).

ITINERARIES

Markthalle IX p46

The Food Scene

For first-time visitors, the culinary scene in Berlin can appear somewhat lacking, especially when compared with global hubs such as London or New York.

So, in navigating the metropolis at mealtimes, where best to hunt down a simple snack, blowout feast or just a sausage? Here, we'll take in venues across the city: grand old dining rooms to traditional afternoon *kaffee und kuchen*, international street food pop-ups to specialist shops, markets and much more. Lack of space precludes anything approaching a comprehensive rundown of what's hot and happening – these pages are just the tip of a very big iceberg.

Breakfast here is a big deal. Whether you're up bright and early and fancy a leisurely morning repast, or you've been partying all night and need a final meal before crashing out, Berlin's breakfast culture will see you right. Perhaps one of the most popular spots for *frühstück* (literally 'morning piece') in town right now is **Chipps** (Jägerstrasse 35, 3644 4588, www. chipps.eu) where the emphasis is on the healthy, hearty and herbaceous. While it's a predominantly vegetarian kitchen, Chipps excels at breakfast. One traditional choice to investigate is the self-explanatory *eier im glas* ('eggs in a glass') which can also function as a hangover cure par excellence.

While that's all very well, an alternative to the usual German breakfast table can be found at one of the city's branches of **La Femme**. Head to its Kreuzberg outlet (Kottbusser Damm 77, 5360 4057, www.lafemmeberlin.de) to savour a smorgasbord of morning delights including white cheese, *sucuk* (sausage), olives, eggs and fresh *simit* (the hard, pretzel-shaped sesame-seeded breadstick).

As the heart of the city's Turkish community, Kreuzberg is home to numerous cafés, shops, restaurants and markets. Lots of markets. In fact, Berlin is teeming with open air markets selling wholesome comestibles from around the world. Some are weekly, some bi-weekly, one or two almost daily. Every Tuesday and Friday for example, you can join locals stocking up on delicious fresh produce, snacks and knick-knacks along the sprawling **Türkischer Markt** on Maybachufer (p145).

From unappetizing, greasy boxes of noodles at seemingly every street corner to exquisite, freshly-prepared bibimbap and bánh mì, Berlin's communist past has infused the city's dining scene with a surfeit of flavours from south-east Asia. One of the German capital's most popular Vietnamese food joints is **Yam Yam** (Alte Schönhauser Strasse 6, 2463 2486, www.yamyam-berlin.de) where bibimbap is king – a bowl of steaming, succulent goodness involving rice, meat, kimchi and a fresh fried egg, all waiting to be mashed into a droolworthy mass of comfort food, topped with lashings of spicy sauce.

Now that you're in the heart of Mitte, subject yourself to the city's famed *Currywurst*, a sliced bratwurst covered in an oleaginous gloop of tomato ketchup with curry powder. Berlin, for some reason, wears its curry-sauce-sausage heritage with pride although there are rumours that the dish actually originates from Hamburg. (It's best not to bring this up.) Go where the locals go – in every sense, judging by the smell – under the Eberswalderstrasse railway arches, and get into the queue at the legendary **Konnopke's Imbiss** (p80), where the speciality has been doled out for decades.

Torstrasse, the long street leading from the heartlands of east Berlin into the city centre, has dozens of lunch options. Try **3 Minutes sur Mer** (Torstrasse 167, 6730 2052, www.3minutessurmer.de), a cosy bistro with a menu of unctuous and sumptuous, French-inflected flavours with a contemporary twist. Speaking of contemporary twists, fewer are more contemporary – if not twisted – as the vast, bright new multipurpose space underneath **Soho House** (p168) on Torstrasse called **The Store** (www.thestore-berlin.com). It serves up delicious organic foods, juices, wines and coffees in a setting that's ideal for a light, laid-back and stylish lunch.

Pretty much every street in the city boasts at least a coffee shop or a bakery and the tradition of taking a leisurely afternoon break is one of the most appealing aspects of Berlin life. For a quirky twist, try Mitte's **Princess Cheesecake** (p66) where the impossibly rich and decadent creations range from beetroot-flavoured chocolate cheesecake to homemade truffles

Konnopke's Imbiss p45

with Earl Grey-flavoured ganache. If you're after something more, well, old-school, then **Anna Blume** (p79) should fit the bill. Of the gazillions of similarly quaint, charming and floral coffee shops that abound, this one seems to have the edge on the competition, thanks to its chocolate-box atmosphere, killer cakes and insanely addictive coffee.

Till recently, Berlin had never quite mastered international cuisine. Just ask anyone who has tried to find a decent curry. Yet these days, a global influx of expats is redefining the parameters of the Berliner palate. Pop-up events such as the fortnightly **Bite Club** (Hoppetosse by Badeschiff, Eichenstrasse 4, biteclub.de) or the colossal array of food stalls and barbecue at Kreuzberg's **Markthalle IX** (p129) are more like open air street parties than conventional dining experiences. And there are some adventurous new menus in town. **Dottir** (p56) is small, appealing and shabby-chic restaurant with a tasting menu inspired by Icelandic cuisine. The cooking and quality of ingredients make for a quietly sensational meal. Across the world, yet less than a kilometre away, is a restaurant creating a real buzz, **Zenkichi** (Johannisstrasse 20, 24 630 810, www.zenkichi.de) which could be described as a subterranean Tokyo brasserie. It's a gustatory experience hitherto unrivalled in the city – and the sake selection is pretty good too.

The culinary revolution has even filtered as far down as shabby Neukölln where the slick, hipster-magnet **Industry Standard** (Sonnenallee 83, 62 72 77 32, www.industry-standard.de) has an esoteric Euro-bistro menu that foregrounds quality and diversity.

With all these cafés, pop-ups, restaurants and shops, Berlin is moving into a new era of enjoyment, fun and quality. Forget the fatty pork knuckles and steamed cabbage mindset of the past – but bring a spare stomach on your next trip.

Berlin by Area

Brandenburger Tor p52

Mitte

Historically, the centre, Mitte – meaning 'middle' – floundered in a no-man's-land between East and West. But now Mitte is right back in the swing of things. It contains many of Berlin's biggest sights: the Brandenburg Gate (Brandenburger Tor), the TV Tower (Fernsehturm) and the magnificent UNESCO World Heritage Site of Museum Island (Museumsinsel), which is in the midst of an epic overhaul, scheduled to be fully completed in 2025. But there's much more to this area than ticking off the sights – cool galleries, shops and bars abound.

Unter der Linden & Museumsinsel

Unter der Linden runs east from the Brandenburg Gate, passing museums and embassies, opera houses and cathedrals. The name comes from the lime trees (Linden) that shade the central walkway. Its 18th- and 19th-century neoclassical and Baroque buildings were mostly rubble after World War II, but the majority have been restored. The Linden arrives at Museumsinsel, the island in the Spree where Berlin was born and now a World Heritage Site. It was also the site of the GDR's parliament complex, the Palast der Republik. After lengthy arguments and occupations, the asbestos-ridden Palast was finally demolished in 2009, to be replaced by a reconstruction of the old Prussian City Palace. At the time of writing, the new Stadtschloss is set to be completed in 2019.

Sights & museums

Alte Nationalgalerie
Bodestrasse 1-3 (266 424242, www.smb. museum/ang). U6, S1, S2, S5, S7, S25, S75 Friedrichstrasse or S5, S7, S75 Hackescher Markt. **Open** 10am-6pm

Tue, Wed, Fri-Sun; 10am-8pm Thur.
Admission €8; €4 reductions.
Map p51 D3 ❶

With its ceiling and wall paintings, fabric wallpapers and marble staircase, the Old National Gallery is a sparkling home to one of the largest collections of 19th-century art and sculpture in Germany. Friedrich Stüler was commissioned to design the building to house the collection of wealthy industrialist JHW Wagener in 1861, who donated it to the Prussian state. The 440 paintings and 80 sculptures span the period from Goethe to the early Modern, with Romantic German artists such as Adolph Menzel, Caspar David Friedrich, Max Liebermann and Carl Spitzweg well represented. There are also some first-rate works from Manet, Monet and Rodin. Although the gallery is worth a visit, don't expect to see any kind of definitive German national collection.

Altes Museum

Lustgarten (266 424242, www.smb. museum/am). U6, S1, S2, S5, S7, S25, S75 Friedrichstrasse or S5, S7, S75 Hackescher Markt. **Open** 10am-6pm Tue, Wed, Fri-Sun; 10am-8pm Thur.
Admission €10; €5 reductions.
Map p51 D3 ❷

Opened as the Royal Museum in 1830, the Old Museum originally housed all the art treasures on Museumsinsel. It was designed by Schinkel and is considered to be one of his finest buildings, with a particularly magnificent entrance rotunda, where vast neon letters declare that 'All Art has been Contemporary'. Now that the Egyptian galleries have moved into the Neues Museum round the corner, this building houses a new exhibition on ancient worlds, with an excellent look at the Etruscans and Romans on the top floor. The main floor shows off the collection of classical antiquities, including a world-class selection of Greek art, pride of place going to the superlative third-century bronze, *The Praying Boy*.

Berliner Dom

Lustgarten 1 (2026 9136, guided tours 2026 9119, www.berliner-dom.de). U6, S1, S2, S5, S7, S25, S75 Friedrichstrasse or S5, S7, S75 Hackescher Markt. **Open** Apr-Sept 9am-7pm Mon-Sat; noon-8pm Sun. Oct-Mar 9am-7pm Mon-Sat; noon-7pm Sun. **Admission** €7; €4 reductions; free under-18s. **Map** p51 D3 ❸

The dramatic Berlin Cathedral, which celebrated its centenary in 2005, is now finally healed of its war wounds. Built in Italian Renaissance style, it was destroyed during World War II and remained a ruin until 1973, when extensive restoration work began. It has always looked fine from the outside, but now that the internal work is complete, it is fully restored to its former glory.

Crammed with detail and containing dozens of statues of eminent German Protestants, its lush 19th-century interior is hardly the perfect acoustic space for the frequent concerts that are held here (even on the colossal organ), but it's worth a visit to see the crypt containing around 90 sarcophagi of notables from the Hohenzollern dynasty, or to clamber up for splendid views from the cupola. Call to book a guided tour.

Bode-Museum

Monbijoubrücke (266 424242, www. smb.museum/bm). U6, S1, S2, S5, S7, S25, S75 Friedrichstrasse or S5, S7, S75 Hackescher Markt. **Open** 10am-6pm Tue, Wed, Fri-Sun; 10am-8pm Thur. **Admission** €8; €4 reductions.
Map p50 C3 ❹

Built by Berlin architect Ernst Eberhard von Ihne in 1904, the Bode-Museum reopened after a thorough renovation in 2006. It was originally intended by Wilhelm von Bode as a home for art from the beginnings of Christendom, and now contains the Byzantine Collection, Sculpture Collection and also the Numismatic Collection. The neo-Baroque great

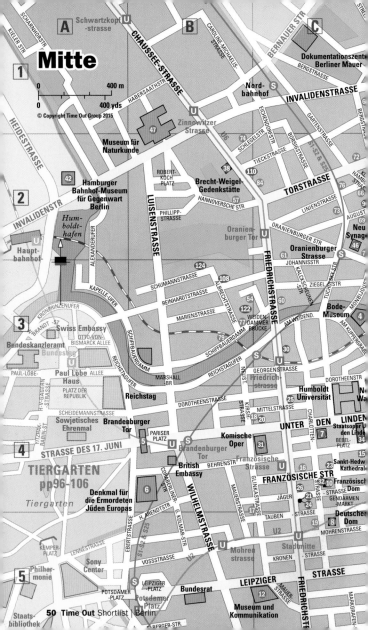

Mitte

	A	B	C

1

Schwartzkopf-strasse

Dokumentationszentrum Berliner Mauer

400 m
400 yds

© Copyright Time Out Group 2015

KIELER STR
SCHARNHORSTR
CHAUSSEE-STRASSE
CAROLINE-MICHAELIS-STRASSE
BERNAUER STR
BERGSTRASSE

HEIDESTRASSE
HABERSAATHSTR
Nord-bahnhof
INVALIDENSTRASSE

47
Zinnowitzer Strasse

Museum für Naturkunde

EICHENDORFFSTR
SCHLEGELSTR
TIECKSTRASSE
GARTENSTRASSE
S-52 & S26

74
110
38
Brecht-Weigel-Gedenkstätte
TORSTRASSE
76
66
9

2

INVALIDENSTR
42
Hamburger Bahnhof-Museum für Gegenwart Berlin
LUISENSTRASSE
ROBERT-KOCH-PLATZ
PHILLIPP-STRASSE
HANNOVERSCHE STR
57
LINIENSTRASSE
AUGUST
69
Neu Synag
46

Humboldt-hafen
ALEXANDERUFER
84
Oranien-burger Tor
ORANIENBURGER STR
Oranienburger Strasse
JOHANNISSTR
KALCKSCHEUNEN-STR
ZIEGEL STR
TUCHOLSKY
MONBIJOUS

Haupt-bahnhof
KRONPRINZENUFER
KAPELLE-UFER
124
SCHUMANNSTRASSE
108
REINHARDTSTRASSE
MARIENSTRASSE
54
122
WEIDEN-DAMMER-BRÜCKE
77
AM WEIDEND.
60
FRIEDRICHSTRASSE
Bode-Museum
AM KUPFERGRABEN
4

3

BRANDT
37
Swiss Embassy
OTTO-VON-BISMARCK ALLEE
SCHIFFBAUERDAMM
SCHIFFBAUERDAMM
REICHSTAGUFER
30
GEORGENSTRASSE
DOROTHEENSTR

Bundeskanzleramt
Bundestag
Paul Löbe Haus
PLATZ DER REPUBLIK
MARSHALL BR
REICHSTAGUFER
Friedrich-strasse
Humboldt Universität
N Wa

PAUL-LÖBE-
OTTO-VON-
REICHSTAGUFER
DOROTHEENSTRASSE
NUST
KIRSH-STRASSE
MITTELSTRASSE
25
CHARLOTTEN-
DOROTHEENSTR

Reichstag
SCHEIDEMANNSTRASSE
18
20
UNTER DEN LINDEN
7
Staatsoper U den Linden
BEBEL-PLATZ
34

4

Sowjetisches Ehrenmal
Brandenburger Tor
5
Pariser Platz
Brandenburger Tor
Komische Oper
31
Französische Strasse
16
Sankt-Hedw Kathedrale

STRASSE DES 17. JUNI

TIERGARTEN
pp96-106
Tiergarten
British Embassy
BEHRENSTR
FRANZÖSISCHE STR
Französisch Dom
26
2
GENDARMEN-MARKT

Denkmal für die Ermordeten Jüden Europas
6
COLA-BERLINER-STR
H. ARENDT-STR
WILHELMSTRASSE
MAUERSTRASSE
GLINKASTRASSE
JÄGER STRASSE
21
24
Deutscher Dom
8

5

Philhar-monie
KEMPER-PLATZ
LENNESTRASSE
Sony Center
POTSDAMER-PLATZ
Potsdamer Platz
EBERTSTRASSE
ST-52 & S25
H. KOLMAR-STR
VOSSSTRASSE
Bundesrat
LEIPZIGER
11
TAUBEN STRASSE
KRONEN-STRASSE
U2
Mohren strasse
Stadtmitte
U
19
MOHRENSTRASSE
STRASSE
FRIEDRICHSTR

Staats-bibliothek
50 Time Out Shortlist | Berlin
BERGER-STR
LEIPZIGER STRASSE
Museum und Kommunikation
12
MAUER STRASSE
MARKGRAFEN

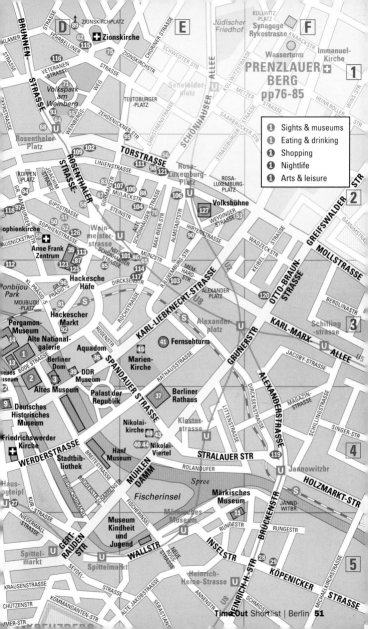

dome, the basilica hall and the glorious cupola have been carefully restored to keep up with modern curatorial standards, but they retain their magnificence. Most impressively, despite having one of the world's largest sculpture collections and more than half a million pieces in the coin collection, the museum somehow retains a totally uncluttered feel, and the sculptures stand free from off-putting glass cases. In particular, make sure you look out for the wall-length Apse Mosaic from AD 545 and the 14th-century Mannheim High Altar.

Brandenburger Tor

Pariser Platz. U55, S1, S2
Brandenburger Tor. **Map** p50 B4 ⑤
The focal point of Unter den Linden's western end is the Brandenburger Tor (Brandenburg Gate). Constructed in 1791, and designed by Carl Gotthard Langhans after the Propylaea gateway into ancient Athens, the gate was built as a triumphal arch celebrating Prussia's capital city. It was initially called the Friedenstor (Gate of Peace) and is the only city gate remaining from Berlin's original 18.

The Quadriga statue, a four-horse chariot driven by Victory and designed by Johann Gottfried Schadow, sits on top of the gate. It has had an eventful life. When Napoleon conquered Berlin in 1806, he carted the Quadriga off to Paris and held it hostage until his defeat in 1814. The Tor was badly damaged during World War II and, during subsequent renovations, the GDR removed the Prussian Iron Cross and turned the Quadriga around so that the chariot faced west.

The current Quadriga is actually a 1958 copy of the 18th-century original, and was stranded in no-man's-land for 30 years. It saw further repair after some overly exuberant youths climbed up on the Tor to celebrate the fall of the Wall. The Iron Cross was replaced and the Quadriga was turned back to face into Mitte again.

Denkmal für die ermordeten Juden Europas

Cora-Berliner-Strasse 1 (2639 4336, www.holocaust-denkmal.de). U2, S1, S2, S25 Potsdamer Platz. **Open** Field of stelae 24hrs daily. Information centre Apr-Sept 10am-8pm daily. Oct-Mar 10am-7pm daily. **Admission** free.
Map p50 B4 ⑥
After many years of controversy, Peter Eisenmann's 'field of stelae' – 2,711 of them, arranged in undulating rows on 19,704sq m (212,000sq ft) of ground – with its attendant information centre to memorialise the Murdered Jews of Europe, was opened in 2005. Each of the concrete slabs has its own foundation, and they tilt at differing angles. The effect is (no doubt deliberately) reminiscent of the packed headstones in Prague's Old Jewish Cemetery. There's no vantage point or overview: to fully engage with the structure you need to walk into it. It's spooky in places, especially on overcast days and near the middle of the monument, where it's easy to feel a sense of confinement. The information centre is at the south-east corner of the site, mostly underground. It's like a secular crypt, containing a sombre presentation of facts and figures about the Holocaust's Jewish victims.

Deutsche Bank KunstHalle

Unter den Linden 13-15 (202 0930, www.deutsche-bank-kunsthalle.de). U6 Französische Strasse. **Open** 10am-8pm daily **Admission** €4; €3 reductions; free under-12s. Free to all Mon.
Map p50 C4 ⑦
Deutsche Bank took over management of this space from the Guggenheim in April 2013 and now holds four shows a year, with guest curators invited to build exhibitions from the bank's vast corporate art collection.

Deutscher Dom

Gendarmenmarkt, entrance in Markgrafenstrasse (2273 0431). U2, U6 Stadtmitte. **Open** May-Sept 10am-7pm

Tue-Sun. Oct-Apr 10am-6pm Tue-Sun. Guided tours every half hour 11am-5pm; call first for English- or French-speaking guide. **Admission** free.
Map p50 C5 ❽

The neoclassical domed tower of this church – and the identical tower of the Französischer Dom on the other side of the square – were built in 1780-85 by Carl von Gontard for Frederick the Great, in imitation of Santa Maria in Montesanto and Santa Maria del Miracoli in Rome. The Deutscher Dom was intended for Berlin's Lutheran community. The dome is topped by a 7m (23ft) gilded statue representing Virtue. Badly damaged by Allied bombing in the war, the church and tower burned down in 1943, and were restored in the 1980s and '90s.

Inside is a permanent exhibition on the history of Germany's parliamentary system, from the 1848 revolution through the suspension of parliamentary politics by the Nazis, up to the present day. Visitors are encouraged to consider the role of parliaments throughout the modern world, but there are no translations, so to get much out of this without a guided tour your German must be up to scratch.

Deutsches Historisches Museum

Zeughaus, Unter den Linden 2 (203 040, www.dhm.de). U6 Französische Strasse.
Open 10am-6pm daily. **Admission** €8; €4 reductions; free under-18s.
Map p51 D4 ❾

The permanent exhibition in the Zeughaus provides an exhaustive blast through German history from 100 BC to the present day, divided chronologically into significant eras. The museum originally had trouble raising the funds to buy historical objects, but there's enough here now for the exhibits to work on their own, without the need for an overarching narrative. German nationalism becomes the focus once you enter the 19th century, and, later on, more than one room is dedicated to the Nazi era. The DHM has succeeded admirably in looking the past straight in the eye, although the attempt to be impartial means that it's sometimes factual to the extreme. Temporary exhibitions are housed in the gorgeous IM Pei building.

BERLIN BY AREA

Hamburger Bahnhof – Museum für Gegenwart p61

Französischer Dom & Hugenottenmuseum

Gendarmenmarkt (229 1760, www. franzoesischer-dom.de). U2, U6 Stadtmitte. **Open** Church noon-5pm Mon-Sat; after service-5pm Sun. Tower 10am-6pm Tue-Sun. **Admission** Church free. Tower €3; €1 reductions. No credit cards. **Map** p50 C4 ⑩

Built in the early 18th century for Berlin's 6,000-plus-strong French Protestant community, the church (known as the Französischen Friedrichstadtkirche) was later given a Baroque domed tower, as was the Deutscher Dom across the square. The tower, with its fine views over Mitte, is purely decorative and unconsecrated – and not part of the modest church, which has a separate entrance at the western end.

An exhibition on the history of the French Protestants in France and Berlin-Brandenburg is displayed within the building. The museum chronicles the religious persecution suffered by Calvinists (note the bust of Calvin on the outside of the church) and their subsequent immigration to Berlin after 1685, at the behest of the Hohenzollerns. The development of the Huguenot community is also detailed, with paintings, documents and artefacts. One part of the museum is devoted to the church's history, particularly the effects of World War II – it was bombed during a Sunday service in 1944 and remained a ruin until the mid 1980s.

Märkisches Museum

Am Köllnischen Park 5 (240 020 171, www.stadtmuseum.de). U2 Märkisches Museum. **Open** 10am-6pm Tue-Sun. **Admission** €5; €3 reductions. Free 1st Wed of mth. **Map** p51 E5 ⑪

This extensive, curious and somewhat old-fashioned museum traces the history of Berlin through a wide range of historical artefacts. Different sections examine themes such as Berlin as a newspaper city, women in Berlin's history, city guilds, intellectual Berlin and the military. There are models of

the city at different times, and some good paintings, including works by members of the Brücke group. It ends with a particularly charming section about traditional toys, with plenty of hands-on exhibits.

Museum für Kommunikation

Leipziger Strasse 16 (202 940, www. mfk-berlin.de). U2 Mohrenstrasse or U2, U6 Stadtmitte. **Open** 9am-8pm Tue; 9am-5pm Wed-Fri; 10am-6pm Sat, Sun. **Admission** €4; €2 reductions; free under-17s. No credit cards. **Map** p50 C5 ⑫

A direct descendant of the world's first postal museum (founded in 1872), this collection covers a bit more than mere stamps. It traces the development of telecommunications up to the internet era, though philatelists might want to head straight to the basement and ogle the 'Blue Mauritius', one of the world's rarest stamps.

Neues Museum

Bodestrasse 1 (266 424242, www.smb. museum/nm). U6, S1, S2, S5, S7, S25, S75 Friedrichstrasse or S5, S7, S75 Hackescher Markt. **Open** 10am-6pm Tue, Wed, Fri-Sun; 10am-8pm Thur. Entry by timed ticket. **Admission** €12; €6 reductions. **Map** p51 D3 ⑬

Reopened in 2009 after extensive remodelling, this stunning building houses the Egyptian Museum & Papyrus Collection, the Museum of Prehistory & Early History and artefacts from the Collection of Classical Antiquities. The most famous object is the bust of the Egyptian queen, Nefertiti (which Germany refuses to return to Egypt despite repeated requests), and the skull of a Neanderthal from Le Moustier, France. The Museum für Vor- und Frühgeschichte (Prehistory & Early History), which traces the evolution of Homo sapiens from 1,000,000 BC to the Bronze Age, has among its highlights reproductions (and some originals) of Heinrich Schliemann's famous treasure of ancient Troy, including works in

Chipperfield's Museum Island

A tapestry of textures.

Considering it catapulted David Chipperfield from merely the front rank of the world's architects into the celebrity realm of the 'starchitect', won the 2011 Mies van der Rohe Award for Architecture and saw its mastermind awarded both a knighthood and a RIBA prize, what's surprising about the restoration of the **Neues Museum** (see p54) is how understated it is. It's the first triumph in his masterplan for the Museumsinsel, which has taken more than 15 years.

Badly damaged by Allied bombing in World War II, the Neues Museum was left to rot under the communist regime despite its prominent location on the capital's Museum Island. Its makeover is breathtakingly elegant, chaste and discreet. The biggest single intervention is a gargantuan, blank, modernist

staircase, but perhaps the most beautiful space is the top deck of the five-storey concrete 'cage' of slim pillars, inserted into an existing courtyard without touching the sides; a light-filled atrium containing a handful of Egyptian busts.

Chipperfield is so beloved in Berlin, he's been described as 'one of Germany's greatest architects' – even though he's British. He continues work on the **James Simon Gallery**, which will act as a new unified entrance and ticket hall for all the museums on the island, and has begun a redesign of the **Neue Nationalgalerie**. His own stark office on Joachimstrasse was awarded a RIBA award in 2013, and fans of his work should check out the imposing, ten-storey **Parkside** apartment block, right on the edge of the Tiergarten, behind Potsdamer Platz.

ceramic and gold, as well as weaponry. Look out also for the sixth-century BC grave of a girl buried with a gold coin in her mouth. Information is available in English. Entry is within a half-hour ticketed time slot, so book online to skip the queues.

Pergamonmuseum

Am Kupfergraben (266 424242, www. smb.museum/pm). U6, S1, S2, S5, S7, S25, S75 Friedrichstrasse or S5, S7, S75 Hackescher Markt. **Open** 10am-6pm Mon-Wed, Fri-Sun; 10am-8pm Thur. **Admission** €12; €6 reductions. **Map** p51 D3 ⑭

One of the world's major archaeological museums. Its treasures, comprising the Antikensammlung (Collection of Classical Antiquities) and the Vorderasiatisches Museum (Museum of Near Eastern Antiquities), contain three major draws. The star attraction is the Hellenistic Pergamon Altar, dating from 170-159 BC; huge as it is, the museum's partial reconstruction is only a third of the original's size. In an adjoining room, and even more architecturally impressive, is the towering Roman Market Gate of Miletus (29m/95ft wide and almost 17m/56ft high), erected in AD 120. This leads through to the third of the big attractions: the extraordinary blue and ochre tiled Gate of Ishtar and the Babylonian Processional Street, dating from the reign of King Nebuchadnezzar (605-562 BC). There are plenty of other gems to see, including some stunning Assyrian reliefs.

The Pergamon is also now home to the Museum für Islamische Kunst (Museum of Islamic Art), which takes up some 14 rooms in the southern wing. The wide-ranging collection includes applied arts, crafts, books and architectural details from the eighth to the 19th centuries. Entrance to the museum is included in the overall admission price, as is an excellent audio guide.

Ongoing renovation means the Pergamon Altar is closed until 2019.

Sankt-Hedwigs-Kathedrale

Bebelplatz (203 4810, www.hedwigs-kathedrale.de). U2 Hausvogteiplatz or U6 Französische Strasse. **Open** 10am-5pm Mon-Sat; 1-5pm Sun. **Admission** free. Guided tours €1.50. **Map** p50 C4 ⑮

Constructed in 1747 for Berlin's Catholic minority, this circular Knobelsdorff creation was bombed out during the war and only reconsecrated in 1963. Its modernised interior contains a split-level double altar with a ribbed dome. The crypt holds the remains of Bernhard Lichtenberg, who preached here against the Nazis, was arrested, and died while being transported to Dachau in 1943.

Eating & drinking

Borchardt

Französische Strasse 47 (8188 6262). U6 Französische Strasse. **Open** 11.30am-late daily. €€€. **Brasserie** **Map** p50 C4 ⑯

People come to Borchardt not for the respectable French food, but for the clannish atmosphere, where you can often spot a film star or politico. Ideal if you fancy a dozen oysters and a fillet of pike-perch or beef after a cultural evening nearby.

Café Nö!

Glinkastrasse 23 (201 0871, www.cafe-noe.de). U6 Französische Strasse. **Open** noon-1am Mon-Fri; 7pm-1am Sat. €€. **Wine bar Map** p50 B/C4 ⑰

This unassuming but right-on wine bar with simple and wholesome meals is owned by a former GDR rock musician now continuing his family's gastronomy tradition. Given the mostly bland or overpriced restaurants in the neighbourhood, this is a genuine pearl.

Dottir

Mittelstrasse 40 (330 060 760, www.dottirberlin.com). U6, S1, S2, S5, S7, S25, S75 Friedrichstrasse. **Open** 6pm-late Tue-Sat. €€€. **Scandinavian** **Map** p50 C4 ⑱

Chef Victoria Eliasdottir (daughter of artist Olafur Eliasson) serves chic New Nordic cuisine, with the accent on light, fresh flavours cut with Icelandic-influenced pickles and vinegars. It's located in one of the last remaining unrenovated buildings in the district, and has managed to keep its impeccable 1950s shabby-chic charm intact.

Newton Bar

Charlottenstrasse 57 (2029 5421, www. newton-bar.de). U6 Französische Strasse. **Open** 10am-late daily. **Bar Map** p50 C5 ⑲
An entire wall of this large bar is dedicated to a series of Helmut Newton's black and white nudes. Stick to the classics, martinis or a good single malt, settle into the cosy seating and watch the world go by from the heated terrace.

Shopping

Berlin Story

Unter den Linden 40 (2045 3842, www. berlin-story.de). U6 Französische Strasse. **Open** 10am-7pm Mon-Sat; 10am-6pm Sun. **Map** p50 C4 ⑳
You won't find a better selection of Berlin-related books in German and English: everything from novels with Berlin settings to non-fiction volumes on the history and culture of the city.

Brille 54

Friedrichstrasse 71 (2094 6060, www. brille54.de). U6 Französische Strasse. **Open** 10am-7pm Mon-Fri; 10am-6pm Sat. **Map** p50 C4 ㉑
This small, sleek space in Quartier 206 was designed by hot young local architects Plajer & Franz. Lots of smart international brands are found here, including Lindberg, Thom Browne and Oliver Peoples.

Contemporary Fine Arts

Am Kupfergraben 10 (288 7870, www. cfa-berlin.com). U6, S1, S2, S3, S5, S7, S75 Friedrichstrasse. **Open** 11am-6pm Tue-Fri; 11am-4pm Sat. No credit cards. **Map** p51 D3/4 ㉒

Bruno Brunnet, Nicole Hackert and Philipp Haverkampf's gallery is among the swishest in Berlin. The museum-like space (designed by David Chipperfield) shows major stars such as Georg Baselitz and Norbert Schwontkowski, alongside YBA luminaries (Cecily Brown, Chris Ofili) and well-known German artists (Daniel Richter, Jonathan Meese).

Corner Berlin

Französische Strasse 40 (2067 0940, www.thecornerberlin.de). U6 Französische Strasse. **Open** 10.30am-7.30pm Mon-Fri; 10am-7pm Sat. **Map** p50 C4 ㉓
Typically plush surroundings for this luxury 'lifestyle' shop. There's designer nightclub clobber for both sexes: Rick Owens biker jackets and studded Christian Louboutin slippers for the boys; silken Lanvin tunics and Balenciaga handbags for the girls.

Departmentstore Quartier 206

Friedrichstrasse 71 (2094 6500, www. dsq206.com). U6 Französische Strasse. **Open** 11am-8pm Mon-Fri; 10am-6pm Sat. **Map** p50 C4 ㉔
This ultra-luxe store occupies the first floor of IM Pei studio's neo-art deco building known for its elaborate Byzantine-style tiled flooring. Definitive pieces are carefully selected from cult labels such as Alexander Wang and Vivienne Westwood, alongside cosmetics and furnishings from the likes of perfumier Jul et Mad and craftsman Alexander Lamont.

Dussmann das KulturKaufhaus

Friedrichstrasse 90 (2025 1111, www. kulturkaufhaus.de). U6, S1, S2, S5, S7, S25, S75 Friedrichstrasse. **Open** 9am-midnight Mon-Fri; 9am-11.30pm Sat. **Map** p50 C4 ㉕
Intended as a 'cultural department store', this spacious five-floor retailer has books, magazines, CDs and DVDs.

The huge English-language section has an excellent selection of cookbooks and travel literature.

Galeries Lafayette

Friedrichstrasse 76-78 (209 480, www. galerieslafayette.de). U6 Französische Strasse. **Open** 10am-8pm Mon-Sat. **Map** p50 C4 ㉖

Galeries Lafayette caters across the board, with sophisticated labels such as Ferragamo and Agnès B for genteel Charlottenburg mums, while French rock-chic from Sandro and the Kooples caters for a younger crowd. As to be expected, the food halls are excellent, with a fine butcher selling Charolais beef and capons from Burgundy.

Schinkel Pavilion

Oberwallstrasse 1 (2088 6444, www. schinkelpavillon.de). U2 Hausvogteiplatz. **Open** 2-8pm Thur, Fri; noon-6pm Sat, Sun. **Map** p51 D4 ㉗

This octagonal pavilion with its wall-to-ceiling glass, designed to DDR specifications in 1969, shows all manner of installation, sculpture and performance art. Philippe Parreno, Douglas Gordon and James Franco have appeared recently.

Nightlife

Sage Club

Köpenicker Strasse 76 (no phone, www. sage-club.de). U8 Heinrich-Heine-Strasse. **Map** p51 F5 ㉘

A labyrinthine complex of half a dozen dancefloors accessed via the north-side entrance to Heinrich-Heine-Strasse U-Bahn station, the Sage Club caters to a relatively young, rock-oriented crowd. It is only reliably open on Thursdays for rock night: an unpretentious affair where skinny jeans and leather jackets is the uniform of choice.

Tresor

Köpenicker Strasse 70 (no phone, www. tresorberlin.de). U8 Heinrich-Heine-Strasse. **Map** p51 F5 ㉙

Galeries Lafayette

Berlin's original techno club is housed in what was formerly the main central-heating power station for East Berlin. The colossal location is breath-taking, but only a tiny portion of the vast space is in use. The experience of the basement floor is one you'll not forget; a black hole occasionally punctuated by flashing strobes with some of the loudest, hardest techno it's humanly possible to hear.

Arts & leisure

Admiralspalast

Friedrichstrasse 101 (tickets 4799 7499, www.admiralspalast.de). U6, S1, S2, S5, S7, S25, S75 Friedrichstrasse.
Map p50 C3 ③⓪
One of the few original Weimar revue theatres left in Berlin, Admiralspalast was home to the GDR Berlin State Opera during the post-war years. Threatened with demolition in the late 1990s, it was restored and, in 2009, was the first venue in Germany to stage Mel Brooks' Nazi-lampooning *The Producers*.

Komische Oper

Behrenstrasse 55-57 (202 600, tickets 4799 7400, www.komische-oper-berlin.de). U6 Französische Strasse.
Map p50 C4 ③①
Despite its name, the Komische Oper puts on a broader range than just comic works. Founded in 1947, it made its reputation by breaking with the old operatic tradition of 'costumed concerts' – singers standing around on stage – and putting an emphasis on 'opera as theatre', with real acting skill demanded of its young ensemble.

Konzerthaus

Gendarmenmarkt 2 (2030 92101, www.konzerthaus.de). U6 Französische Strasse. **Map** p50 C4 ③②
This 1821 architectural gem by Schinkel was all but destroyed during the war. Lovingly restored, it reopened in 1984 with three main concert spaces. Organ recitals in the large hall are a treat, played on the massive 5,811-pipe Jehmlich organ.

Maxim Gorki Theater

Am Festungsgraben 2 (2022 1115, www.gorki.de). U6, S1, S2, S5, S7, S25, S75 Friedrichstrasse. **Map** p50 C3 ③③

Expect new interpretations of classical and modern dramas, as well as adaptations from films and novels, with the result that the atmosphere alone is often enough to transcend the language barrier.

Staatsoper Unter den Linden

Unter den Linden 7 (203 540, tickets 2035 4555, www.staatsoper-berlin.de). U2 Hausvogteiplatz. **Map** p50 C4 ③④
The Staatsoper was founded as Prussia's Royal Court Opera in 1742 and designed by Knobelsdorff along the lines of a Greek temple. Although the present building dates from 1955, the façade faithfully copies the original, twice destroyed in World War II. Ongoing renovation should end in October 2017; until then the company are performing at the Schiller Theater in Charlottenburg (Bismarckstrasse 110).

Alexanderplatz & the Scheunenviertel

While the part of Mitte south of the River Spree has a little more in the way of Berlin's iconic sights, the north bank is the better side of the river for eating and drinking. The shopping's pretty good as well.

Sights & museums

Anne Frank Zentrum

Rosenthaler Strasse 39 (288 865 610, www.annefrank.de). U8 Weinmeisterstrasse. **Open** 10am-6pm Tue-Sun. **Admission** €5; €3 reductions; €12 families; free under-10s. No credit cards. **Map** p51 D2 ③⑤
This permanent exhibition about the life and death of Anne Frank opened in 2006 and is a co-project with the Anne Frank House in Amsterdam. Pictures, collages, films and special objects describe the world of the diarist and her family in the context of National Socialism, the persecution of the Jews and World War II.

AquaDom & Sea Life

*Spandauer Strasse 3 (992 800, www.
visitsealife.com/berlin). S5, S7, S75
Hackescher Markt.* **Open** 10am-6pm
daily. **Admission** €17.50; €12.50
reductions. **Map** p51 D3 ③⑥

Billed as two attractions in one, both
involving lots of water and plenty
of fish. Sea Life leads you through 13
themed aquaria offering fish in different habitats. The AquaDom is the
world's largest free-standing aquarium – a space age tuboid that looks
like it might have just landed from
some alien planet. A lift takes you
up through the middle of this giant
cylindrical fishtank – a million litres
of saltwater that is home to 2,500
colourful creatures, and enfolded by
the atrium of the Radisson Blu hotel
(p167). Unfortunately, only the staff
are allowed to scuba-dive through the
tank to feed the fish.

Berliner Rathaus

*Rathausstrasse 15 (guided tours
9026 2411). U2, U5, U8, S5, S7, S75
Alexanderplatz.* **Open** 9am-6pm Mon-
Fri. Guided tours by appointment.
Admission free. **Map** p51 E4 ③⑦

This magnificent building was constructed of terracotta brick during
the 1860s in an Italian Renaissance
pastiche. The history of Berlin up
to that point is illustrated in a series
of 36 reliefs on the façade. During
Communist times, it served as East
Berlin's town hall – which made its old
nickname, Rotes Rathaus ('Red Town
Hall'), after the colour of the façade,
doubly fitting. West Berlin's city government workers moved here from
their town hall, Rathaus Schöneberg, in
1991. Entry is restricted to small parts
of the building; bring some ID.

Brecht-Weigel-
Gedenkstätte

*Chausseestrasse 125 (200 571 844,
www.adk.de/de/archiv/gedenkstaetten).
U6 Oranienburger Tor.* **Open** Guided
tours (every 30mins) 2-3.30pm Tue;

5-6.30pm Thur; 10am-3.30pm Sat;
11am-6pm Sun; and by appointment.
Admission €5; €2.50 reductions.
No credit cards. **Map** p50 B2 ③⑧

Brecht's home from 1948 until his death
in 1956 has been preserved exactly as
he left it. Tours of the house (phone in
advance for an English tour) give interesting insights into the life and reading
habits of the playwright. The window
at which he worked overlooked the
grave of Hegel in the neighbouring
cemetery. Brecht's wife, actress Helene
Weigel, continued living here until her
death in 1971. The Brecht archives are
kept upstairs.

DDR Museum

*Karl Liebknecht Strasse 1 (847 123
731, www.ddr-museum.de). S5, S7, S75
Hackescher Markt.* **Open** 10am-8pm Mon-
Fri, Sun; 10am-10pm Sat. **Admission**
€6; €4 reductions. **Map** p51 D3 ③⑨

Bright blue neon signage and a
Trabant in the window welcome you
into 'one of Europe's most interactive
museums!' This is Ostalgia in action.
Touchscreens, sound effects and even
the 'DDR Game' mean that the more dis-
tasteful aspects of East German life are
cheerfully glossed over. The museum is
essentially a collection of GDR memorabilia, from travel tickets to Palast der
Republik serviettes. Climb inside the
Trabi or sit on a GDR couch in a GDR
living room where you can watch GDR
TV. Even the much feared Stasi get the
interactive family treatment too – you
can pretend to be a Stasi officer and lis-
ten in on a bugged flat. Take it all with a
large pinch of salt.

Ephraim-Palais

*Poststrasse 16 (2400 2162, www.
stadtmuseum.de). U2, U5, U8, S5,
S7, S75 Alexanderplatz.* **Open** 10am-
6pm Tue, Thur-Sun; 10am-8pm Wed.
Admission €5; €3 reductions; free
under-18s. Free 1st Wed of mth.
No credit cards. **Map** p51 E4 ④⓪

Built in the 15th century as a lavish
townhouse, remodelled in late Baroque

style in the 18th century, demolished by the Communists, and then rebuilt by them close to its original location for the 750th anniversary of Berlin in 1987, the Ephraim-Palais is today home to temporary exhibitions about Berlin's history drawn from the city's collection. Soft chandelier lighting and parquet floors lend a refined air to the place.

Fernsehturm

Panoramastrasse 1A (242 3333, www.berlinerfernsehturm.de). U2, U5, U8, S5, S7, S75 Alexanderplatz. **Open** Mar-Oct 9am-midnight daily. Nov-Feb 10am-midnight daily. **Admission** €12.50; €8 reductions; free under-3s. **Map** p51 E3 ㉛

See p75 **Tower of the Hour.**

Hamburger Bahnhof – Museum für Gegenwart

Invalidenstrasse 50-51 (3978 3439, www.hamburgerbahnhof.de). U55, S5, S7, S75 Hauptbahnhof. **Open** 10am-6pm Tue, Wed, Fri-Sun; 10am-8pm Thur. **Admission** (incl temporary exhibitions) €10; €5 reductions. **Map** p50 A2 ㉜

This contemporary art museum opened in 1997 within this vast, grand neoclassical ex-train station. Outside is a stunning fluorescent light installation by Dan Flavin. Inside, the biggest draw is the controversial Friedrich Christian Flick Collection: some 2,000 works from around 150 artists (mainly from the late 20th century), with key pieces by Bruce Nauman and Martin Kipperberger. Flick, from a steel family whose fortune was earned partly from Nazi-era slave labour, paid for the refurbishment of the adjacent Rieckhalle warehouse to house the (many large-scale) works, which are doled out in temporary, themed exhibitions. There are other shows too – Tomás Saraceno installed a network of interactive gigantic bouncy balloons for his Cloud Cities show – plus one of Berlin's best art bookshops.

Hanf Museum

Mühlendamm 5 (242 4827, www. hanfmuseum.de). U2, U5, U8, S5, S7, S75 Alexanderplatz. **Open** 10am-8pm Tue-Fri; noon-8pm Sat, Sun. **Admission** €4.50, €3 reductions; free under-10s. No credit cards. **Map** p51 E4 ㊸

The world's largest hemp museum aims to teach the visitor about the uses of the plant throughout history, as well as touching on the controversy surrounding it. The café (doubling as a video and reading room) serves cakes made with hemp, as well as those without it.

Knoblauchhaus

Poststrasse 23 (240 020 171, www. knoblauchhaus.de). U2, U5, U8, S5, S7, S75 Alexanderplatz. **Open** 10am-6pm Tue-Sun. **Admission** free. **Map** p51 E4 ㊹

This neoclassical mid 18th-century townhouse was once home to the influential Knoblauch family and contains an exhibition about some of their more prominent members. However, the real draw is the house's striking interior. The first floor contains an exhibition about the increasingly sophisticated middle-class tastes of post-Napoleonic Germany, while the second floor hosts temporary exhibitions about 19th-century cultural history.

Marienkirche

Karl-Liebknecht-Strasse 8 (2475 9510, www.marienkirche-berlin.de). U2, U5, U8, S5, S7, S75 Alexanderplatz. **Open** 10am-6pm daily. **Admission** free. **Map** p51 E3 ㊺

Begun in 1270, the Marienkirche is one of Berlin's few remaining medieval buildings. Just inside the door is a wonderful 'Dance of Death' fresco dating from 1485, and the 18th-century Walther organ here is considered his masterpiece. Marienkirche hit the headlines in 1989 when the East German civil rights movement chose it for one of their first sit-ins, since churches were among the few places where people could congregate without state permission.

Neue Synagoge

Centrum Judaicum, Oranienburger Strasse 28-30 (8802 8316, www.centrum judaicum.de). S1, S2, S25 Oranienburger Strasse. **Open** Mar-Oct 10am-8pm Mon, Sun; 10am-6pm Tue-Thur; 10am-2pm Fri. Nov-Feb 10am-6pm Mon-Thur, Sun; 10am-2pm Fri. **Admission** €3.50; €3 reductions. No credit cards. **Map** p51 C2 ㊻

Built in 1857-66 as the Berlin Jewish community's showpiece, it was the New Synagogue that was attacked during Kristallnacht in 1938, but not too badly damaged – Allied bombs did far more harm in 1945. The façade remained intact and the Moorish dome has been rebuilt. Inside is a permanent exhibition about Jewish life in Berlin and a glassed-in area protecting the ruins of the sanctuary.

Museum für Naturkunde

Invalidenstrasse 43 (2093 8551, www. naturkundemuseum-berlin.de). U6 Naturkundemuseum. **Open** 9.30am-6pm Tue-Fri; 10am-6pm Sat, Sun. **Admission** €5; €3 reductions. **Map** p51 B1/2 ㊼

Berlin's recently renovated Natural History Museum is a real trove. The biggest (literally) draw is the skeleton of a Brachiosaurus dinosaur, which weighed 50 tons at death and is as high as a four-storey house. 'Oliver' – as the dinosaur is nicknamed – is one of the world's largest known land animals and was discovered in the early 1900s. Don't miss the creepy Forschungssammlungen (research collections), which show off some of the museum's store of over a million pickled animals suspended in jars of alcohol. Berlin's most famous polar bear, Knut, who died in 2011, is now stuffed and on display.

Nikolaikirche

Nikolaikirchplatz (240 020 171, www. stadtmuseum.de). U2, U5, U8, S5, S7, S75 Alexanderplatz. **Open** 10am-6pm daily. **Admission** €5; €3 reductions; free under-18s. Free 1st Wed of mth. **Map** p51 E4 ㊽

Inside Berlin's oldest congregational church is an interesting collection chronicling the city's development until 1648. Old tiles, tapestries, and stone and wood carvings – even punishment devices – are on display. There are fascinating photos of wartime damage, plus examples of how the stones melted together in the heat of bombardment.

Ramones Museum

Krausnickstrasse 23 (7552 8890, www.ramonesmuseum.com). S1, S2, S25 Oranienburger Strasse. **Open** noon-10pm daily. **Admission** €3.50. No credit cards. **Map** p51 D2 ㊾

Run by a German Ramones' maniac, Flo Hayler, this compact museum houses a vast collection of memorabilia, including childhood photos, gig set lists, flyers and concert T-shirts. There are also movie screenings, acoustic shows, Ramones-related special events and a small in-house record label.

Sammlung Hoffmann

Sophienstrasse 21 (2849 9121, www. sophie-gips.de). U8 Weinmeisterstrasse. **Open** (by appointment only) 11am-4pm Sat. **Admission** €8. No credit cards. **Map** p51 D2 ㊿

Erika and Rolf Hoffmann's private collection of international contemporary art includes a charming floor installation by Swiss video artist Pipilotti Rist, a luxurious art library, and work by Lucio Fontana, Frank Stella, Douglas Gordon, Felix Gonzalez-Torres and AR Penck. The Hoffmanns offer guided tours every Saturday by appointment – felt slippers supplied. Every summer, the entire display changes.

Eating & drinking

Altes Europa

Gipsstrasse 11 (2809 3840, www.alteseuropa.com). U8 Weinmeisterstrasse. **Open** noon-1am daily. No credit cards. **Bar** **Map** p51 D2 ㋛

Barcomi's

The gentle minimalism of the decor – big picture windows, basic furnishings and nothing but a few old maps and prints on the walls – is a relief in an increasingly touristy neighbourhood, and this inviting place is good for anything from a mid-afternoon drink to a rowdier night out with friends.

Barcomi's

Sophie-Gips-Höfe, Sophienstrasse 21 (2859 8363, www.barcomis.de). U8 Weinmeisterstrasse. **Open** 9am-9pm Mon-Sat; 10am-9pm Sun. **Café Map** p51 D2 ⓼
Berlin's very own domestic goddess, Cynthia Barcomi, opened her first café, in Kreuzberg, back in 1997. The American expat brought her nation's sweet treats to Berlin, doling out blueberry pancakes and whoopee pies as well as bagels. The café is situated in a quiet courtyard near Hackescher Markt, and locals flock to the outdoor tables.

Bar 3

Weydingerstrasse 20 (9700 5106). U2 Rosa-Luxemburg-Platz. **Open** 9pm-late Tue-Sat. No credit cards.
Bar Map p51 E2 ⓼
Located in a backstreet off Torstrasse, this cosy bar is a favourite of Mitte

media types. With a large horse shoe-shaped bar dominating the room, it's bar stools or standing only, as this place seriously packs out with a slick, bespectacled clientele and the occasional actor or celebrity.

Berliner Ensemble Kantine

Bertolt-Brecht-Platz 1 (2840 8117). U6, S1, S2, S5, S7, S25, S75 Friedrichstrasse. **Open** 9am-midnight Mon-Sat; 4pm-midnight Sun. **€. German Map** p50 B3 ⓼
Eat passable, hearty German fare with the jovial cast and crew at the canteen of Brecht's Berliner Ensemble. It's tucked around the back of the theatre, down some steps in the courtyard. The three daily specials cost around €5 or less, and always include a good veggie option.

Café Fleury

Weinbergsweg 20 (4403 4144). U8 Rosenthaler Platz. **Open** 8am-10pm Mon-Sat; 10am-8pm Sun. **€€.** No credit cards.
Café Map p51 D1 ⓼
This wildly popular French café at the bottom of the hill up to Prenzlauer Berg provides the perfect perch from which to people-watch over a buttery croissant and café au lait.

Mogg p66

Chelsea Bar

*Torstrasse 59 (0176 3225 2652, www.
thechelsea bar.info). U2 Rosa-Luxemburg-
Platz.* **Open** 7pm- late daily. **Bar**
Map p51 E2 ⑤⑥
A recent addition to the thriving
Torstrasse scene, this is an appeal-
ingly scuzzy, down-at-heel joint that's
yet to be overrun by the city's hipsters.

Chicago-Williams

*Hannoverschestrasse 2 (2804 2422,
www.chicagowilliamsbbq.com). U6
Oranienburger Tor.* **Open** 5pm-midnight
daily. €€. **Barbecue** Map p50 B2 ⑤⑦
At Berlin's first real attempt at aping
a Southern-style barbecue shack, plat-
ters of smoked meats come piled high
on plastic trays. The unctuous ribs are
a particular highlight, but pulled pork,
pastrami, steak and other favourites
are all available. There's an extensive
menu of craft beers, IPAs, pale ales and
dark beers. The place gets rowdy as the
night progresses.

CôCô

*Rosenthalerstrasse 2 (2463 0595, www.
co-co.net). U8 Rosenthaler Platz.* **Open**
11am-10pm Mon-Thur; 11am-midnight
Fri, Sat; noon-10pm Sun. €. No credit
cards. **Vietnamese** Map p50 D2 ⑤⑧
There's been a banh mi explosion in
Berlin. This Vietnamese speciality
combines fatty pâté and roast pork
slices, offset by coriander and zingy
pickled daikon and carrot, all in an
airy-light baguette. CôCô's choice of
sandwich fillings includes banh mi thit
nuong (with lemongrass meatballs)
and banh mi chay (with tofu), as well as
the classic variety.

Cordobar

*Grosse Hamburger Strasse 32 (2758
1215, www.cordobar.net). S1, S2,
S25 Oranienburger Strasse or U8
Rosenthaler Platz.* **Open** 5pm-2am
Tue-Sat. **Winebar** Map p50 D2 ⑤⑨
The wine-bar-with-small-plates model
has become extremely popular in recent
years, and Mitte finally has an excellent

example. The list focuses on southern
German and Austrian wines, with many
unsulphured 'natural' bottles. Hot and
cold dishes such as blood-sausage pizza
or smoked eel with brussels sprouts, are
also available.

Grill Royal

*Friedrichstrasse 105B (2887 9288, www.
grillroyal.com). U6, S1, S2, S5, S7, S25,
S75 Friedrichstrasse.* **Open** 6pm-1am
daily. €€€. **Steakhouse** Map p50 C3 ⑥⑩
Grill Royal is a stylish, friendly and
profoundly meaty experience. Not
for vegetarians or those on a diet or

BERLIN BY AREA

budget, Grill is as compelling for its people-watching potential as it is for its (stoutly priced) steaks, seafood and accoutrements. The walls are adorned with rather striking soft-porn art from the owner's collection.

House of Small Wonder

Johannisstrasse 20 (2758 2877, www.houseofsmallwonder.de). U6 Oranienburger Tor. **Open** 9am-5pm Mon-Fri; 10am-4pm Sat, Sun. €€. **Japanese** Map p50 C2 ⑥①

HOSW serves Japanese food, given an American twist. The menu offers unlikely juxtapositions of Eastern and Western flavours in an airy and suitably eccentric setting.

Kapelle

Zionskirchplatz 22-24 (4434 1300, www.cafe-kapelle.de). U8 Rosenthaler Platz. **Open** 9am-3am daily. No credit cards. **Bar** Map p51 D1 ⑥②

A comfortable, high-ceilinged café-bar at the corner of the Zionskirchplatz, Kapelle takes its name from Die Rote Kapelle, 'the Red Orchestra'. This was a clandestine anti-fascist organisation, and in the 1930s and '40s the Kapelle's basement was a secret meeting place for the Resistance.

Katz Orange

Bergstrasse 22 (983 208 430, www. katzorange.com). U8 Rosenthaler Platz. **Open** 6pm-3.30am Mon-Sat. €€€. **Modern German** Map p50 C1 ⑥③

Set off the street in a handsome 19th-century red-brick ex-brewery, Katz Orange is a grown-up restaurant for locavore dining with an excellent late-night cocktail bar attached. They take pains to source local produce from trusted farmers and suppliers to create a short menu of seasonal dishes.

Kim

Brunnenstrasse 10 (no phone, www.kim-in-berlin.com). U8 Rosenthaler Platz. **Open** 9pm-late daily. No credit cards. **Bar** Map p51 D1 ⑥④

Kim's door is unmarked: look for an all-glass façade and crowds of people sporting billowy monochrome clothing. Cheap drinks and a rotating roster of neighbourhood DJs add to the don't-give-a-damn aesthetic.

Lebensmittel im Mitte

Rochstrasse 2 (2759 6130). U8 Weinmeisterstrasse. **Open** noon-4pm, 5-11pm Mon-Sat. €€. No credit cards. **German/Austrian** Map p51 E3 ⑥⑤

This deli/restaurant is a little journey into southern German and Austrian cuisine. The deli at the front offers fine cheeses, rustic bread, organic veg, sausages and even Austrian pumpkin-seed oil. But you can also settle on to long wooden benches beneath the antlers on the wall, and dine on high-fat, carb-loaded dishes such as Leberkäse, tongue, rösti and cheese Spätzle. Laptops not allowed.

Das Lokal

Linienstrasse 160 (2844 9500, http://lokal-berlin.blogspot.co.uk). S1, S2, S25 Oranienburger Strasse. **Open** 6pm-midnight Mon, Sat, Sun; noon-4pm, 6pm-midnight Tue-Fri. €€€. **Modern German** Map p50 C2 ⑥⑥

Das Lokal's weekly changing seasonal menu might feature starters of pigeon with chestnuts, mussels in broth or asparagus croquettes – all designed to demonstrate the superior flavour of well-sourced produce. It's also an oasis for offal dishes and game, with which Berlin's surrounding forests abound.

Maxime

Gormannstrasse 25 (6583 3962, www.vins-cochonneries.com). U8 Weinmeisterstrasse. **Open** 6pm-1am Tue-Sat. **Winebar** Map p50 D2 ⑥⑦

Maxime has a rotating menu of around 20 wines by the glass, as well as an extensive list of bottles from France, Spain and Italy. Naturally, where there's wine, there's cheese – with pungent raw-milk brillat-savarin and bûche des pyrénées on offer.

BERLIN BY AREA

Mein Haus am See

Brunnenstrasse 197-198 (2388 3561, www.mein-haus-am-see.blogspot.com). U8 Rosenthaler Platz. **Open** 9am-late daily. No credit cards. **Bar Map** p51 D1 ❻❽

This hugely popular split-level joint is situated a stone's throw from busy Rosenthaler Platz. There are exhibitions, readings and DJs, and it almost never closes, so whether you want another beer, a sobering coffee or a panino at 4.30am, this is the place to come. Excellent breakfasts too.

Mogg

Auguststrasse 11-13 (330 060 770, www.moggandmelzer.com). U6 Oranienburger Tor. **Open** 8am-late Mon-Fri; 10am-late Sat, Sun. **€€**. **Deli Map** p50 C2 ❻❾

This New York-style deli is a lunchtime hotspot for local galleristas, where all the necessaries are pitch-perfect: the pickles pack a hefty crunch; fresh coleslaw is just the right side of creamysour; and the toasted rye bread reveals a fluffy interior.

Monsieur Vuong

Alte Schönhauser Strasse 46 (3087 2643, www.monsieurvuong.de). U8 Weinmeisterstrasse. **Open** noon-midnight daily. **€**. No credit cards. **Vietnamese Map** p51 E2 ❼⓿

Monsieur Vuong offers two daily specials (usually something saucy with rice or noodles), plus a short regular menu of noodle salads and pho soups – a large bowl of broth with glass noodles, topped with chicken or beef and crunchy beansprouts, a generous helping of chopped coriander and a squirt of lime.

Nola's am Weinberg

Veteranenstrasse 9 (4404 0766, www.nola.de). U8 Rosenthaler Platz. **Open** 10am-1am daily. **€€**. **Swiss Map** p51 D1 ❼❶

This former park pavilion has a fabulous terrace overlooking the park slope, as well as a bar and dining room.

Expect artery-hardening Swiss fare, such as venison goulash with mushrooms and spinach noodles, or cheese and spinach rösti.

Noto

Torstrasse 173 (2009 5387, www.noto-berlin.com). U8 Rosenthaler Platz. **Open** 6pm-midnight Mon-Sat. **€€€€**. **Haute cuisine Map** p50 C2 ❼❷

Noto exemplifies contemporary Berlin dining: a laid-back setting, with the chef-owner cooking traditional German produce made modern through creative techniques. The succinct menu changes weekly.

Princess Cheesecake

Tucholskystrasse 37 (2809 2760, www.princess-cheesecake.de). U2 Senefelderplatz. **Open** 10am-7pm daily. **Café Map** p50 C2 ❼❸

Here you can try the venerable 'Kaffee und Kuchen' tradition – Germany's equivalent of afternoon tea. Try a classic baked cheesecake or one of the more adventurous numbers such as 'Mi Cariño Suave', laden with candied almonds and toffee and topped with quark cream.

Reinstoff

Edison-Höfe, Schlegelstrasse 26C (3088 1214, www.reinstoff.eu). U6 Naturkundemuseum. **Open** 7pm-midnight Tue-Sat. **€€€€**. **Haute cuisine Map** p50 B2 ❼❹

Chef Daniel Achilles uses meticulously sourced, mostly organic, ingredients to create 'taste adventures'. You choose from two menus: the ganznah (quite near) and weiter-draussen (far away), each playing with the notion of taste memory and texture, but utilising a distinctly different palette of ingredients.

Sababa

Kastanienallee 50-51 (4050 5401, www.sababahummus.de). U2 Senefelderplatz or U8 Rosenthaler Platz. **Open** 11am-10pm daily. **€**. No credit cards. **Israeli Map** p51 D1 ❼❺

Israeli chef Ze'ev brings a taste of one of the Middle East's uniting features – rich and creamy houmous – plus plenty of pitta to mop it up with. You'll also find shakshuka, a breakfast favourite of two eggs baked in tomato sauce; zingy salads; and assorted omelettes.

Schwarzwaldstuben

Tucholskystrasse 48 (2809 8084). S1, S2, S25 *Oranienburger Strasse.* **Open** 9am-midnight daily. €€. No credit cards. **German Map** p50 C2 🟨

Some of the best German cooking comes from Swabia, but Swabian restaurants tend to be filled with teddy bears and knick-knacks. This place, however, is casually chic, and wears its mounted deer head ironically. Food is excellent: the soups are hearty; stellar main courses include the Schäuffele with sauerkraut and potatoes.

Ständige Vertretung

Schiffbauerdamm 8 (282 3965, www. staev.de). U6, S1, S2, S5, S7, S25, S75 *Friedrichstrasse.* **Open** 9am-1.30am daily. **Bar Map** p50 B3 🟨

The knick-knack-filled Ständige commemorates the still controversial decision to move the German capital from Bonn to Berlin after reunification. Due to the pub's proximity to the government quarter, you get the odd politician popping in for some draught Kölsch. There's a lovely terrace by the river.

Tadshikische Teestube

KunstHof, Oranienburger Strasse 27 (204 1112, www.tadshikische-teestube. de). S1, S2, S25, *Oranienburger Strasse* or U6 *Oranienburger Tor.* **Open** 4pm-midnight Mon-Fri; noon-midnight Sat, Sun. €€. **Café Map** p50 C2 🟨

Originally the Soviet pavilion at the 1974 Leipzig Fair, this charming Tajik tearoom was lovingly preserved and for many years operated out of the grander Palais on the Moat. It's had to move – but a new owner has arrived to continue this Berlin oddity at a new location in an old art gallery.

Tausend

Schiffbauerdamm 11 (2758 2070, www. tausendberlin.com). U6, S1, S2, S5, S7, S25, S75 *Friedrichstrasse.* **Open** 9pm-late Tue-Sat. **Bar Map** p50 B3 🟨

With its unmarked entrance – look for the iron door under the train overpass – and strict entrance policy, this grown-up bar is as exclusive as Berlin gets. This is where the well-heeled come to be seen sipping innovative drinks in a tubular, steel-ceilinged interior lit by eerily eye-like 3D installations.

Trois Minutes sur Mer

Torstrasse 166 (6730 2052, www. 3minutessurmer.de). U8 *Rosenthaler Platz.* **Open** 11.30am-midnight Mon-Fri; 10am-midnight Sat, Sun. €€€. **French Map** p50 C2 🟨

Here, the traditional Parisian bistro aesthetic (art deco bar stools, paper tablecloths) sits alongside Nouveau Berlin touches (GDR light fittings and funky red bar stools). There are excellent fish options and more gutsy dishes as well.

Trust

Neue Promenade 10 (no phone, www. trust-berlin.com). S5, S7, S75 *Hackescher Markt.* **Open** 10pm-5am Thur-Sat. No credit cards. **Bar Map** p51 D3 🟨

All the spirits here are sold in Trust-branded bottles and the idea is to band together with friends (especially if just made at the bar) to booze the night away. It's owned by Cookie, a local club legend, but watch out for the moody doorman. Local DJs spin on weekends.

ULA-Berlin

Anklamer Strasse 8 (8937 9570, www.ulaberlin.jimdo.com). S1, S2, S25 *Nordbahnhof.* **Open** 6pm-midnight Tue-Sun. €€€. **Japanese Map** p50 C1 🟨

Head to ULA for an elegant alternative to budget sushi joints. The kitchen is headed by Taro Fujita, who was previously chef at the Japanese ambassador's residence. The high-concept menu and fine sakés are matched by the sleek, black interior.

Weinbar Al Contadino Sotto le Stelle

Gormannstrasse 10 (2759 2102, www. alcontadino.eu). U8 Weinmeisterstrasse. **Open** 6pm-midnight Tue-Sat. €€.
Italian Map p51 D2 ⑬

Skip the overpriced main restaurant and instead head to the cosy wine bar for some of the city's best Emilia-Romagnan cooking, which follows Slow Food guidelines for sourcing produce.

Weinbar Rutz

Chausseestrasse 8 (2462 8760, www. rutz-weinbar.de). U6 Naturkundemuseum. **Open** 6.30-10.30pm Tue-Sat. €€€.
German Map p50 C2 ⑭

The impressive ground-floor bar has a whole wall showcasing wines from around the globe. There are hearty meals in the bar downstairs (pig's stomach with sauerkraut and mustard-seed sauce, anyone?), while the second-floor restaurant serves a limited nouvelle menu from Michelin-starred chef Marco Müller.

Shopping

14 oz. Berlin

Neue Schönhauser Strasse 13 (4920 3750, www.14oz-berlin.com). U8 Weinmeisterstrasse. **Open** 1-8pm Mon-Sat. **Map** p51 D3 ⑮

This menswear (mainly) shop caters for the rugged high-end heritage look, but also stocking quality leather footwear from English cobblers Trickers and eye-wateringly expensive Nigel Cabourne jackets.

Acne Studios

Weinmeisterstrasse 2 (9700 5187, www. acnestudios.com). U8 Weinmeisterstrasse. **Open** 11am-8pm Mon-Sat. **Map** p51 E2 ⑯

Sweden's Acne just keeps going from strength to strength, having completed its transformation from cult jeans label to fully-fledged global empire with its slinky draping and quality materials.

Ampelmann Galerie Shop

Rosenthaler Strasse 40-41 (4404 8801, www.ampelmann.de). S5, S7, S75 Hackescher Markt. **Open** 9.30am-8pm Mon-Sat (summer until 10pm); 10.30am-7pm Sun. **Map** p51 D3 ⑰

You'll find a huge variety of stuff emblazoned with the old East's enduring symbol, the jaunty red and green traffic-light men. They've become unofficial city mascots and have started colonising West Berlin road crossings too.

APC

Mulackstrasse 36 (2844 9192, www. apc.fr). U2 Rosa-Luxemburg-Platz or U8 Weinmeisterstrasse. **Open** 11.30am-7.30pm Mon-Fri; noon-6pm Sat. **Map** p51 D3 ⑱

Tucked away on a side street that boasts Mitte's finest couture shops, this popular Parisian brand offers mensand womenswear essentials: chunky woollens, leather boots and Japanese denim jeans.

Arkonaplatz Flohmarkt

Arkonaplatz (786 9764, www. troedelmarkt-arkonaplatz.de). U8 Bernauer Strasse. **Open** 10am-4pm Sun. **Market Map** p51 D1 ⑲

A broad array of retro gear – ranging from vinyl to clothing, books to trinkets, bikes to coffee tables – is all available here at moderate prices. The golden rule of flea markets applies: the best stuff gets snapped up early.

Blush

Rosa-Luxemburg-Strasse 22 (2809 3580, www.blush-berlin.com). U2 Rosa-Luxemburg-Platz or U8 Weinmeisterstrasse. **Open** noon-8pm Mon-Fri; noon-7pm Sat. **Map** p51 E2 ⑳

There's all sorts of silk and lace goodies at this lingerie shop, including underwear, pyjamas and even hot water bottle covers.

Bonbon Macherei

Oranienburger Strasse 32 (4405 5243, www.bonbonmacherei.de). S1, S2, S25

Oranienburger Strasse. **Open** noon-8pm Wed-Sat. No credit cards. **Map** p50 C2 ㉛
A nostalgic candy shop that offers sweet, sour and everything in between. Katja Kolbe and Hjalmar Stecher produce their boiled sweets in the on-site workshop using vintage equipment and traditional recipes.

Buchhandlung Walther König
Burgstrasse 27 (2576 0980, www. buchhandlung-walther-koenig.de). S5, S7, S75 Hackescher Markt. **Open** 10am-8am Mon-Sat. **Map** p51 D3 ㉜
Cologne-based Walther König is Germany's top art publisher; this flagship store by Museumsinsel heaves with beautifully reproduced catalogues and a comprehensive range of critical-theory literature.

Civilist
Brunnenstrasse 13 (8561 0715, www. civilistberlin.com). U8 Rosenthaler Platz. **Open** noon-8pm Mon-Fri; 11am-6pm Sat. **Map** p51 D1 ㉝
No self-respecting Berlin skater would be seen in anything other than a Civilist wool beanie. This neatly designed shop focuses on limited-edition collaborations and mature skate labels including HUF and aNYthing.

Do You Read Me?
Auguststrasse 28 (6954 9695, www. doyoureadme.de). U8 Rosenthaler Platz or S1, S2, S25 Oranienburger Strasse. **Open** Summer 10am-9.30pm Mon-Sat. Winter 10am-7.30pm Mon-Sat. **Map** p51 D2 ㉞
On Mitte's main art drag, this small shop's shelves heave with glossy picks of global fashion, style, art and design print media. The magazines are attractively presented, and there's a small selection of books in the back.

DSTM
Torstrasse 161 (4920 3750, www.dstm. co). U8 Rosenthaler Platz. **Open** 1-8pm Mon-Sat. **Map** p51 E2 ㉟

Canadian-born Jen Gilpin's label, Don't Shoot The Messenger, is the definitive city look. Local influences can be read from all over: shades of Marlene Dietrich's austere raunchiness and even the complex fastenings of fetish-ware are apparent in the billowy clothing, made mostly in fine black silk and leather.

Fun Factory
Oranienburger Strasse 92 (2804 6366, www.funfactory.com). S5, S7, S75 Hackescher Markt. **Open** 11am-8pm Mon-Thur; 11am-9pm Fri, Sat. **Map** p51 D3 ㊱
Berlin's temple to adult toys lies slap-bang in the middle of Hackescher Markt's central shopping area. With an interior designed by American futurist Karim Rashid, the two-floor shop caters to a mixed gay/straight crowd.

Galerie Eigen Art
Auguststrasse 26 (280 6605, www.eigen-art.com). U8 Rosenthaler Platz or S1, S2, S25 Oranienburger Strasse. **Open** 11am-6pm Tue-Sat. **Map** p51 D2 ㊲
A stalwart of the old Auguststrasse art strip, this is where man-about-town Gerd Harry 'Judy' Lybke continues his longstanding relationship with New Leipzig School star painters Matthias Weischer and Neo Rauch.

Happy Shop
Torstrasse 67 (0157 7847 3620 mobile, www.happyshop-berlin.com). U2 Rosa-Luxemburg-Platz. **Open** 11am-7pm Tue-Sat. **Map** p51 E2 ㊳
This spacious boutique features a cool op-art façade, racks and mannequins dangling from the ceiling, and a selection of wonderfully unique pieces by funky Japanese designer Tsumori Chisato and Bernhard Wilhelm.

KW Institute for Contemporary Art
Auguststrasse 69 (243 4590, www. kw-berlin.de). U6 Oranienburger Tor or S1, S2, S25 Oranienburger Strasse.

KW Institute for Contemporary Art p69

Open noon-7pm Tue, Wed, Fri-Sun; noon-9pm Thur. **Admission** €6; €4 reductions. **Map** p50 C2 ❾❾

Housed in a former margarine factory, KW has been a major non-profit showcase since the early 1990s. It gets involved with other local galleries and projects, such as Berlin Art Week and the cheerfully never-less-than-controversial Berlin Biennale.

LaLa Berlin

Mulackstrasse 7 (2576 2924, www. lalaberlin.com). U8 Weinmeisterstrasse. **Open** noon-8pm Wed-Sat. **Map** p51 E2 ❿⓿⓿

Iranian-born Leyla Piedayesh knocks out stylish and cosy knitwear at her Mitte boutique. She's become well known, thanks to famous fans such as Claudia Schiffer and Cameron Diaz.

Made in Berlin

Neue Schönhauser Strasse 19 (2123 0601). U8 Weinmeisterstrasse. **Open** 11am-8pm Mon-Sat. **Map** p51 E2 ❿⓿❶

Another branch of the Kleidermarkt clothes empire, where the 'better stuff'

supposedly goes – vintage Barbour, Burberry and Lacoste, for example. It's still pretty cheap, though, and offers a ton of great no-name 1980s gear.

Moebel Horzon

Torstrasse 106 (0176 6273 0874, www.modocom.de). U8 Rosenthaler Platz. **Open** varies. No credit cards. **Map** p51 D2 ❿⓿❷

Artist? Writer? Businessman? It's hard to define what Rafael Horzon really does. But the fact is that he invented simple shelves that are easy on the eye and can be admired in his showroom.

Mykita

Rosa-Luxemburg-Strasse 6 (6730 8715, www.mykita.com). U2, U5, U8, S5, S7, S75 Alexanderplatz. **Open** 11am-8pm Mon-Fri; noon- 6pm Sat. **Map** p51 E3 ❿⓿❸

This Berlin-based glasses label has been a mainstay for fashion-conscious locals since 2004, but the brand has hit the big time since some of its more experimental frames were picked up by the likes of Lady Gaga.

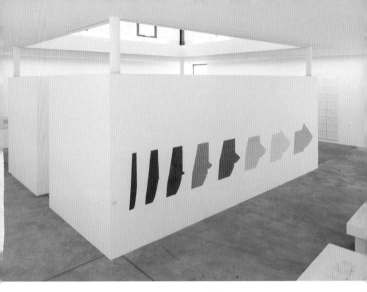

Das Neue Schwarz

Mulackstrasse 38 (2787 4467, www.dasneueschwarz.de).U2Rosa-Luxemburg-Platz or U8 Weinmeisterstrasse. **Open** 11am-8pm Mon-Sat. **Map** p51 E2 ⓙ

Mulackstrasse is full of expensive designer boutiques, so Das Neue Schwarz ('the new black') is a great alternative for those looking for a (relative) bargain. The hand-selected stock offers almost-new designer pieces from past seasons, most still with tags. There's stuff for both boys and girls: chunky Céline handbags, flashy Bernard Willhelm bomber jackets, Chloé wedges and Dries Van Noten suits, to name just a few.

Oona

Auguststrasse 26 (2804 5905, www.oona-galerie.de). S1, S2, S25 Oranienburger Strasse or U8 Rosenthaler Platz. **Open** 2-6pm Tue-Fri; 1-6pm Sat. **Map** p51 D2 ⓙ

In addition to its permanent collection, this 'gallery for contemporary jewellery' features work by young creatives from Japan, Australia and Europe.

Pro QM

Almstadtstrasse 48-50 (2472 8520, www.pro-qm.de). U2 Rosa-Luxemburg-Platz. **Open** 11am-8pm Mon-Sat. **Map** p51 E2 ⓙ

This art bookshop has the rarified design of a white cube, but don't let that put you off – inside the ambience is extremely welcoming, with staff encouraging lengthy browsing.

RSVP

Mulackstrasse 14 (2809 4644, www.rsvp-berlin.de). U8 Weinmeisterstrasse. **Open** noon-7pm Mon-Thur; noon-8pm Fri, Sat. **Map** p51 D2 ⓙ

Stationery for the aesthete: art deco scissors, exotic erasers, weighty Rivoli writing paper, Polish notebooks and Koh-I-Noor mechanical pencils.

Sammlung Boros

Reinhardtstrasse 20 (no phone, www.sammlung-boros.de). U6 Oranienburger Tor. **Open** by appointment. No credit cards. **Map** p50 B3 ⓙ

More akin to a museum than an actual gallery, this concrete World War II bunker has been transformed into a 3,000sq m space containing the formidable collection of advertising mogul Christian Boros and his wife Karen. Tours are on weekends by appointment only; book your place through the website.

Shusta

Rosenthaler Strasse 72 (7621 9780, www.shusta.de). U8 Rosenthaler Platz. **Open** 11am-8pm Mon-Sat. **Map** p51 D2 **109**

In this high-ceilinged store, you'll find stylish leather shoes imported from all over the world by Tedros and Fidel, the shop's very cool and friendly owners.

Smart Deli

Chausseestrasse 5 (2068 7037, www.smartdeli.org). U6 Oranienburger Tor. **Open** 10am-10pm Mon-Sat. **Map** p50 B2 **110**

This is one of the best places in Berlin to buy specific Japanese products such as the cult Kewpie mayonnaise and curry paste.

Soto

Torstrasse 72 (2576 2070, www.sotostore.com). U2 Rosa-Luxemburg-Platz. **Open** noon-8pm Mon-Fri; 11am-8pm Sat. **Map** p51 E2 **111**

One for the boys, with a curated selection of cult labels on offer: limited-edition Flyknit Nikes, soft woollen slacks from Norse Projects or fine knitwear from Acne.

Sprüth-Magers

Oranienburger Strasse 18 (2888 4030, www.spruethmagers.com). S5, S7, S75 Hackescher Markt. **Open** 11am-6pm Tue-Sat. **Map** p51 D3 **112**

This is now the main space for Cologne powerhouses Monika Sprüth and Philomene Magers (alongside their London gallery). They've been key in developing the careers of such international figures as Peter Fischli and David Weiss, Andreas Gursky and Cindy Sherman.

Whisky & Cigars

Sophienstrasse 8-9 (282 0376, www.whisky-cigars.de). S5, S7, S75 Hackescher Markt. **Open** 11am-7pm Mon-Fri; 11am-6pm Sat. **Map** p51 D2 **113**

Two friends with a love of single malts are behind this shop, which stocks 450 whiskies, plus cigars from Cuba, Jamaica and Honduras, among other sources. Regular tastings too.

Wood Wood

Rochstrasse 4 (2804 7877, www.woodwood.dk). U2, U5, U8, S5, S7, S75 Alexanderplatz. **Open** noon-8pm Mon-Fri; noon-7pm Sat. **Map** p51 E3 **114**

An avant-garde design collective from Copenhagen, Wood Wood offers beautiful, angular and sometimes outrageous street fashion, sneakers and accessories.

Zionskirchplatz Farmers' Market

Zionskirchplatz (394 4073). U2 Senefelderplatz or U8 Rosenthaler Platz. **Open** 11am-6.30pm Thur. **Map** p51 D1 **115**

Regional growers sell fruit and vegetables, fresh fish, home-made jams, assorted breads, and organic cheese from Berliner Käsehandel. Farmers set up on the cobbled walkway surrounding one of Berlin's most beautiful churches, making this a truly picturesque market.

Nightlife

Acud

Veteranenstrasse 21 (4435 9498, www.acud.de). U8 Rosenthaler Platz or S1, S2, S25 Nordbahnhof. **Map** p51 D1 **116**

A massive complex, containing a cinema, theatre and gallery, operated by a friendly Berlin arts collective. There's also a party floor with a playlist mainly devoted to reggae, breakbeat and drum 'n' bass. The cinema programme is interesting, consisting mostly of independent and low-budget films.

Oona p71

Bohannon

*Dircksenstrasse 40 (6950 5287, www.
bohannon.de). U2, U5, U8, S5, S7, S75
Alexanderplatz.* **Map** p51 E3 ⑰
The club's name, a nod to US funk
legend Hamilton Bohannon, indicates
its driving musical principle. Billed as
offering 'soulful electronic clubbing',
this basement location features two
dancefloors, regular sets by the likes of
dancehall DJ Barney Millah and excellent Saturday night soul parties.

Clärchen's Ballhaus

*Auguststrasse 24 (282 9295, www.
ballhaus.de). S1, S2, S25 Oranienburger
Strasse.* **Map** p51 D2 ⑱
Dance hall Clärchen's Ballhaus has
been frequented by fleet-footed
Berliners since it was established by
Clara Haberman in 1913. Since 2005,
it's been under new management and
is more popular than ever. People come
to tango on Tuesdays, learn to swing on
Wednesdays, attend the 'pasta opera'
nights in the Mirror Salon, or even
find the love of their lives on weekend
nights. Some come to have an inexpen-
sive oven-baked pizza, served inside
or in the beautiful front garden. But
the magic never fails: after midnight,

both ballrooms teem with all types in a
free-for-all that begins with live music
and then segues into Michael Jackson,
the Beach Boys, old German Schlager
music, or all of the above.

Golden Gate

*Corner of Dircksenstrasse &
Schicklerstrasse (5770 4278, www.
goldengate-berlin.de). U8, S5, S7, S75
Jannowitzbrücke.* **Map** p51 F4 ⑲
Once home to a rather hit-and-miss
music policy, with the occasional live
show, this grimy little club has now set-
tled firmly into a series of all-weekend
techno parties. Its location – smack dab
in the middle of a motorway – means it
has no issue with noise. The Thursday
night parties are particularly raucous,
with the club carrying on until pretty
much Monday afternoon.

House of Weekend

*12th floor, Alexanderplatz 5 (2589 9366,
www.houseofweekend.berlin). U2, U5,
U8, S5, S7, S75 Alexanderplatz.* **Map**
p51 F3 ⑳
Weekend's home is at the top of one of
Alexanderplatz's many Communist-
era tower blocks. The roof terrace
is a big draw, combining a decent

booking policy with spectacular views. It recently rebranded itself as a VIP venue, which means upmarket barbecues on the terrace from 7pm and a buttoned-down club experience two floors below from 11pm.

Kaffee Burger & Old CCCP

Torstrasse 60 (2804 6495, www. kaffeeburger.de). U2 Rosa-Luxemburg-Platz. **Map** p51 E2 ⓑ

Proudly boasting 200 concerts and 364 parties a year, Kaffee Burger's programme runs the cultural gamut. Early evenings may see readings, lectures, films or live music. Later on, DJs play anything from old-school country to Balkan beats, or even flamboyant Israeli pop at the 'unkosher Jewish night' Meschugge. Adjoining Kaffee Burger is the Russian-themed late bar, Old CCCP.

Arts & leisure

Berliner Ensemble

Bertolt-Brecht-Platz 1 (2840 8155, www.berliner-ensemble.de). U6, S1, S2, S5, S7, S25, S75 Friedrichstrasse. **Map** p50 B3 ⓑ

Thanks to its historical association with Bertolt Brecht this is probably Berlin's most famous theatre. Under current artistic director Claus Peymann, it is regarded by Germans as a place where older, formerly radical directors go to work. You can still see the late Heiner Müller's 20-year-old staging of *The Resistable Rise of Arturo Ui*, along with productions by Robert Wilson and Peter Stein.

Chamäleon

Hackesche Höfe, Rosenthaler Strasse 40-41 (tickets 400 0590, www. chamaeleonberlin.de). S5, S7, S75 Hackescher Markt. **Map** p51 D3 ⓑ

This beautiful old theatre with a touch of decadence is located in the courtyards of the Hackesche Höfe. The focus is on stunning acrobatics combined with music theatre.

Deutsches Theater

Schumannstrasse 13A (284 410, tickets 2844 1221, www.deutsches theater.de). U6, S1, S2, S5, S7, S25, S75 Friedrichstrasse. **Map** p50 B3 ⓑ

Of all the theatres in Berlin, the Deutsches Theater behaves most like a state theatre in any other German city, offering a Spielplan of new interpretations of works by Goethe and Schiller alongside Shakespeare, Aeschylus and a smattering of new plays.

Hackesche Höfe Kino

Rosenthaler Strasse 40-41 (283 4603, www.hoefekino.de). U8 Weinmeisterstrasse or S5, S7, S75 Hackescher Markt. No credit cards. **Map** p51 D3 ⓑ

Being a four-storey walk up hasn't stopped this place from becoming one of the area's best-attended cinemas. It shows mostly foreign films, with documentaries and occasional indie features in English.

Sophiensaele

Sophienstrasse 18 (2789 0030, tickets 283 5266, www.sophiensaele.com). U8 Weinmeisterstrasse. No credit cards. **Map** p51 D2 ⓑ

Hidden on a quiet side road near Hackescher Markt and set back behind a little courtyard, it's easy to miss Sophiensaele. However, it's here, over four floors, that you're likely to see some of the most cutting-edge performances in Berlin, in some of the most atmospheric performance spaces the city has to offer.

Volksbühne

Rosa-Luxemburg-Platz (2406 5777, www.volksbuehne-berlin.de). U2 Rosa-Luxemburg-Platz. **Map** p51 E2 ⓑ

Built in 1914, the experimental Volksbühne is Berlin's most imposing theatre. Tate Modern's Chris Dercon will take over from current artistic director Frank Castorf in 2017.

Tower of the Hour

Berliners have learned to love the Fernsehturm.

Built in the late 1960s at a time when relations between East and West Berlin were at their lowest ebb, the 365m (1,198ft) Television Tower – its ball-on-spike shape visible all over the city – was intended as an assertion of Communist dynamism and modernity. Construction began in 1965, and the **Fernsehturm** (p61) finally opened on 7 October 1969 – the 20th anniversary of the founding of the GDR.

It marked the very centre of the city in the manner of a medieval church tower, allowed the second GDR TV station to commence broadcasting, and advertised the thrusting triumph of socialism in a form visible for miles around, in particular all over West Berlin. Equipped with a viewing platform at 203 metres (668 feet) and a revolving restaurant one floor above, it was also a handy tourist attraction.

At last, the city had a politically neutral but versatile symbol that could be used in all sorts of different ways. Soon it was making appearances on tourist brochures and party calendars, commemorative stamps and political posters, city maps and menu covers, shopping bags and official invitations. Easily anthropomorphised with a smiley face added to the ball, and often depicted with garlands of flowers, it also served as a perfect canvas for literature addressed to socialist youth. In the heyday of East Berlin, it was as inescapable as a graphic icon as it was as a towering landmark.

The Fernsehturm nearly didn't survive reunification: it was so closely associated with the outgoing Communist regime that there were calls to tear it down. But it remains useful and is still a major tourist draw, and Berliners have once again learned to love the thing. The restaurant still revolves, and the tower is still the fourth-tallest free-standing structure in Europe. What more could you ask of an icon?

Zeiss-Grossplanetarium

Prenzlauer Berg

Prenzlauer Berg is the area that has been most visibly transformed by Berlin's history. From 19th-century roots as a working-class district, it's become the most desirable neighbourhood for hip young families, the bijou children's clothing shops speaking nothing of its previous life as a centre of GDR dissidence or post-Wall bohemia. There aren't many major museums or sights, but there's some fine late 19th-century civic architecture, Berlin's biggest flea market and lots of great shopping. A blend of old and new, sleekly modern and charmingly quaint, Prenzlauer Berg is ideal for a weekend's exploring.

The focal point is leafy **Kollwitzplatz**, which is lined with bars, cafés and restaurants, and hosts an organic market on Thursdays. Heading south-east from the square, Knaackstrasse leads to one of the district's main landmarks, the **Wasserturm**. This water tower, constructed by English architect Henry Gill in 1852-75, provided running water for the first time in Germany. The Nazis used its basement as a prison and torture chamber. A plaque commemorates their victims; the tower has been converted into swanky apartments.

Opposite the Wasserturm on Rykestrasse is the **Synagoge Rykestrasse**, a neo-romanesque turn-of-the-20th-century structure that was badly damaged during Kristallnacht in 1938. After renovation in 1953, it was the only working synagogue in East Berlin. Nearby is the **Jüdischer Friedhof**, Berlin's oldest Jewish cemetery, and fairly gloomy due to its closely packed stones and canopy of trees. Now it stands peacefully in gentrified surrounds. To learn more about the district's history, look in at the **Prenzlauer Berg Museum**.

Knaackstrasse extends north-west from Kollwitzplatz to the vast complex of the **Kulturbrauerei**, an old brewery that now houses a concert space, galleries, artists' studios, a market, a cinema and a museum. South-west from here, the area around Kastanienallee has plenty of good bars, shops and restaurants. To the north-east is the 'LSD' area – around Lychener Strasse, Stargarder Strasse and Dunckerstrasse – which is what passed for the GDR's druggy zone, and **Helmholtzplatz**, popular with young families.

On the other side of Prenzlauer Allee is **Ernst-Thälmann-Park**, named after the leader of the pre-1933 German Communist Party. In its north-west corner stands the

Zeiss-Grossplanetarium, a fantastic GDR space that once celebrated Soviet cosmonauts and is currently being renovated (it should reopen in 2016). On the Greifswalder Strasse side of the park, just north of the Danziger Strasse corner, is a bombastic 1980s statue of Ernst Thälmann himself, raising a Communist fist – after the Wall fell, only pre-GDR figures remained memorialised in street names and monuments. The statue has a contemporary feature: a heated nose to melt any accumulating snow.

Sights & museums

Eating & drinking

Shopping

Nightlife

Arts & leisure

© Copyright Time Out Group 2015

Prenzlauer Berg

Mauerpark

Sights & museums

Gethsemanekirche

Stargarder Strasse 77 (445 7745, www. gethsemanekirche.de). U2, S8, S9, S41, S42, S85 Schönhauser Allee. **Open** *Services* 11am Sun. **Map** p77 B1 ❶

Situated just south of Schönhauser Allee S-Bahn, this striking neo-Gothic church built in August Orth's typical red-brick style is best known for its central role as a meeting place for GDR dissidents in the late 1980s. A statue outside commemorates their sacrifice.

Mauerpark

Bernauer Strasse (no phone, www. mauerpark.info). U2 Eberswalder Strasse. **Open** 24hrs daily. **Admission** free. **Map** p77 A1 ❷

The site of an old train station, this area became a 'death strip' when the Wall went up, with a viewing platform for West Berliners to look into the East. It became a community space in the 1990s, with two sports halls, a graffiti-daubed section of the Wall and a popular Sunday flea market. It's a lovely place to spend a summer afternoon among the drum circles, circus performers and assorted hippy types.

Museum in the Kulturbrauerei

Kulturbrauerei, Schönhauser Allee 36 (4677 7790, www.hdg.de/berlin). U2 Eberswalderstrasse. **Open** 10am-6pm Tue, Wed, Fri-Sun; 10am-8pm Thur. **Admission** free. **Map** p77 B2 ❸

Permanent exhibition 'Everyday Life in the GDR' is fascinating. Examples of leisure time include a Trabi roof-mounted tent and a mocked-up GDR living room.

Prenzlauer Berg Museum

Prenzlauer Allee 227 (902 953 917). U2 Senefelderplatz, or tram M2. **Open** 9am-7pm Tue, Wed, Fri; noon-8pm Thur. **Admission** free. **Map** p77 B3 ❹

A small but interesting exhibition (lots of old photos) examines local history and culture, with an emphasis on the area's development before and after the Wall went up.

Eating & drinking

8MM

Schönhauser Allee 177B (4050 0624, www. 8mmbar.com). U2 Senefelderplatz. **Open** 9pm-late daily. No credit cards. **Bar** **Map** p77 B3 ❺

Sometimes the 4/4 techno beat can seem inescapable in Berlin, so head to this dive bar for an alternative. Weekends get raucous with DJs playing punk and new-wave staples. Drinks are very reasonable, making it just the place for your umpteenth nightcap.

A Magica

Greifenhagener Strasse 54 (2280 8290, www.amagica.de). U2, S8, S9, S41, S42, S85 Schönhauser Allee. **Open** noon-midnight Mon-Fri; 4pm-midnight Sat, Sun (Oct-Mar 4-10pm Sat, Sun). **€. Pizza Map** p77 B1 ⑥

An oasis of democratic Italian nosh, this pizzeria has been packing them in since 2007. It's very popular with local young families, and for good reason: their Roman-style base is thin and flavoursome, and pizzas start at just €5.

Anna Blume

Kollwitzstrasse 83 (4404 8749, www.cafe-anna-blume.de). U2 Eberswalder Strasse. **Open** 8am-midnight daily. **€. Café Map** p77 B2 ⑦

This café-cum-florist is named after a poem by Kurt Schwitters. There are expensive but high-quality pastries, plus sweet and savoury crêpes, soups and hot dishes. The terrace is lovely in summer, and the interior, not surprisingly, smells of flowers.

Antipodes

Fehrbelliner Strasse 5 (0176 3834 0118 mobile). U2 Senefelderplatz. **Open** 8am-5pm Wed-Fri; 9am-5pm Sat, Sun. **€. Café Map** p77 B3 ⑧

This tiny café doles out all-day breakfast classics and, as to be expected from Kiwi ownership, great coffee, whether creamy flat whites or punchy espressos. Cutesy decor and beaming service complete the welcoming atmosphere.

Babel

Kastanienallee 33 (4403 1318). U2 Eberswalder Strasse. **Open** 10am-1am daily. **€.** No credit cards. **Lebanese Map** p77 A2 ⑨

Babel offers Lebanese shawarma wraps filled with grilled chicken, halloumi or crispy falafel. The *teller* (plates) are big enough to share, coming with fresh houmous, tabbouleh, pickled radish and their famous green chilli sauce.

Barn Roastery

Schönhauser Allee 8 (0151 2410 5136 mobile, www.thebarn.de). U8 Rosenthaler Platz. **Open** 8.30am-6pm Tue-Fri; 10am-6pm Sat, Sun. **€.** No credit cards. **Café Map** p77 B3 ⑩

The Barn is a shrine to the coffee bean. When owner Ralf Kueller opened this second, more spacious branch (the first is in Mitte), customers were bemused by the industrial bollard set in the doorway. Ralf was taking a rather humourless stand against the area's 'yummy mummy' invasion by banning prams (and laptops and dogs), so there are no distractions from the bean.

Beckett's Kopf

Pappelallee 64 (0162 237 9418 mobile, www.becketts-kopf.de). U2 Eberswalder Strasse. **Open** 8pm-late daily. No credit cards. **Bar Map** p77 B1 ⑪

This long-running cocktail bar is a source of fine drink in rather sparsely served Prenzlauer Berg. It follows the classic 'speakeasy' model: enter via an unmarked door and find yourself in rooms draped in red velvet. One of the two rooms caters for non-smokers, a relative rarity in Berlin's bar scene.

Bird

Am Falkplatz 5 (5105 3283, www.thebirdinberlin.com). U2, S8, S9, S41, S42, S85 Schönhauser Allee. **Open** 6pm-midnight Mon-Thur; 5pm-midnight Fri; noon-midnight Sat, Sun. **€€€.** No credit cards. **North American Map** p77 A1 ⑫

The Bird's burgers are mighty: 250g of freshly minced meat smothered in molten cheese and caramelised onions, with a toasted English muffin on top. Alongside this glistening beauty lies an enormous pile of hand-cut fries, one of the restaurant's highlights.

BERLIN BY AREA

Bonanza

Oderberger Strasse 35 (0171 563 0795 mobile, www.bonanzacoffee.de). U2 Eberswalder Strasse. **Open** 8.30am-6pm Mon-Fri; 10am-6pm Sat, Sun. €. No credit cards. **Café Map** p77 A2 ⑬

Bonanza serves some of the best coffee in Berlin. The bar is dominated by a handmade Synesso Cyncra machine, and seating is minimal. The cake selection is small but high grade.

Café Anita Wronski

Knaackstrasse 26-28 (442 8483). U2 Senefelderplatz. **Open** 9am-1am daily. €. No credit cards. **Café Map** p77 B2 ⑭

This is a friendly café on two levels, with scrubbed floors, beige walls, hard-working staff and as many tables crammed into the space as the laws of physics allow. Quiet in the afternoon, it's a good spot in which to sit and read.

Le Croco Bleu

Prenzlauer Allee 242 (0177 443 2359 mobile, www.lecrocobleu.com). U2 Senefelderplatz. **Open** 6pm-late Thur-Sat. **Bar Map** p77 B3 ⑮

Le Croco Bleu is the baby of Berlin drinks king Gregor Scholl. Housed in the old machine rooms of the 19th-century Bötzow Brewery, its name derives from an apocryphal story about a pair of Berlin Zoo crocodiles who were given shelter in a basement pool at the end of World War II. Try the Acu Acu, a potent blend of aged rums, orgeat (almond syrup) and absinthe.

Dairy

Raumerstrasse 12 (0176 2273 7551 mobile, www.thedairy.de). U2 Eberswalder Strasse. **Open** 8am-6pm Mon-Fri; 9am-6pm Sat, Sun. €. No credit cards. **Café Map** p77 B1 ⑯

One of the first places to open in the great wave from Down Under, this Kiwi-run café does all sorts of wonderful Anglo goodies, from scones and mince pies, to more substantial lunch offerings of cottage pie or avocado and chicken salad.

Dr Pong

Eberswalder Strasse 21 (no phone, www.drpong.net). U2 Eberswalder Strasse. **Open** 8pm-late Mon-Sat; 7pm-late Sun. No credit cards. **Bar Map** p77 B1/2 ⑰

Bring your table-tennis bat (or hire one) and prepare for drunken ping-pong carnage. The action doesn't start until around midnight, when you can expect 30 or so players – some good, some bad – to surround the table in one almighty round-the-world session. There's a bar and, oddly, Twiglets for nourishment. Opening hours are unreliable.

Fischfabrik

Danziger Strasse 24 (6431 4581, www.fischfabrikberlin.de). U2 Eberswalder Strasse. **Open** 10am-10pm Mon-Sat; 2-10pm Sun. €. No credit cards. **Fish & chips Map** p77 B2 ⑱

This fish shop does a pretty decent chip supper, with Sarson's malt vinegar on every table. The fish is as fresh as it gets in Berlin, nicely steamed within a crispy shell, and the chips hit the spot even if they aren't really cut thickly enough. Perfect with a glass of the crisp house riesling.

Gugelhof

Knaackstrasse 37 (442 9229, www.gugelhof.de). U2 Senefelderplatz. **Open** 4pm-midnight Mon-Fri; 10am-midnight Sat, Sun. €€. **Alsatian Map** p77 B2 ⑲

Gugelhof pioneered the Kollwitzplatz scene in the 1990s. Food is refined but filling, service is formal but friendly, and the furnishings are comfortably worn. The *Backöfe* – lamb, pork and beef marinated in riesling, stewed and served in an earthenware pot with root vegetables and a bread-crust lid – displays the peasant flourishes of Alsace's regional cooking.

Konnopke's Imbiss

Under U-Bahn tracks, Schönhauser Allee 44B, at Danziger Strasse (442 7765). U2 Eberswalder Strasse. **Open** 9am-8pm Mon-Fri; 11.30am-8pm Sat. €. No credit cards. **Imbiss Map** p77 B2 ⑳

This venerable sausage stand has been in the same family since 1930. After coming up with a secret recipe for ketchup (not available after the Wall was erected), it was the first place to offer Currywurst in East Berlin, and still serves probably the most famous – if not the best – Currywurst in the city.

Lucky Leek

Kollwitzstrasse 54 (6640 8710, www. lucky-leek.de). U2 Senefelderplatz. **Open** 6-11pm Wed-Sun. **€€.** No credit cards. **Vegan Map** p77 B2/3 ㉔
Chef Josita Hartanto started out at Charlottenburg's haute-cuisine La Mano Verde, and now has quite a following for her inventive vegan food. She's pushed the boundaries through clever plating and textural contrast, with dishes such as filo-spinach pockets of seitan with macadamia dumpling and brussels-sprout praline.

Neue Odessa Bar

Torstrasse 89 (0171 839 8991 mobile, www.neueodessabar.de). U8 Rosenthaler Platz. **Open** 7pm-late daily. No credit cards. **Bar Map** p77 A3 ㉒
Acting as the unofficial hub for the hip 'SoTo' set – the area south of Torstrasse

– this bar serves a mean cocktail. It's populated by local fashionistas and media-industry expats, who come here after doing the rounds of nearby gallery openings. DJs appear at weekends.

Oderquelle

Oderbergerstrasse 27 (4400 8080, www. oderquelle.de). U2 Eberswalder Strasse. **Open** 6pm-1am Mon-Sat; noon-1am Sun. **€€. Austrian/German Map** p77 A2 ㉓
This simple yet cosy spot might be a tad more expensive than its rivals, but that's because it's better than them. Typical dishes are goose leg stuffed with vegetables on red-wine risotto or vegetable strudel in tomato sauce.

Osmans Töchter

Papelallee 15 (3266 3388, www.osmans toechter.de). U2 Eberswalder Strasse. **Open** 5.30pm- midnight daily. **€€.** No credit cards. **Turkish Map** p77 B1 ㉔
Exposed light bulbs and mismatched wooden chairs are a Berlin cliché these days, but the look is still unusual for a Turkish restaurant. A network of Turkish housewives helps produce the range of meze salads and dips, as well as the *manti*, meat dumplings smothered in a garlicky yoghurt sauce.

Bonanza

BERLIN BY AREA

Pasternak

*Knaackstrasse 22-24 (441 3399,
www.restaurant-pasternak.de). U2
Senefelderplatz.* **Open** 9am-1am daily.
€€. Russian Map p77 B2/3

A small bar and restaurant that
became home to the wave of Russian
immigrants, many of them Jewish,
following the fall of the Soviet
Union. Food focuses on Russian and
Ashkenazi classics such as sweet and
sour brisket or beef stroganoff. The
lively atmosphere can get a little much
sometimes – ask for a table in the small
side room.

Prater

*Kastanienallee 7-9 (448 5688, www.
pratergarten.de). U2 Eberswalder Strasse.*
Open 6-11pm Mon-Sat; noon-11pm Sun.
No credit cards. **Bar Map** p77 B2

This rowdy beer garden, which lies
across a courtyard from an old ballroom of the same name, has been
doing Berliners a brisk service since
1852. The enthusiastic beer-swilling,
big wooden tables and platefuls of
Bratwurst and *Bretzeln* (pretzels)
almost make you feel like you've been
teleported down south to Munich.

Sasaya

*Lychener Strasse 50 (4471 7721, www.
sasaya-berlin.de). U2 Eberswalder
Strasse.* **€€.** No credit cards.
Japanese Map p77 B1

Berlin's infamous lack of fresh fish
poses a challenge for Japanese restaurants; there are scores of pan-Asian
places serving 'discount' sushi, but
the real thing is hard to come by. An
authentic menu and a bustling atmosphere have kept Sasaya a long-term
fave. The sashimi is eye-poppingly
fresh, and fine cooked dishes include
grilled horse mackerel and *kakuni*
(braised pork belly). Booking essential.

Sauvage

*Winsstrasse 30 (3810 0025, www.
sauvageberlin.com). S8, S9, S41, S42,*

Prater

*S85 Greifswalder Strasse, or tram M2,
M4, M10.* **Open** 6pm-midnight Wed-Fri;
11am-3.30pm, 6pm-midnight Sat, Sun.
€€€. No credit cards. **French Map** p77
C2

Rodrigo and Boris Leite-Poço were well
ahead of the curve when they opened
Europe's first Paleo restaurant in 2011.
Local produce features in dishes such
as hare terrine, or herb-crusted pike-
perch with fennel and celeriac gratin.

Schwarze Pumpe

*Choriner Strasse 76 (449 6939,
www.schwarzepumpe-berlin.de). U2
Senefelderplatz, or U8 Rosenthaler
Platz.* **Open** 10am-1am daily. No
credit cards. **Bar Map** p77 A3

One of the first places to open after
the Wall fell, Schwarze Pumpe is still
a popular low-key neighbourhood
bar, which has seen the street go from
reclaimed derelict housing to luxury
apartment living. It serves reasonably
priced magnums of wine, draught beer
and a decent menu of bar snacks.

Si An

Rykestrasse 36 (4050 5775, www.sian-berlin.de). U2 Senefelderplatz, or tram M2, M10. **Open** noon-midnight daily. **€.** No credit cards. **Vietnamese Map** p77 C2 ③⓪
One of the first Viet restaurants to really up the ante on decor while making an effort to cook everything fresh. There are assorted phos and usually a combination of curry, rice and meats heaped with fresh herbs and veg.

La Soupe Populaire

Prenzlauer Allee 244 (4431 9680, www. lasoupepopulaire.de). U2 Senefelderplatz. **Open** noon-2.30pm, 5.30-10.30pm Thur-Sat. **€€. German Map** p77 B3 ③①
Michelin-starred local hero Tim Raue opened this high-end 'canteen' to serve local German classic dishes reimagined. The restaurant is in the hulking Bötzow brewery – all exposed piping and industrial walkways – overlooking a large art gallery, and a special menu is created for each new exhibition.

Les Valseuses

Eberswalder Strasse 28 (7552 2032, www.lesvalseuses.de). U2 Eberswalder Strasse. **Open** 6.30pm-midnight daily. **€€.** No credit cards. **French Map** p77 B1/2 ③②
This modern French bistro is very good value: the 200g steak frites with béarnaise is a very reasonable €13.50. The specials board changes weekly – expect the likes of steak tartare with smoked garlic or chicken with lemon and green olives. Team your meal with a 'natural' wine from the Languedoc.

Wohnzimmer

Lettestrasse 6 (445 5458, www. wohnzimmer-bar.de). U2 Eberswalder Strasse. **Open** 10am-late daily. No credit cards. **Bar Map** p77 B1 ③③
Behind the door of this shabbily elegant 'living room' is a bar-like structure assembled from kitchen cabinets and assorted GDR furniture. Even if not the bohemian destination it used to be, it still provides a sanctuary for hip

young Helmholtzplatz mothers during the day, and for local barflies at night who come for the strong cocktails.

Shopping

D.nik

Wörther Strasse 14 (3064 8628, www. dnik-berlin.de). U2 Senefelderplatz. **Open** 10am-7pm Mon-Fri; 10am-6pm Sat. **Map** p77 B2 ③④
The name spells 'child' backwards in German. You'll find modular Tukluk, which can be folded into gigantic colourful geometric structures, playful furniture from young Swedish designers Little Red Stuga and cardboard building blocks.

Fein & Ripp

Kastanienallee 91-92 (4403 3250, www.feinundripp.de). U2 Eberswalder Strasse. **Open** noon-7pm Mon-Sat. **Map** p77 B2 ③⑤
A curious shop, which started out selling old stock discovered in a Swabian clothes factory – primarily cotton underwear from the 1920s to the '70s. They've now expanded into brands that continue traditional production methods: Frye's heavy leather prison boots and Pike Brothers' stiff blue denim.

Goldhahn & Sampson

Dunckerstrasse 9 (no phone, www. goldhahnundsampson.de). U2 Eberswalder Strasse. **Open** 8am-8pm Mon-Fri; 9am-8pm Sat. **Map** p77 B/C1 ③⑥
A charming deli that sells all sorts, from locally roasted Andraschko coffee to imported Japanese mayonnaise. Also, international cookbooks and specialist cookery classes, such as macaroon baking or festive Jewish cuisine.

Goo

Oderbergerstrasse 45 (4403 3737, www. paulsboutiqueberlin.de). U2 Eberswalder Strasse. **Open** noon-8pm Mon-Sat. **Map** p77 A2 ③⑦
This tiny shop sets itself apart from the usual vintage store by specialising

in almost-new designer clobber from big labels such as Comme des Garçons, Wood Wood and Y-3.

Kollwitzplatz Farmers' Market

Kollwitzplatz (organic market 4433 9137, farmers' market 0172 327 8238 mobile). U2 Senefelderplatz. **Open** noon-7pm Thur; 9.30am-5pm Sat. **Map** p77 B2 ⊕

The Saturday farmers' market is popular with gourmets stocking up on weekend food supplies and with locals out for a stroll and a snack. You'll find chocolates by Martin Franz, locally made tofu, fresh pasta and a Turkish-run stand selling the best *Gözleme* in town. The Thursday market is smaller and exclusively organic.

Lunettes Brillenagentur

Dunckerstrasse 18 (4471 8050, www. lunettes-selection.de). S8, S9, S41, S42, S85 Prenzlauer Allee, or tram M2. **Open** noon-8pm Mon, Tue, Thur, Fri; 10am-8pm Wed; noon-6pm Sat. **Map** p77 C1 ⊕

Owner Uta Geyer has a knack for getting her hands on hard-to-find vintage spectacles frames, ranging from sleek 1920s pieces to rockabilly cat-eyes, classic aviators to glitzy Jackie Os. Prices are affordable.

Manufacture Délicate

Rykestrasse 7 (6891 3699, www. manufacture-delicate.de). U2 Senefelderplatz, or tram M2. **Open** 7am-6pm Tue-Fri; 8am-6pm Sat, Sun. **Map** p77 B2 ⊕

A 2013 addition to the Prenzlauer Berg bakery scene, Manufacture Délicate distinguishes itself with a variety of hard-crust sourdough loaves, fruit tarts and sweet pastries.

Mauerpark Flohmarkt

Bernauer Strasse 63-64 (0176 2925 0021 mobile). U8 Bernauer Strasse. **Open** 7am-5pm Sun. **Map** p77 A2 ⊕

One of the biggest and busiest flea markets in Berlin, selling everything from local designer clothes to cardboard boxes of black-market CDs. This is also the venue for the immensely popular weekly outdoor singing session, Bearpit Karaoke, where thousands flock in summer to have a go on the mobile sound system.

Onkel Philipp's Spielzeugwerkstatt

Choriner Strasse 35 (449 0491, www. onkel-philipp.de). U2 Senefelderplatz. **Open** 9.30am-6.30pm Tue, Wed, Fri; 11am-8pm Thur; 11am-4pm Sat. **Map** p77 B2 ⊕

A toy-repair shop full of aged playthings, wooden toys, puzzles, trains, puppets and more. If you ask nicely, owner Philipp Schünemann might let you view his private GDR toy collection.

Saint George's

Wörther Strasse 27 (8179 8333, www.saintgeorgesbookshop.com). U2 Senefelderplatz, or tram M2. **Open** 11am-8pm Mon-Fri; 11am-7pm Sat. **Map** p77 B/C2 ⊕

Founded by English twins Paul and Daniel Gurner, Saint George's harks back to the heyday of London's Charing Cross Road. Housing around 10,000 English-language books, it's also reliable for second-hand books in good condition.

Shakespeare & Sons

Raumerstrasse 36 (4000 3685, www. shakesbooks.de). U2 Eberswalder Strasse. **Open** 9am-8pm Mon-Sat; 10am-8pm Sun. **Map** p77 C1 ⊕

Nothing to do with Paris's famous Shakespeare and Co, but an offshoot of a pair of bookshops in Prague. It has French and English books, both new and used, in every genre, but specialises in eastern European literature in English translations.

Temporary Showroom

Kastanienallee 36A (6220 4564, www.temporaryshowroom.com). U2 Senefelderplatz. **Open** 11am-7pm Mon-Sat. **Map** p77 A2 ⊕

This is both a boutique stocking cult labels and a creative agency for young designers. There's technical shoeware from Adidas's experimental SLVR line to go with your patterned tracksuit from Switzerland's Julian Zigerli.

VEB Orange

Oderbergerstrasse 29 (9788 6886, www.veborange.de). U2 Eberswalder Strasse. **Open** 11am-7pm Mon-Sat. **Map** p77 A2 ㊻

The tagline claims they sell 'everything but fruit' – and you're sure to find a wide range of original 1960s and '70s furniture, lighting and clothes.

Nightlife

Bassy Cowboy Club

Schönhauser Allee 176A (281 8323, www.bassy-club.de). U2 Senefelderplatz. **Open** 9pm-late Tue, Fri; 10pm-late Sat. No credit cards. **Map** p77 B3 ㊼

A move from Hackescher Markt, and a more diverse music programme has done wonders for Bassy's reputation. It has a pre-1969 music policy, with concerts of rockabilly, beat, surf or hot jazz starting at 11pm.

Saint George's

Duncker

Dunckerstrasse 64 (445 9509, www.dunckerclub.de). S8, S9, S41, S42 Prenzlauer Allee. **Open** 9pm-late Mon; 10pm-late Thur; 11pm-late Fri, Sat. No credit cards. **Map** p77 C1 ㊽

Duncker is located in a neo-Gothic church on a nondescript side street. While the tail end of the week focuses on new wave, dark wave and indie, it's the Dark Monday goth party that is the club's bread and butter.

Roadrunner's Paradise

Saarbrückerstrasse 24 (7808 2991, www.roadrunners-paradise.de). U2 Senefelderplatz. **Open** varies. No credit cards. **Map** p77 B3 ㊾

RP is tucked away next to a motorcycle repair shop, in a courtyard of the former Königstadt brewery – a suitably greasy location for this butch venue. On offer is a tasty but irregular mixture of live shows and DJ sets, focusing on garage, blues-rock, rockabilly and surf.

Arts & leisure

Ballhaus Ost

Pappelallee 15 (4799 7474, www.ballhaus ost.de). U2 Eberswalderstrasse. **Tickets** €15; €8 reductions. **Map** p77 B1 ㊿

This dilapidated ex-ballroom hosts art, performance art, dance and concerts, offering a unique and authentic cultural evening. There's also a lounge and bar populated by a very cool crowd.

Kulturbrauerei

Schönhauser Allee 36 (4431 5100, www.kulturbrauerei.de). U2 Eberswalderstrasse. **Open** varies. **Map** p77 B2 (51)

With its assortment of venues, outdoor bars and barbecues, this cultural centre housed in an enormous former brewery can resemble a cross between a medieval fairground and a school disco.

East Side Gallery

Friedrichshain & Lichtenberg

Berlin's alternative squat community migrated to Friedrichshain in the 1990s and politicised this working-class district. Much of the area is pretty bleak, dominated by big Communist-era housing blocks and slashed through by railway tracks. It's also home to East Berlin's first massive post-war civic building project – a broad boulevard that was originally named Stalinallee, and then Karl-Marx-Allee.

East of Friedrichshain, Lichtenberg isn't the most attractive of neighbourhoods, but it does contain a couple of key former Stasi strongholds and East Berlin Zoo.

Friedrichshain

The best way to get a feeling for both Friedrichshain and the old GDR is to head east from Alexanderplatz down Karl-Marx-Allee, which is the site of the **Computerspiele Museum** and GDR icon **Café Sybille**. From Lichtenberger Strasse onwards, the street truly impresses in its Communist monumentalism, with rows of grand apartment blocks draped in stone and Meissen tiles stretching beyond the twin towers of Frankfurter Tor.

On Mühlenstrasse along the north bank of the Spree, is the **East Side Gallery**, a stretch of former Wall that was turned into a mural memorial in 1990. The industrial buildings are now home to loft spaces, offices and studios. Both Universal Music and MTV-Europe have moved their German HQ here, as part of the vast Mediaspree complex, which has met much opposition. Some of Berlin's best nightlife can be found around Ostkreuz at places such as **Salon zur Wilden Renate** and the infamous **Homopatik** (://about blank).

North-west is the **Volkspark Friedrichshain**. This huge park is scattered with socialist-realist art, and has an open-air stage, a fountain of fairy-tale characters and the popular **Café Schönbrunn**. Graves of fighters who fell in March 1848 in the battle for German unity are here too. It's a popular gay cruising zone at night.

Sights & museums

Computerspiele Museum

Karl-Marx-Allee 93A (6098 8577, www.computerspielemuseum.de). U5 Weberwiese. **Open** 10am-8pm Mon, Wed-Sun. **Admission** €8; €5 reductions. **Map** p89 A1 ❶
This excellent museum traces the history of the video-game industry, from early arcade classics such as Pong to groundbreaking genre-definers like Sim City.

East Side Gallery

Mühlenstrasse (no phone, www. eastsidegallery-berlin.de). U1, S5, S7, S75 Warschauer Strasse or S5, S7, S75 Ostbahnhof. **Open** 24hrs daily. **Admission** free. **Map** p89 A3 ❷
The largest remaining section of Wall still standing, where, in 1990, international artists came together to produce 101 paintings across its side. Dmitri Vrubel's striking portrait depicting Brezhnev and Hönecker's kiss – a Soviet sign of great respect – is easily its most iconic image.

Eating & drinking

Antlered Bunny

Oderstrasse 7 (6640 5300, www. auntbenny.com). S3, S5, S7, S41, S42, S75 Ostkreuz. **Open** 6pm- 2am Tue-Sat. No credit cards. **Bar Map** p89 E2 ❸
The Canadian siblings behind the excellent Aunt Benny have created this capsule cocktail bar (installed behind their café). Drinks include the Rosebud – Bulleit rye, rose syrup, maple syrup and calvados – and you can even get freshly shucked oysters at weekends.

Café Schönbrunn

Volkspark Friedrichshain (4530 56525, www.schoenbrunn.net). Bus 200. **Open** 10am-late daily. €€. **Café**
A couple of years ago, this lakeside place sold basic coffee and snacks to an elderly crowd. With a change of management, the food (and music) improved dramatically. The concrete front is unchanged, while the (new) lounge furniture is pure 1970s.

Café Sybille

Karl-Marx-Allee 72 (2935 2203, www. cafe-sibylle-berlin.de). U5 Weberwiese. **Open** 10am-8pm Mon-Wed; 10am-10pm Thur, Fri; noon-10pm Sat, Sun. €. No credit cards. **Café Map** p89 A1 ❹
The perfect pit stop when doing some GDR sightseeing, this opened as a milk bar in the 1950s and was one of East Berlin's most popular cafés. They serve ice-cream sundaes, coffee, cake and, of course, beer. There's also a roof terrace accessible by reservation and a free exhibition on local history.

CSA

Karl-Marx-Allee 96 (2904 4741, www.csa-bar.de). U5 Weberweise. **Open** 7pm-late daily. No credit cards. **Bar Map** p89 A1 ❺
This ultra-modern bar is housed in the old Czech Airlines building; the angular furniture and white plastic fittings contrast magnificently with its shabby location and the vast concrete sweep of Karl-Marx-Allee. Expect a relaxed atmosphere, a design-conscious crowd and excellent drinks.

Dirty South

Krossener Strasse 18 (2936 0555, www. dirtysouthberlin.de). U5 Samariterstrasse. **Open** 5pm-4am Mon-Fri; noon-4am Sat, Sun. €. No credit cards. **Tex-Mex Map** p89 C2 ❻
A Tex-Mex dive offering late-night cocktails and boozy weekend brunches. The tacos, burritos and quesadillas are excellent, as is the bloody mary. The decor is Edwardian saloon.

Goodies

Warschauer Strasse 69 (0151 5376 3801 mobile, www.goodies-berlin.de). U1, S5, S7, S75 Warschauer Strasse. **Open** 7am-8pm Mon-Fri; 9am-8pm Sat, Sun. **€**. No credit cards. **Vegetarian Map** p89 C2 **7**

Visit the original branch of the veggie Goodies chain for tofu bagels and super-food smoothies. Friendly staff and comfortable sofas facilitate lingering.

Hops & Barley

Wuhlischstrasse 22-23 (2936 7534, www.hopsandbarley-berlin.de). U1, S5, S7, S75 Warschauer Strasse. **Open** 5pm-3am daily. No credit cards. **Bar Map** p89 D2 **8**

Interesting hop varieties are used here to produce traditional German beers, such as the top-fermenting *Weiz* (wheat) and *Dunkles* (dark), as well as *Apfelwein* (apple wine – cider, to you and me), a drink rarely seen in Berlin pubs. The heavy wooden bar is matched with fine green and white tiling, with the large brewing kettles in pride of place along one side.

Kater Mikesch

Proskauerstrasse 13 (2804 1950, www.kater-mikesch.com). U5 Samariterstrasse or Frankfurter Tor. **Open** 5pm-midnight Mon-Fri; noon-midnight Sat, Sun. **€€**. No credit cards. **Czech Map** p89 D1 **9**

Hearty Bohemian specialities – goulash, dumplings (both bread and potato), paprika chicken and other Czech favourites – are served in this modern restaurant. The unfiltered Svijany beer on tap is excellent.

Monster Ronson's Ichiban Karaoke

Warschauer Strasse 34 (8975 1327, www.karaokemonster.de). U1, S5, S7, S75 Warschauer Strasse. **Open** 7pm-midnight daily. No credit cards. **Bar Map** p89 B3 **10**

This karaoke bar is now packed most nights. Aspiring divas can belt out songs in several different booths, some small and intimate, others with their own stage area, where transsexual hosts often compere on weekends.

Mutzenbacher

Libauerstrasse 11 (9561 6788, www.mutzenbacher-berlin.de). U1, S5, S7, S75 Warschauer Strasse. **Open** noon-midnight Mon-Fri; 10am-midnight Sat, Sun. **€€**. No credit cards. **Austrian Map** p89 C2 **11**

The restaurant takes its name from fictional Viennese prostitute Josephine Mutzenbacher, star of a famous 1906 erotic novel, and offers inventive Austrian cuisine, in surroundings befitting Friedrichshain's punkier vibe. A mounted boar's head made from glass shards looks over as fetching waitstaff in *Lederhosen* bring out *Rindsvögerl* (braised beef rolls) with red cabbage or *Fleischkäse* (meatloaf).

Nil

Grünberger Strasse 52 (2904 7713, www.nil-imbiss.de). U5 Frankfurter Tor. **Open** 11am- midnight daily. **€**. No credit cards. **Imbiss Map** p89 C2 **12**

In a city full of vegetarians, mini chain Nil was an instant hit with its Sudanese spin on the falafel wrap: fried to order for extra crispness; plenty of fresh salad; and the magic ingredient, a creamy peanut sauce.

Paule's Metal Eck

Krossener Strasse 15 (291 1624). U1, S5, S7, S75 Warschauer Strasse. **Open** 7pm-5am daily. No credit cards. **Bar Map** p89 C2 **13**

Eck attracts a young crowd with relentless metal videos, a decent selection of beers, and both pool and table football. The interior is half gloomy mausoleum, half pastiche medieval style.

Schneeweiss

Simplonstrasse 16 (2904 9704, www.schneeweiss-berlin.de). U1, S5, S7, S75 Warschauer Strasse. **Open** 6pm-1am Mon-Fri; 10am-1am Sat, Sun. **€€**. **Southern German/Austrian Map** p89 C2 **14**

Friedrichshain

Sights & museums

Eating & drinking

Shopping

Nightlife

Arts & leisure

KREUZBERG
pp123-139

East Side Gallery

O2 World

© Copyright Time Out Group 2015

This understated place, done out in minimalist white, offers 'Alpine' dishes – essentially a fusion of Italian, Austrian and south German ideas. There are daily lunch and dinner menus, plus a breakfast, and snacks, shakes and schnitzels throughout the day. Booking advisable.

Schwarzer Hahn

Seumestrasse 23 (2197 0371, www. schwarzerhahn-heimatkueche.de). U5 Samariterstrasse or tram M13. **Open** 5.30-11pm Mon-Sat. **€€€**. No credit cards. **Modern German Map** p89 D2
What Berlin does so well – a great kitchen that's been discreetly knocking out fantastic regional German cuisine for years. It's excellent value too. Try their pickled suckling-pig cheek with cauliflower and barley salad or the potato and chanterelle strudel.

Sigiriya

Grünberger Strasse 66 (2904 4208, www.restaurant-sigiriya.de). U5 Frankfurter Tor. **Open** noon-midnight daily. **€**. No credit cards. **Sri Lankan Map** p89 C2
Sigiriya is a hit with British expats for its authentic curries. Organic or free-range meat and dairy are used, and the kitchen does plenty of interesting vegetarian dishes, such as green mung-bean curry.

Spätzle & Knödel

Wühlischstrasse 20 (2757 1151, www. spaetzle knoedel.de). U1, S5, S7, S75 Warschauer Strasse or tram M13. **Open** 5-11pm Mon-Fri; 3-11pm Sat, Sun. **€€**. No credit cards. **Bavarian Map** p89 D2
A bare-bones eaterie – literally a brick-walled room with wooden tables – catering to southern German appetites with plates piled high with cheesy *Spätzle* or dumplings, topped with goulash, roast pork or mushroom sauce.

Supamolly

Jessner Strasse 41 (2900 7294, www. supamolly.de). U5, S8, S9, S41, S42, S85 Frankfurter Allee. **Open** 8pm-late Tue-Sat. No credit cards. **Bar Map** p89 E2

Schneeweiss p88

With the few remaining Berlin squats now tourist sites, Supamolly soldiers on as a punk-music venue, bar, cinema and general activist meeting point. It retains its grimy charm, the candlelit bar welcoming all for cheap beer at all hours of the night.

Süss War Gestern

Wühlischstrasse 34 (0176 2441 2940 mobile). U5 Samariterstrasse or tram M13. **Open** 7pm-4am Mon, Tue; 7pm-5am Wed; 7pm-6am Thur; 7pm-8am Fri, Sat. No credit cards. **Bar Map** p89 D2 ⑲
Berlin's nightlife can sometimes seem aggressively all-or-nothing, but this Friedrichshain DJ bar provides a welcome middle ground, with free entry, cheap beer and two floors with DJs.

Trattoria Libau

Libauer Strasse 10 (2576 8529). U1, S5, S7, S75 Warschauer Strasse. **Open** 4pm-midnight Tue-Sun. €. No credit cards. **Italian Map** p89 C2 ⑳
A little Italian gem, serving Roman-style pizzas big enough to share, salads and the ubiquitous tiramisu, all at very reasonable prices. Service can be gruff.

Tres Cabezas

Boxhagener Strasse 74 (2904 7470, www.trescabezas.de). S3, S5, S7, S41, S42, S75 Ostkreuz. **Open** 8.30am-7.30pm daily. €. No credit cards. **Café Map** p89 E2 ㉑
So much more than a cute neighbourhood café. Owner Robert Stock has control over every step of the production chain, from owning a Fairtrade plantation in Costa Rica to servicing the Kees van der Westen espresso machines they exclusively stock. Their custom blends are freshly roasted on-site.

Shopping

Big Brobot

Kopernikusstrasse 19 (7407 8388, www.bigbrobot.com). U5 Frankfurter Tor. **Open** 11am-8pm Mon-Fri; 11am-6pm Sat. **Map** p89 C2 ㉒

A paradise for graphics nerds, with hundreds of collectible toys, comics and books on tattoo art or vintage typography. Big Brobot also stocks high-end skate labels such as Stüssy and Kid Robot.

Flohmarkt am Boxhagener Platz

Boxhagener Platz (fleamarket 0162 292 3066 mobile, farmers' market 0178 476 2242 mobile). U5 Samariterstrasse. **Open** 9am-3.30pm Sat; 10am-6pm Sun. No credit cards. **Map** p89 C2 ㉓
The Boxi market now offers a thriving farmers' market on Saturdays and craft fare on Sundays (when you may also find some cheap vintage clothing).

Olivia

Wühlischstrasse 30 (6050 0368, www.olivia-berlin.de). U1, S5, S7, S75 Warschauer Strasse. **Open** noon-7pm Mon-Sat; 1-6pm Sun. No credit cards. **Map** p89 C2 ㉔
A cutesy boutique of a chocolatier with beautiful hand-painted biscuits, lots of cocoa varieties and their signature cakes, which come baked in a jar.

Stil Raum Berlin

Eldenaer Strasse 21 (4679 4857, www.stilraumberlin.de). S8, S9, S41, S42, S85 Storkower Strasse. **Open** noon-7pm Tue-Fri; noon-4pm Sat. No credit cards.
The owners of this beautiful furniture showroom make regular trips to Copenhagen and bring back Danish design classics.

Nightlife

://about blank

Markgrafendamm 24C (no phone, http://aboutparty.net). S3, S5, S7, S8, S9, S41, S42, S75 Ostkreuz. No credit cards. **Map** p89 D3 ㉕
Particularly famed for its open-air parties, this club near Ostkreuz station is a favourite with the city's more adventurous hedonists – not least for its monthly blowout Homopatik night.

Urban Spree

Berghain/Panorama Bar

Am Wriezener Bahnhof (no phone, www.berghain.de). U1, S3, S5, S7, S75 Warschauer Strasse. No credit cards. **Map** p89 A2 ㉖

The hippest and hardest electronic music club in Berlin, if not Europe. The building is a Communist-era power station transformed into a concrete cathedral of techno on two floors, with the mixed Panorama Bar upstairs and Berghain below. The latter is awash with pumped-up, shirtless gay men sweating it out on the dancefloor (or in the darkroom at the back) from Saturday night well into Sunday afternoon. In summer, the party pours over into the garden chill-out area, bar and dancefloor. Arrive after 6am to avoid the massive queues. Cameras are prohibited – they're taken at the door and returned later.

Kater Blau

Holzmarktstrasse 25 (no phone, www. katerblau.de). S5, S7, S75 Ostbahnhof. This is the X-rated part of the expansive, family-friendly Holzmarkt development. With a moored boat, roaring fire at night and many hammock-like structures, the potential for alfresco relaxing is very high. At the business end of proceedings, a fine roster of electronic DJs spin away unendingly – sometimes for four days straight. The vibe is more crusty than chic, and increasingly so as the weekend unravels. If you have the stamina (and courage) to last well into Monday afternoon, expect to encounter some of Berlin's strangest creatures.

K17

Pettenkofer Strasse 17A (4208 9300, www.k17-berlin.de). U5, S8, S9, S41, S42 Frankfurter Allee. No credit cards. Goth, EBM, industrial and metal are undead and well in this three-floor club. Parties hit full pelt at the weekend and the occasional live shows feature hardcore, nu-metal and crossover bands. The Dark Hostel offers goth-friendly accommodation.

Rosi's

Revaler Strasse 29 (no phone, www.rosis-berlin.de). S3, S5, S7, S8, S9, S41, S42, S75 Ostkreuz. No credit cards. **Map** p89 D3 ㉗

A typical Berlin club, Rosi's is a tumbledown, DIY affair: all bare bricks and mismatched flea-market furniture. The atmosphere is very relaxed and the crowd tends to be young and studenty.

noise, with an emphasis on the experimental and DIY. Summertime bonus: an expansive suntrap of a beer garden.

YAAM

Schillingbrücke, at Stralauer Platz (no phone, www.yaam.de). S5, S7, S75 Ostbahnhof.

YAAM was evicted from its previous home, but quickly found another riverside spot, so it's business as usual for this legendary beach bar and cultural centre. By day, there might be kids playing and a laid-back game of volleyball in progress, with a jerk chicken stall on the side. As the light fades, things ease up a notch or two with concerts and parties bouncing to an Afro-Caribbean beat.

Arts & leisure

Astra Kulturhaus

Revaler Stasse 99 (2005 6767, www. astra-berlin.de). U1 Warschauer Strasse. **Map** p89 C2 ㉙

Berlin's premier alternative venue, this is part of the large RAW Tempel complex on old industrial warehouse grounds that's somewhat reminiscent of Christiania in Copenhagen. Arrive early as it gets crowded, and pillars can mean tricky sightlines. The likes of Bill Callahan, Godspeed You! Black Emperor, Death Cab for Cutie and Damon Albarn have played here.

Filmtheater Am Friedrichshain

Bötzowstrasse 1-5 (4284 5188, www.yorck.de). Bus 200.

This charming five-screen cinema is on the park and has a lovely beer garden.

Fritzclub im Postbahnhof

Strasse der Pariser Kommune 8 (698 1280, www.fritzdub.com). S5, S7, S75 Ostbahnhof. No credit cards. **Map** p89 A2 ㉚

This restored industrial building is relatively young in comparison to other venues, but its association with Radio

---

Live acts are a regular feature, DJs spin mainly electro and rock, and the beer garden is popular on summer nights.

Salon zur Wilden Renate

Alt-Stralau 70 (2504 1426, www.renate. cc). S3, S5, S7, S8, S9, S41, S42, S75 Ostkreuz.

Students and ravers press up against refugees from Mitte in this knackered old house, where the reliably crowded rooms are set up like the flats they once were – complete with the odd bed. On languid summer afternoons, the club hops across the river to an intimate open-air wonderland called Else.

Urban Spree

Revaler Strasse 99 (7407 8597, www. urbanspree.com). U1, S5, S7, S75 Warschauer Strasse. **Map** p89 C2 ㉓

This new arts centre is doing much to revive the somewhat moribund (and tacky) area by Revaler Strasse that's known as the 'clubbing mile'. Created by the French crew behind the much-missed .HBC complex, it houses an art gallery, concert hall, studio spaces, bookshop and food trucks. There are frequent performances and concerts, ranging from free-form jazz to acid-folk and improvised instrumental

Fritz gives it the clout to stage the likes of Arcade Fire, Paloma Faith and Fun Lovin' Criminals, as well as regular indie student parties.

Radialsystem V

Holzmarktstrasse 33 (288 788 588, www.radialsystem.de). S5, S7, S75 Ostbahnhof. No credit cards.
This warren of rooms in a former pumping station by the river was opened in 2006 by Jochen Sandig, partner of choreographer Sasha Waltz, whose company, Sasha Waltz & Guests, is based here. It promotes one-off music and performance events, and attracts a well-heeled crowd.

Lichtenberg

Lichtenberg is generally unappealing, but it does contain the **Tierpark Berlin-Friedrichsfelde** (Zoo) and both the **Stasi Museum** and the **Gedenkstätte Berlin-Hohenschönhausen**, a former Stasi prison turned chilling exhibit of state oppression. The **Museum Berlin-Karlshorst** documents the troubled history of Russian-German relations during the last century.

Sights & museums

Forschungs- und Gedenkstätte Normannenstrasse (Stasi Museum)

Ruschestrasse 103 (553 6854, www. stasimuseum.de). U5, S8, S9, S41, S42, S85 Frankfurter Allee. **Open** 10am-6pm Mon-Fri; noon-6pm Sat, Sun. **Admission** €5; €4 reductions. No credit cards.
In what used to be part of the Stasi HQ, you can look around the former offices of secret police chief Erich Mielke and see displays of bugging devices and spy cameras concealed in books, plant pots and car doors. A new exhibition explores the Stasi's structure, methods and activities. Tours are also offered of the Stasi Archives next door.

Gärten der Welt Marzahn

Eisenacher Strasse 99, Marzahn (700 906 699, www.gruen-berlin.de). S7 Marzahn then bus 195. **Open** 9am-sundown daily. **Admission** €4.
A sparkling collection of specialist gardens. The Chinese garden is the largest in Europe; and there are similarly authentic Korean, Balinese and Italian gardens. Kids will love the fiendish hedge maze.

Gedenkstätte Berlin-Hohenschönhausen

Gensler Strasse 66 (9860 8230, www. stiftung-hsh.de). Tram M5, M6. **Open** see website for details. **Admission** €5; €2.50 reductions. No credit cards.
A former remand prison run by the Stasi, this building has a vicious history. The inmates were all political prisoners, from the leaders of the 1953 workers' uprising to critical students. Excellent and highly personal guided tours by ex-prisoners take 90 minutes. The experience is bleak, but offers a potent insight into how the Stasi operated.

Mies van der Rohe Haus

Oberseestrasse 60 (9700 0618, www.mies vanderrohehaus.de). Tram M5, 27. **Open** 11am-5pm Tue-Sun. **Admission** free.
Ludwig Mies van der Rohe designed this L-shaped modernist gem in 1933. It now hosts art exhibitions.

Museum Berlin-Karlshorst

Zwieseler Strasse 4 (5015 0810, www. museum-karlshorst.de). S3 Karlshorst. **Open** 10am-6pm Tue-Sun. **Admission** free.
After the Soviets took Berlin, they commandeered this former German officers' club as HQ for the military administration. It was here, on the night of 8-9 May 1945, that German commanders signed the unconditional surrender, ending the war in Europe. This stern museum surveys over 70 years of German-Soviet relations. Buy an English guide, as the exhibits are labelled in German and Russian.

Tierpark Berlin-Friedrichsfelde

Am Tierpark 125 (515 310, www. tierpark-berlin.de). U5 Tierpark. **Open** Late Mar-mid Sept 9am-6pm daily. Mid Sept-late Mar 9am-5pm daily.
Admission €12; €6-€8 reductions.
East Berlin's zoo is still one of Europe's largest, with an impressive amount of roaming space for the herd animals, although others are still kept in rather small cages. One of the continent's biggest snake farms is here. In the northwest corner is the baroque Schloss Friedrichsfelde.

Shopping

Dong Xuan Center

Herzbergstrasse 128-139 (5321 7480, www.dongxuan-berlin.de). Tram M8, 21.
Open 10am-8pm Mon, Wed-Sun.
Four cavernous warehouses stand on the former site of an enormous coal and graphite processing plant. Tradesmen hawk all sorts of wares for businesses affiliated with the Vietnamese community, from wholesale nail-salon supplies to glitzy chandeliers, but of most interest are the enormous food halls.

Sammlung Haubrok

Herzbergstrasse 40-43 (0172 210 9525 mobile, www.haubrok.org). Tram M8, 21. **Open** By appointment. **Admission** €80 donation per group.
With over 750 works, spanning painting, sculpture, photography and video pieces, Barbara and Axel Haubrok's collection is regarded as one of Berlin's best.

Nightlife

Sisyphos

Hauptstrasse 15 (9836 6839, www. sisyphos-berlin.net). S3 Rummelsburg.
No credit cards.
The party begins on Friday and runs non-stop until Monday. Vast indoor and outdoor spaces at this former dog-biscuit factory help create a festival-like spirit. Music ranges from pumping techno to more housey tunes.

Dong Xuan Center

BERLIN BY AREA

Tiergarten

A mish-mash of districts plus the grand green park that gives it its name, Tiergarten straddles the centre of Berlin; it's home to dozens of embassies as well as the iconic Reichstag parliament building. Tiergarten was once hemmed in on the east by the Wall, but these days it's right at the heart of things again, stretching from the Hauptbahnhof in the north to the Zoo in the south-west. South of the park is the rejuvenated commercial centre of Potsdamer Platz, the museums and venues of the Kulturforum, and Potsdamer Strasse, the former red-light drag that is now experiencing something of a revival.

The park & the Reichstag

A hunting ground for the Prussian electors since the 16th century, **Tiergarten** was opened to the public in the 18th century. It was badly damaged during World War II; in the desperate winter of 1945-46, almost all the surviving trees were cut down for firewood, and it wasn't until 1949 that Tiergarten started to recover. Today, joggers, nature lovers, gay cruisers and picnickers pour into the park in fair weather.

Its main thoroughfare, **Strasse des 17 Juni** (the date of the East Berlin workers' strike of 1953), is one of the few pieces of Hitler's plan for 'Germania' that actually got built – a grand east–west axis, lined with Nazi lamp-posts and linking Unter den Linden to Neu-Westend. The **Sowjetisches Ehrenmal** (Soviet War Memorial) is at its eastern end.

At the north-eastern corner of the park stands the **Reichstag** – a must-do on any visitor's itinerary. The post-war **Englischer Garten** was landscaped in the style of Capability Brown and filled with plants donated by the English royal family and various horticultural societies. Within the loop of the Spree north of the garden is the **Hansaviertel**, a post-war housing project designed by a who's who of architects as part of the 1957 Interbau Exhibition for the 'city of tomorrow'. It's of great interest to lovers of concrete modernism.

Sights & museums

Gaslaternen-Freilichtmuseum Berlin

Strasse des 17 Juni (9025 4124, www.museumsportal-berlin.de). S5, S7, S75 Tiergarten. **Open** 24hrs daily. **Admission** free. **Map** p98 B3 ❶
A charming little oddity right by the Tiergarten S-Bahn station, this open-air gas-lamp museum has over 90 examples of historic streetlights.

Reichstag

Platz der Republik (2270, www. bundestag.de). U55, S1, S2, S25 Brandenburger Tor. **Open** 8am-midnight daily (last entry 10pm). **Admission** free. **Map** p99 F2 ❷
The imposing Reichstag was controversial from the beginning. Architect Paul Wallot struggled to find a style that would symbolise German national identity at a time – 1884-94, shortly after unification – when no such style or identity existed. It was burned on 17 February 1933; the Nazis blamed Dutchman Marius van der Lubbe, a Communist, and used it as an excuse to begin their seizure of power. But since its celebrated renovation by Lord Foster, the Reichstag again houses the Bundestag (Federal Parliament). Foster conceived of it as a 'dialogue between old and new': graffiti scrawled by Russian soldiers in 1945 has been left on view, and there's no attempt to deny the building's turbulent history.

No dome appeared on Foster's original plans, but the German government insisted upon one as a sop to conservatives. Foster then insisted that unlike the original dome (damaged in the war and demolished in the 1950s), the new dome must be open to visitors as a symbol of political transparency; due to the materials used, it ended up costing even more than a replica would have done.

A lift whisks you up to the roof; ramps then lead to the top of the dome, from where there are fine views of the city. At the centre is a funnel of mirrors, angled so as to shed light on the workings of democracy below, but also lending an almost funhouse effect to the dome. An excellent (free) audio guide points out all the surrounding landmarks.

Note that you must book in advance by filling in an online form and suggesting three possible time-slots at least three working days in advance: www. bundestag.de/besuche/kuppel.html.

Siegessäule

Strasse des 17 Juni (391 2961). S5, S7, S75 Bellevue. **Open** *Summer* 9.30am-6.30pm Mon-Fri; 9.30am-7pm Sat, Sun. *Winter* 10am-5pm Mon-Fri; 10am-5.30pm Sat, Sun. **Admission** €3; €2.50 reductions; free under-5s. No credit cards. **Map** p98 C3 ❸
Tiergarten's biggest monument was built in 1871-73 to commemorate Prussian campaigns against Denmark (1864), Austria (1866) and France (1870-71). Originally positioned in front of the Reichstag, it was moved by Hitler to form a centrepiece of the east–west axis connecting western Berlin with the palaces and ministries of Mitte. On top of the column is a gilded goddess of victory by Friedrich Drake; captured French cannons and cannonballs, sawn in half and gilded, decorate the column itself. It's an arduous 285 steps up to the viewing platform.

Eating & drinking

Balikci Ergün

Lüneburger Strasse 382 (397 5737). S5, S7, S75 Bellevue. **Open** 5pm-midnight Mon; 3pm-midnight Tue-Sun. **€.** No credit cards. **Turkish Map** p99 D2 ❹

Tiergarten

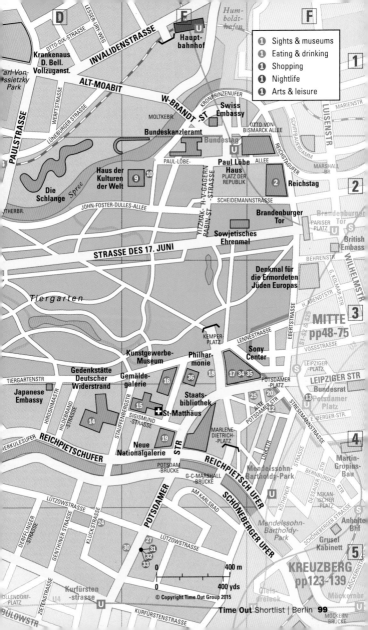

Krankenaus D. Bell. Vollzuganst.

arl-Von-ssietzky Park

OTTO-DIX-STRASSE

LESSER-URY-WEG

INVALIDENSTRASSE

Haupt-bahnhof

Humboldt-hafen

① Sights & museums
① Eating & drinking
① Shopping
① Nightlife
① Arts & leisure

ALT-MOABIT

W-BRANDT-ST

KRONPRINZENUFER

Swiss Embassy

OTTO-VON-BISMARCK-ALLEE

LUISENSTR

MARIENSTR

MARSHALL-BR

PAULSTRASSE

WERFTSTRASSE

LÜNEBURGER STRASSE

MOLTKEBR.

Bundeskanzleramt

Bundestag

SCHIFFBAUERDAMM

Die Schlange

Spree

Haus der Kulturen der Welt

PAUL-LÖBE-

Paul Löbe Haus

PLATZ DER REPUBLIK

Reichstag

REICHSTAGUFER

2

9 **10**

UTHERBR.

JOHN-FOSTER-DULLES-ALLEE

YITZHAK RABIN-STR

H.-V.-GAGERN-STRASSE

SCHEIDEMANNSTRASSE

Brandenburger Tor

PARISER PLATZ

Brandenburger Tor

British Embass

WILHELMSTR

Sowjetisches Ehrenmal

BEHRENSTR.

G. KOLMAR-STR.

STRASSE DES 17. JUNI

Tiergarten

Denkmal für die Ermordeten Jüden Europas

EBERTSTRASSE

H.-ARENDT-STR

MITTE pp48-75

3

VOSSSTRASSE

LEIPZIGER PLATZ

LEIPZIGER STR

Bundesrat

KEMPER-PLATZ

LENNESTRASSE

Kunstgewerbe-Museum

Philharmonie

Sony Center

POTSDAMER PLATZ

S

Gedenkstätte Deutscher Widerstand

Gemälde-galerie

TIERGARTENSTR.

16

36 **18**

17 **34** **35**

25

ALTE POTSDAMER STR

20

STRESEMANNSTRASSE

Potsdamer Platz

E. BERGER-STR.

Bundesrat

HIROSHIMASTR

HILDEBRAND STRASSE

Japanese Embassy

15

STAUFFENBERGSTR

St-Matthäus

Staatsbibliothek

MARLENE-DIETRICH-PLATZ

LINKSTR

13

Martin-Gropius-Bau

DESSAUER STR

14

SIGISMUND-STRASSE

Neue Nationalgalerie

19

POTSDAMER STR

REICHPIETSCH UFER

SCHÖNEBERGER UFER

Mendelssohn-Bartholdy-Park

BERNBURGER STR

ASKAN-ISCHER PLATZ

HERKULESUFER

REICHPIETSCHUFER

POTSDAM-BRÜCKE

G-C-MARSHALL-BRÜCKE

AM KARLSBAD

KÖTHENER

24

LÜTZOWSTRASSE

DERFFLINGER STRASSE

GENTHINER STRASSE

KLUCKSTRASSE

30

27

31

32

33

LÜTZOWSTRASSE

Mendelssohn-Bartholdy-Park

SCHÖNEBERGER STRASSE

Anhalter Bhf

S

Grusel Kabinett

KREUZBERG pp123-139

5

4

ULLENDORFPLATZ

Kurfürsten-strasse

U

KURFÜRSTENSTRASSE

0   400 m

0   400 yds

© Copyright Time Out Group 2015

Gleis dreieck

U

Möcker

MÖCKERN

Time Out Shortlist | Berlin **99**

Siegessäule p97

This is as close to an Anatolian fish shack as you'll find in Berlin. The formula is simple but effective: daily fresh fish charred on the grill, zingy side salads and plenty of cold beer. It's tucked away beneath a railway arch.

Café am Neuen See

Lichtensteinallee 2 (254 4930, www. cafeamneuensee.de). S5, S7, S75 *Tiergarten.* **Open** 9am-late daily. No credit cards. **Bar Map** p98 C3 ❺
Hidden away by a small lake in western Tiergarten, this café, beer garden and brasserie rolled into one is among Berlin's most idyllic spots. In summer, there are rowing boats for hire.

Konditorei Buchwald

Bartningallee 29 (391 5931, www. konditorei-buchwald.de). S5, S7, S75 *Bellevue.* **Open** 8am-6pm Mon-Sat; 9am-6pm Sun. **€.** No credit cards. **German Map** p99 C1 ❻
One Berlin institution (afternoon coffee and cake) celebrated by another: Buchwald, which has been in business

for over 160 years. The premises are charming and old-fashioned. The cakes are legendary.

Teehaus im Englischen Garten

Altonaer Strasse 2 (3948 0400, www. teehaus-tiergarten.com). S5, S7, S75 *Bellevue.* **Open** 10am-11pm daily. **€€.** No credit cards. **German Map** p98 C2 ❼
This 1950s garden in the north-west of the Tiergarten was designed to commemorate Anglo-German relations during the blockade of Berlin. The thatched teahouse serves seasonal specialities such as venison stew.

Shopping

Kunst und Trödel Markt

Strasse des 17 Juni 110-114 (2655 0096, www.berliner-troedelmarkt.de). U2 Ernst-Reuter-Platz, or S5, S7, S75 *Tiergarten.* **Open** 10am-5pm Sat, Sun. **Map** p98 A3 ❽
This second-hand market lies west of Tiergarten S-Bahn station. You'll find good-quality, early 20th-century objects (with prices to match) alongside a jumble of vintage clothing, old furniture, records and books.

Arts & leisure

Haus der Kulturen der Welt

John-Foster-Dulles-Allee 10 (3978 7175, www.hkw.de). S5, S7, S75 *Bellevue.* **Map** p99 E2 ❾
Set up in 1989 to promote the arts of developing countries, the 'House of World Cultures' features a lively programme of concerts, exhibitions and symposia centred on global cultural questions. Housed in Hugh Stubbins' oyster-like building, erected in 1957 as America's contribution to the Interbau Exhibition, this is a treasured Berlin cultural institution.

Tipi am Kanzleramt

Grosse Queralle, between Bundeskanzleramt & Haus der Kulturen

der Welt (3906 6550, www.tipi-am-kanzleramt.de). Bus 100, 248.
Map p99 E2 ➓

A circus tent in the Tiergarten, with cool international performers presenting comedy, dance and cabaret shows.

Potsdamer Platz & south of the park

At the south-east corner of the Tiergarten is the resurrected **Potsdamer Platz**, intended to be the reunified city's new commercial centrepiece. In the 1920s, it was one of Europe's busiest squares. Like much of Berlin, it was bombed flat in World War II; during the Cold War, it became a grim no-man's-land bisected by the Wall.

Immediately to its west is one of the city's major concentrations of museums, galleries and cultural institutions. Collectively known as the **Kulturforum** and built in anticipation of reunification, it was based on the designs of Hans Scharoun. There are numerous museums in the vicinity, while a short walk away is the less highbrow attraction of the **Zoologischer Garten & Aquarium** and the hub of West Berlin around Bahnhof Zoo and the Ku'damm.

Sights & museums

Bauhaus Archiv – Museum für Gestaltung

Klingelhöferstrasse 13-14 (254 0020, www.bauhaus.de). U1, U2, U3, U4 Nollendorfplatz. **Open** 10am-5pm Mon, Wed-Sun. **Admission** Mon, Sat, Sun €7; €4 reductions. Wed-Fri €6; €3 reductions. **Map** p98 C4 ➑

Walter Gropius, founder of the Bauhaus school, designed the white building that now houses this absorbing design museum. The permanent exhibition has furniture, ceramics, prints, sculptures, photographs and sketches created in the Bauhaus workshop between 1919 and 1933, when the school was closed down by the Nazis. There are also first-rate temporary exhibitions and a good gift shop.

Daimler Contemporary

Haus Huth, Alte Potsdamer Strasse 5 (2594 1420, www.sammlung.daimler. com). U2, S1, S2, S25 Potsdamer Platz. **Open** 11am-6pm daily. Guided tours 4pm 1st Sat of mth. **Admission** free. **Map** p99 F4 ➒

Daimler's collection is serious stuff. It sticks to 20th-century abstract and geometric art; the collection numbers around 1,800 works from artists such as Josef Albers, Max Bill, Walter de Maria, Jeff Koons and Andy Warhol.

Dalí – Die Ausstellung

Leipziger Platz 7 (0700 325 423 7546, www.daliberlin.de). U2, S1, S2, S25 Potsdamer Platz. **Open** noon-8pm Mon-Sat; 10am-8pm Sun. **Admission** €12.50; €9.50 reductions; free under-6s. **Map** p99 F4 ➓

There is no obvious reason why Berlin boasts a Salvador Dalí museum, let alone one as good as this. Opened in 2009, it has more than 400 Dalí originals, including drawings, lithographs, etchings, woodcuts, illustrated books, graphics and complete portfolios.

Gedenkstätte Deutscher Widerstand

Stauffenbergstrasse 13-14 (2699 5000, www.gdw-berlin.de). U2, S1, S2, S25 Potsdamer Platz. **Open** 9am-6pm Mon-Wed, Fri; 9am-8pm Thur; 10am-6pm Sat, Sun. Guided tours 3pm Sun. **Admission** free. **Map** p99 D4 ➓

The Memorial to the German Resistance chronicles the German resistance to National Socialism. At the back is a memorial to the conspirators killed during their attempt to assassinate Hitler at this site on 20 July 1944. Regular guided tours are in German only, but you can book an English tour four weeks in advance.

Gemäldegalerie

Stauffenbergstrasse 40 (266 424242, www.smb.museum/gg). U2, S1, S2, S25 Potsdamer Platz. **Open** 10am-6pm Tue, Wed, Fri-Sun; 10am-8pm Thur. **Admission** €10; €5 reductions. **Map** p99 E4 ⑮

The Picture Gallery is a first-rate early European collection with many fine Italian, Spanish and English works on display, but the real highlights are the superb Dutch and Flemish pieces. Fans of Rembrandt can indulge themselves with around 20 paintings, the best of which include a portrait of preacher and merchant Cornelis Claesz Anslo and his wife, and an electric Samson confronting his father-in-law. Two of Franz Hals' finest works are here – the wild, fluid, almost impressionistic *Malle Babbe* (Mad Babette) and the detailed portrait of the one-year-old Catharina Hooft and her nurse. Other highlights include a couple of unflinching portraits by Robert Campin (early 15th century), a version of Botticelli's *Venus Rising*, and Corregio's brilliant *Leda with the Swan*. Look out too for a pair of Lucas Cranach Venus and Cupid paintings and his *Fountain of Youth*. Pick up the excellent (free) English-language audio guide.

Kunstgewerbemuseum

Matthäikirchplatz 40 (266 424242, www. smb.museum/kgm). U2, S1, S2, S25 Potsdamer Platz. **Open** 10am-6pm Tue-Fri; 11am-6pm Sat, Sun. **Admission** €8; €4 reductions. **Map** p99 E3/4 ⑯

This place reopened in late 2014 after a two-year revamp. Its collection of European arts and crafts stretches from the Middle Ages through Renaissance, Baroque and rococo to Jugendstil and art deco. New features include an impressive fashion gallery, covering 150 years of fashion history.

Museum für Film und Fernsehen

Sony Center, Potsdamer Strasse 2 (300 9030, www.deutsche-kinemathek.de).

U2, S1, S2, S25 Potsdamer Platz. **Open** 10am-6pm Tue, Wed, Fri-Sun; 10am-8pm Thur. **Admission** €7; €4.50 reductions. No credit cards. **Map** p99 E/F3 ⑰

The Deutsche Kinemathek has been amassing films, memorabilia, documents and antique film apparatus since 1963. Striking exhibits include the two-storey-high video wall of disasters from Fritz Lang's adventure films and a morgue-like space devoted to films from the Third Reich, but the main attraction is the Marlene Dietrich collection of personal effects, home movies and designer clothes.

Musikinstrumentenmuseum

Tiergartenstrasse 1 (254 810, www. sim.spk-berlin.de). U2, S1, S2, S25 Potsdamer Platz. **Open** 9am-5pm Tue, Wed, Fri; 9am-8pm Thur; 10am-5pm Sat, Sun. **Admission** €6; €3 reductions; free under-17s. No credit cards. **Map** p99 E3 ⑱

More than 3,200 string, keyboard, wind and percussion instruments are crammed in here. Museum guides play obsolete instruments such as the Kammerflugel; on Saturdays at noon, the largest Wurlitzer organ in Europe – salvaged from an American silent movie house – is cranked into action.

Neue Nationalgalerie

Potsdamer Strasse 50 (266 424242, www.smb.museum/nng). U2, S1, S2, S25 Potsdamer Platz. **Map** p99 E4 ⑲

This stark glass and steel pavilion designed in the 1960s by Mies van der Rohe was built to house 20th-century German and international artworks. There are key pieces by Kirchner, Picasso, Gris and Léger. The Neue Sachlichkeit is well represented, while the Bauhaus contribution includes work from Paul Klee and Wassily Kandinsky. It's currently closed for a major renovation (the first in its history), masterminded by David Chipperfield under the guiding principle 'as much Mies as possible'. It should reopen in summer 2020.

Zoologischer Garten & Aquarium

Panoramapunkt

Kollhoff Tower, Potsdamer Platz 1, entrance on Alte Potsdamer Strasse (2593 7080, www.panoramapunkt.de). U2, S1, S2, S25 Potsdamer Platz. **Open** *Summer* 10am-8pm daily. *Winter* 10am-6pm daily. **Admission** €6.50. No credit cards. **Map** p99 F4 ⑳

What's billed as 'the fastest elevator in Europe' shoots up to the 100m (328ft) viewing platform in the Kollhoff Tower. The building's north-east corner is precisely at the point where the borders of Tiergarten, Mitte and Kreuzberg all meet – and also on what was the line of the Wall. There are good views to the south and west; looking north, the DB Tower gets in the way.

Zoologischer Garten & Aquarium

Hardenbergplatz 8 (254 010, www.zoo-berlin.de). U2, U9, S5, S7, S75 Zoologischer Garten. **Open** *Zoo* Summer 9am-7pm daily. Winter 9am-5pm daily. *Aquarium* 9am-6pm daily. **Admission** *Zoo or Aquarium* €13; €6.50-€10 reductions. *Both* €20; €10-€15 reductions. **Map** p98 B4 ㉑

Germany's oldest zoo (opened in 1841) is also one of the world's largest (almost 14,000 creatures) and most important. Beautifully landscaped, it has lots of architectural oddities, and there are plenty of places for a coffee, beer or snack. You can access the aquarium from the zoo or through its own entrance on Olof-Palme-Platz by the Elephant Gate. On the ground floor are the fish (including some impressive sharks); on the first you'll find reptiles (the crocodile hall is the highlight); while insects and amphibians occupy the second.

Eating & drinking

Café Einstein

Kurfürstenstrasse 58 (2639 1918, www.cafeeinstein.com). U1, U2, U3, U4 Nollendorfplatz. **Open** 8am-midnight daily. €€€. **Austrian Map** p98 C5 ㉒

Victoria Bar

This Nollendorfplatz institution is set in an 1870s neo-Renaissance villa; red leather banquettes, parquet flooring and wooden chairs all contribute to the historic Viennese café experience. Come for breakfast (herb omelette with feta cheese and spinach, say) or an afternoon treat of apple strudel and a *Wiener Melange* (a creamy Austrian coffee), all served with a flourish by the charming uniformed waiters.

Cinco

Das Stue Hotel, Drakestrasse 1 (311 7220, www.5-cinco.com). S5, S7, S75 Tiergarten. **Open** 7-10.30pm Tue-Sat. **€€€€. Spanish** Map p98 C3 ㉓
Chef Paco Pérez gained another Michelin star (his fifth) within Cinco's first year of opening. He supposedly keeps a camera trained on the kitchen 24/7, so he can quality-control all the way from Spain. The menu combines Catalan traditional cooking and the inventive plating of Spain's *nueva cocina*. Expect deconstructed classics along the lines of *ajo blanco* (garlic soup) and Iberian suckling pig. Booking is advisable.

Edd's

Lützowstrasse 81 (215 5294, www.edds-thai restaurant.de). U1 Kurfürstenstrasse. **Open** 11.30am-3pm, 6pm-midnight Mon-Fri; 5pm-midnight Sat; 2pm-midnight Sun. **€€€. No credit cards. Thai** Map p99 D5 ㉔
A comfortable, elegant Thai run by a husband-and-wife team. Try the banana flower and prawn salad or the double-cooked duck no.18. Best to book.

Facil

Mandala, Potsdamer Strasse 3 (590 051 234, www.facil.de). U2, S1, S2, S25 Potsdamer Platz. **Open** noon-3pm, 7-11pm Mon-Fri. **€€€€. Haute cuisine** Map p99 F4 ㉕
Upstairs at the plush Mandala hotel is a pavilion-like structure walled off by a row of verdant chestnut trees, its trim white furnishings and impeccable service perfectly complimenting Michael Kempf's complex cooking. Expect rustic ingredients such as veal hearts and salsify spun into culinary gold.

Hugos

Hotel InterContinental Berlin, Budapester Strasse 2 (2602 1263, www.hugos-restaurant.de). U2, U9, S5, S7, S75 Zoologischer Garten. **Open** 6.30-10.30pm Tue-Sat. **€€€€. Haute cuisine Map** p98 B4 **26**

One of Berlin's best restaurants, and with the awards to prove it. Chef Thomas Kammeier juxtaposes classic French technique – the silver Christofle cheese trolley is a sight to behold – with New German flair. Try the wagyu short rib, cooked sous-vide and served with buckwheat and truffles, or the perfectly poached turbot enriched with mussels and jerusalem artichoke.

Joseph-Roth-Diele

Potsdamer Strasse 75 (2636 9884, www.joseph-roth-diele.de). U1 Kurfürstenstrasse. **Open** 10am-midnight Mon-Fri. **€.** No credit cards. **Café Map** p99 E5 **27**

A traditional Berlin book café that pays homage to the life and work of interwar Jewish writer Joseph Roth. Decorated in ochre tones and with comfortable seating, it offers tea, coffee, wine, beer, snacks and great-value lunch specials such as meatloaf with mash.

Lebensstern

Kurfürstenstrasse 58 (2639 1922, www.lebens-stern.de). U1, U2, U3, U4 Nollendorfplatz. **Open** 7pm-2am daily. **Bar Map** p98 C5 **28**

This smart bar above Café Einstein became a second home for Quentin Tarantino when he was in Berlin to film *Inglourious Basterds*. Some scenes were even filmed here. There are 800 or so rums to try, over 200 gins and excellent cocktails too.

Nordic Embassies Canteen

Rauchstrasse 1 (305 0500, www.nordicembassies.org). U2, U9, S5, S7, S75 Zoologischer Garten. **Open** 1-3pm Mon-Fri. **€.** No credit cards. **Scandinavian Map** p98 C4 **29**

The striking Nordic embassy complex, clad in maplewood and glass, houses an excellent lunch secret. The canteens of Berlin's civic buildings are all open

to the public, so after 1pm you can tuck into the excellent subsidised food provided for the Scandinavian diplomats.

Victoria Bar

Potsdamer Strasse 102 (2575 9977, www.victoriabar.de). U1 Kurfürstenstrasse. **Open** 6.30pm-3am Mon-Thur, Sun; 6.30pm-4am Fri, Sat. No credit cards. **Bar Map** p99 E5 **30**

Artworks by Sarah Lucas and Martin Kippenberger adorn the walls of this sleek bar. The menu is divided by liquor type: go fully decadent with an Alfonso, a mix of Dubonnet, sugar, bitters and champagne, or try a Rosemary's Baby, an aged tequila sour with rosemary and sage.

Shopping

Andreas Murkudis

Potsdamer Strasse 81E (680 798 306, www.andreasmurkudis.com). U2, S1, S2, S25 Potsdamer Platz. **Open** 10am-8pm Mon-Sat. **Map** p99 E5 **31**

The Murkudis brothers are a design duo with the Midas touch. This concept store (designed by one brother and housed in the former Tagesspiegel complex, whose move caused a mini-renaissance for Potsdamer Strasse a few years ago) is white, stark and immense, with neon strip lighting. Clothes (by the other brother, as well as the likes of Dries van Noten and Maison Martin Margiela) are displayed amid contemporary furniture, porcelain and homewares.

BlainSouthern

Potsdamer Strasse 77-87 (644 931 510, www.blainsouthern.com). U2, S1, S2, S25 Potsdamer Platz. **Open** 11am-6pm Tue-Sat. **Map** p99 E5 **32**

The curator duo behind London's influential Haunch of Venison gallery set up in Berlin a few years ago. Their gallery (housed in the same complex as Andreas Murkudis) uses the vast space to powerful effect. Big-name artists include Bill Viola, Damian Hirst and Berlin-based Douglas Gordon.

Galerie Guido W Baudach

Potsdamer Strasse 85 (3199 8101, www.guidowbaudach.com). U2, S1, S2, S25 Potsdamer Platz. **Open** 11am-6pm Tue-Sat. **Map** p99 E5 33

Pioneering gallery Baudach joined the Tagesspiegel complex in 2013 to show influential contemporary German artists such as Andreas Hofer, Thilo Heinzmann and Andy Hope.

Arts & leisure

Arsenal

Potsdamer Strasse 2 (2695 5100, www.arsenal-berlin.de). U2, S1, S2, S25 Potsdamer Platz. No credit cards.
Map p99 E/F3 34

Berlin's own cinematheque offers brazenly eclectic programming, ranging from classic Hollywood to contemporary Middle Eastern cinema. It shows plenty of English-language films, and is a core venue for the annual Berlin International Film Festival.

CineStar IMAX Sony Center

Potsdamer Strasse 4 (2606 6400, www.cinestar.de). U2, S1, S2, S25 Potsdamer Platz. **Map** p99 E/F3 35

CineStar's eight screens show mainstream films in their original language, mostly English. Major releases tend to appear here, shown in both 3D and 2D versions on its massive IMAX screen.

Philharmonie

Herbert-von-Karajan Strasse 1 (254 880, tickets 2548 8999, www.berliner-philharmoniker.de). U2, S1, S2, S25 Potsdamer Platz. **Map** p99 E3 36

Berlin's most famous concert hall is also its most architecturally daring. Designed by Hans Scharoun, the golden building with its distinctive vaulting roof opened in 1963. Its reputation for superb acoustics is accurate, but it does depend on where you sit.

It's home to the Berliner Philharmoniker, which gives about 100 performances in the city during its August to June season. Founded in 1882, the orchestra has been led by some of the world's greatest conductors, most notably Herbert von Karajan (1955-89), as well as by composers such as Richard Strauss and Gustav Mahler. Since 2002, it's been under the leadership of Sir Simon Rattle.

Philharmonie

Schloss Charlottenburg p116

Charlottenburg & Schöneberg

The old heart of West Berlin runs all the way from the Tiergarten to Spandau, from Tegel Airport in the north to wealthy, residential Wilmersdorf in the south. Often derided as staid and stagnant in comparison to its eastern neighbours, Charlottenburg is undeniably bourgeois – the fur coat/small dog quotient is high – but it's far from boring. As well as some charming hotels and lovely squares, it boasts Schloss Charlottenburg, the shopping street of Kurfürstendamm and a few museums. Schöneberg is also well heeled and residential, and home to Berlin's long-established gay scene.

Bahnhof Zoo & the Ku'damm

Immortalised in song by U2 and a centrepiece of the film *Christiane F*, Bahnhof Zoo (Zoo station or Bahnhof Zoologischer Garten, to give it its full name) was long the main entry point to the West. During the Cold War, it was a spooky anomaly – slap in the middle of West Berlin but policed by the East, which controlled the intercity rail system – and a seedy hangout for junkies and winos. The most notable landmark nearby is the fractured spire of the **Kaiser-Wilhelm-Gedächtnis-Kirche**. On the other side of the station is the entrance to the **Zoologischer Garten** itself, which is in Tiergarten. Attempts to glam up the area continue apace with two large new developments, including the enormous Bikini Berlin complex.

This is also the gateway to the **Kurfürstendamm** (or Ku'damm, as it's universally known), the main shopping street of western Berlin. For more shops, chic restaurants and cafés, explore Kantstrasse, leafy Savignyplatz and Bleibtreustrasse.

Kaiser-Wilhelm-Gedächtnis-Kirche

Sights & museums

Beate-Uhse Erotik-Museum

*Joachimstaler Strasse 4 (886 0666,
http://erotikmuseum.beate-uhse.com).
U2, U9, S5, S7, S75 Zoologischer
Garten.* **Open** 9am-10pm Mon-Wed;
9am-midnight Thur-Sat; 11am-10pm
Sun. **Admission** (over-18s only) €9;
€16 couples. **Map** p109 D2 ①

This three-floor collection (housed
above a large Beate-Uhse sex store)
contains oriental prints, some daft
showroom-dummy tableaux, and glass
cases displaying such delights as
early Japanese dildos, Andean penis
flutes, 17th-century chastity belts and
a giant coconut that looks like an arse.
Bizarrely, it feels more like a dusty old
regional museum than anything racy.

C/O Berlin Amerika Haus

*Hardenbergstrasse 22-24 (2844 4160,
www.co-berlin.org). U2, U9, S5, S7, S75
Zoologischer Garten.* **Open** 24hrs daily.
Admission €10; €5 reductions. **Map**
p109 D2 ②

Built by the US in the 1950s to promote transatlantic cultural exchange,

Amerika Haus contained embassy
offices until 2006. It reopened in 2014
after extensive renovations and is now
the home of much-loved photography
gallery C/O Berlin.

Kaiser-Wilhelm-Gedächtnis-Kirche

*Breitscheidplatz (218 5023, www.
gedaechtniskirche.com). U2, U9, S5,
S7, S75 Zoologischer Garten.* **Open**
9am-7pm daily. Guided tours 10.15am,
11am, noon, 1.15pm, 2pm, 3pm Mon,
Fri, Sat; 1.15pm, 2pm, 3pm Tue-Thur.
Admission free. **Map** p109 D2 ③

The Kaiser Wilhelm Memorial Church
is one of Berlin's best-known sights,
and one of its most dramatic at night.
The neo-romanesque structure was
built in 1891-95 by Franz Schwechten
in honour of – you guessed it – Kaiser
Wilhelm I. Much of the building was
destroyed during an Allied air raid in
1943. These days, the church serves
as a stark reminder of the damage
done by the war, although some might
argue it improved what was originally
a profoundly ugly building. Inside
the rump of the church is a glittering art nouveau-style ceiling mosaic
depicting members of the House of
Hohenzollern on pilgrimage towards
the cross. There's also a cross made
from nails from Coventry's war-de-
stroyed cathedral, and photos of the
church before and after the war. The
wrap-around blue stained glass in the
chapel is quite stunning. Guided tours
in English can be booked.

Käthe-Kollwitz-Museum

*Fasanenstrasse 24 (882 5210,
www.kaethe-kollwitz.de). U1, U9
Kurfürstendamm.* **Open** 11am-6pm
daily. **Admission** €6; €3.50 reductions.
No credit cards. **Map** p109 C3 ④

Käthe Kollwitz's powerful, deeply
empathetic work embraces the full
spectrum of life, from the joy of moth-
erhood to the pain of death (with a
particular fascination for the latter).
The collection includes her famous

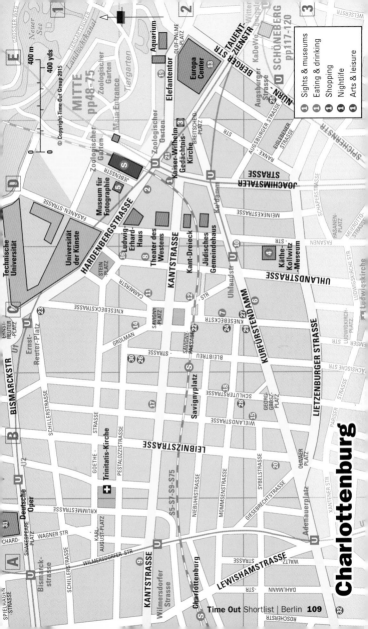

Charlottenburg

Sights & museums

Eating & drinking

Shopping

Nightlife

Arts & leisure

MITTE pp48-75

SCHÖNEBERG pp117-120

lithograph *Brot!*, as well as charcoal sketches, woodcuts and sculptures, all displayed to impressive effect in this grand villa off the Ku'damm. Some labelling is in English.

Museum für Fotografie

Jebensstrasse 2 (266 424242, www.smb. museum/mf). U2, U9, S5, S7, S75 Zoologischer Garten. **Open** 10am-6pm Tue, Wed, Fri-Sun; 10am-8pm Thur. **Admission** €10; €5 reductions. **Map** p109 D1/2 ❺

Shortly before his death in 2004, Berlin-born Helmut Newton donated over 1,000 of his nude and fashion photographs to the city and provided funds for the creation of a new gallery. This museum was the result. Six colossal nudes, modelled on 1930s Nazi propaganda photos, glare down at you on entering the building, and set the tone for the big, garish, confrontational pieces that dominate the exhibits. The top floor has changing shows on the history of photography, drawn from the Berlin State Museums.

Story of Berlin

Kurfürstendamm 207-208 (8872 0100, www.story-of-berlin.de). U1 Uhlandstrasse. **Open** 10am-8pm daily; last entry 6pm. **Admission** €12; €5-€9 reductions. **Map** p109 C3 ❻

This huge space tells Berlin's story from its founding in 1237 to the present day. The 20 themed displays are labelled in both German and English. Underneath all this is a massive nuclear bunker. Built by the Allies in the 1970s, it's still fully functional – guided tours are included in the admission price.

Eating & drinking

1900 Café Bistro

Knesebeckstrasse 76 (8871 5871). S5, S7, S75 Savignyplatz. **Open** 8am-7pm Mon-Sat; 11am-7pm Sun. €. No credit cards. **Café Map** p109 C2 ❼

Booking is recommended for weekend breakfast at this kitschy café, when plates overflow with cold cuts, cheese and fruit. Tray-baked crumble cakes and salads are also available.

Arirang

Uhlandstrasse 194 (4502 1248). U2, U9, S5, S7, S75 Zoologischer Garten. **Open** noon-11pm daily. €€. No credit cards. **Korean Map** p109 C2 ❽

This fabulous restaurant used to be a closely guarded secret in a shabby Wedding location, but in 2014 it moved to Charlottenburg. As is the norm in Korea, dishes come with a selection of kimchi, pickled salads and rice – so don't over-order. The fiery kimchi and noodle stew and spring onion and seafood pancakes are perfect for sharing.

Aroma

Kantstrasse 58 (3759 1628). S5, S7, S75 Savignyplatz. **Open** noon-2.30am daily. €€. No credit cards. **Chinese Map** p109 A2 ❾

Enjoy assorted dumplings in the traditional, genteel tea-time style of yum cha or as part of a full dinner. Go with classics such as *har gao* (steamed shrimp dumplings), fried turnip cakes or *cheong fun*, pillowy steamed rice noodle rolls stuffed with prawn or beef.

Café im Literaturhaus

Fasanenstrasse 23 (882 5414, www.literaturhaus-berlin.de). U1 Uhlandstrasse. **Open** 9.30am-1am daily. €. No credit cards. **Café Map** p109 D2 ❿

This café is in the Literaturhaus villa, which has a bookshop and runs lectures and readings. Sit in the greenhouse-like winter garden or the salon rooms, and tuck into a breakfast of scrambled eggs and smoked salmon, or a *tramezzini* sandwich at lunchtime.

Dicke Wirtin

Carmerstrasse 9 (312 4952, www.dicke-wirtin.de). S5, S7, S75 Savignyplatz. **Open** noon-2am daily. No credit cards. **Bar Map** p109 C2 ⓫

The name means 'fat landlady', and this is a proper German pub: nine beers on tap, bizarre house schnapps and dirt-cheap prices for the area. If you get the munchies, try a plate of bread smothered in *Schmalz* (lard) for €2.60.

Diener Tattersall

Grolmanstrasse 47 (881 5329). S5, S7, S75 Savignyplatz. **Open** 6pm-2am daily. No credit cards. **Bar Map** p109 C2 ⑫
Ex-boxer Franz Diener took this place over in 1954 and with his artist friends turned it into one of the central hubs of West Berlin cultural life. In a city fascinated with Ostalgie and the rapid rhythms of gentrification, raise a toast (or four) to this previous age of West Berlin bohemians.

First Floor

Hotel Palace, Budapester Strasse 45 (2502 1020, www.firstfloor.palace.de). U2, U9, S5, S7, S75 Zoologischer Garten. **Open** 6.30-11pm Tue-Sat. €€€€. **Haute cuisine Map** p109 E2 ⑬
In just a few years, chef Matthias Diether has scooped up a load of awards and a Michelin star. Come here

for refined French dishes, such as sea bass with Périgord truffle.

Florian

Grolmanstrasse 52 (313 9184, www. restaurant-florian.de). S5, S7, S75 Savignyplatz. **Open** 6pm-3am daily. €€€. **German Map** p109 C2 ⑭
Florian has served southern German classics on this quietly posh street for a couple of decades. The cooking is hearty, the decor impeccable. In typical bistro fashion, staff can switch from congenial to arctic at the drop of a hat.

Galerie Bremer

Wielandstrasse 29 (881 4908, www. galerie-bremer.de). S5, S7, S75 Savignyplatz. **Open** 8pm-late Mon-Sat. No credit cards. **Bar Map** p109 B3 ⑮
Supposedly Berlin's oldest cocktail bar, designed in 1946 by Hans Scharoun as a salon to the adjoining art gallery (4-8pm Tue-Fri), this is a great hidden spot for drinking in period style.

Glass

Uhlandstrasse 195 (5471 0861, www. glassberlin.com). U2, U9, S5, S7, S75

Café im Literaturhaus

BERLIN BY AREA

Zoologischer Garten. **Open** 7-11pm
Tue-Sat. **€€€€**. **Haute cuisine**
Map p109 C2 ⑯

Inside a brutalist apartment building,
chef Gal Ben-Moshe has been spinning
straw into culinary gold. Starters come
impaled on smoking cinnamon sticks;
soups are adorned with savoury sor-
bets; and, most impressively, the showpiece 'Candybox' dessert reimagines
the staff's favourite childhood sweets
– there's Snickers snow, passionfruit
Gummy Bears, popping candy and a
flash-frozen chocolate mousse.

Lon Men's Noodles

Kantstrasse 33 (3151 9678). S5, S7,
S75 Savignyplatz. **Open** noon-midnight
daily. **€**. No credit cards. **Taiwanese**
Map p109 B2 ⑰

This tiny hole-in-the-wall spot knocks
out Taiwanese classics such as noodle
soups and *gua bao* (rice buns filled with
duck) as well as more esoteric plates of
sliced pigs' ears with rice noodles.

Marjellchen

Mommsenstrasse 9 (883 2676). www.
marjellchen-berlin.de). S5, S7, S75
Savignyplatz. **Open** 5pm-midnight
daily. **€€**. No credit cards. **German**
Map p109 B2 ⑱

Not many places like Marjellchen exist
any more. It serves specialities from
East Prussia, such as Masurian jugged
game or beef with prunes, in an atmosphere of old-fashioned *gemütlichkeit*
(homely cosiness). The beautiful bar
and great service are further draws,
and the larger-than-life owner recites
poetry and sometimes sings.

Neni

25hours Hotel Bikini Berlin, Budapester
Strasse 40 (120 2210, www.25hours-
hotels.com). U2, U9, S5, S7, S75
Zoologischer Garten. **Open** noon-
10.30pm Mon-Thur, Sun; noon-11.30pm
Fri, Sat. **€€**. No credit cards. **Middle**
Eastern Map p109 E2 ⑲

Yet another top-floor hotel restaurant,
this time in Charlottenburg's newest

boutique hotel. The menu encour-
ages diners to share plates of Middle
Eastern-style food, such as *sabich*
(fried aubergine, houmous and salad),
chraime (cod in tomato stew) or slow-
roasted lamb shoulder.

Nussbaumerin

Leibnizstrasse 55 (5017 8033, www.
nussbaumerin.de). U7 Adenauerplatz.
Open 5pm-midnight Mon-Sat. **€€**. No
credit cards. **Austrian Map** p109 B3 ⑳

Service is warm and welcoming at this
old-fashioned Austrian restaurant,
which is surprisingly good value for its
interesting variations on the Schnitzel
– the 'Salzburger' comes stuffed with
feta, and the 'Kaiser' with cream sauce
and potato dumplings.

Les Solistes by Pierre Gagnaire

Waldorf Astoria Berlin,
Hardenbergstrasse 28 (814 000,
www.waldorfastoriaberlin.com).
U2, U9, S5, S7, S75 Zoologischer Garten.
Open 6.30-10.30pm Tue-Sat. **€€€€**.
Haute cuisine Map p109 D2 ㉑

The anodyne luxe-hotel interior is
quickly forgotten once the splendid
tasting menu begins. French classics,
changing seasonally, are reinterpreted
with panache by head chef Roel
Lintermans – witness roasted pigeon
in a blackcurrant and cherry compote,
its leg served atop a heavenly dome of
offal jelly, or a foie gras custard with
sautéed squid.

Shopping

Bücherbogen

Stadtbahnbogen 593, Savignyplatz
(3186 9511, www.buecherbogen.com).
S5, S7, S75 Savignyplatz. **Open**
10am-8pm Mon-Fri; 10am-6pm Sat.
No credit cards. **Map** p109 C2 ㉒

This bookshop takes up three whole
railway arches, with row upon row of
books on art, design and architecture,
plus exhibition catalogues and lots of
rare or out-of-print volumes.

Manufactum

Hardenbergstrasse 4-5 (2403 3844, www.manufactum.de). U1, U2 Ernst-Reuter-Platz. **Open** 10am-8pm Mon-Fri; 10am-6pm Sat. **Map** p109 C1 ㉓
Founded in 1988 by a high-profile Green Party politician as a counterpoint to cheap mass production, Manufactum developed a cult following for its ironic catalogue blurbs and impeccable selection of products. It continues in the same vein today with an emphasis on high production quality, classic designs and sustainable materials, with a particular German focus. Prices reflect the quality. There's also an on-site bakery, and a café serving almond croissants, small lunch dishes and plates of charcuterie.

Marga Schoeller Bücherstube

Knesebeckstrasse 33 (881 1112). S5, S7, S75 Savignyplatz. **Open** 9.30am-7pm Mon-Wed; 9.30am-8pm Thur; 9.30am-6pm Sat. **Map** p109 C2 ㉔
This bookshop (established 1930) won renown when owner Marga shook a fist at the Nazi regime by removing all Nazi-related texts from her shelves. It relocated in the '70s down the road from its original Ku'damm spot. It goes further than most to provide new non-fiction titles, from philosophical and political texts to theatre studies.

Michas Bahnhof

Nürnberger Strasse 24A (218 6611, www.michas-bahnhof.de). U3 Augsburger Strasse. **Open** 10am-6.30pm Mon-Fri; 10am-3.30pm Sat. **Map** p109 E3 ㉕
Unsurprisingly in such an engineering-mad country, Berlin has some fantastic model-train shops and Michas Bahnhof is one of the best.

P&T

Bleibtreustrasse 4 (9561 5468, www.paperandtea.com). S5, S7, S75 Savignyplatz. **Open** 11am-8pm Mon-Sat. **Map** p109 C2 ㉖
Japanese and Korean green teas, Taiwanese mountain tea and white jasmine-bud tea, as well as fine Asian ceramics for serving.

Steiff Galerie in Berlin

Kurfürstendamm 38-39 (8862 5006, www.steiff.de). U1 Uhlandstrasse. **Open** 10am-8pm Mon-Fri; 10am-7pm Sat. **Map** p109 C3 ㉗
Inventor of the teddy bear, Steiff has been in business since the late 19th century. The company's whole range of artisan animals (not just bears) are here. Prices are aimed at adult hobbyists rather than kids.

Taschen

Schlüterstrasse 39 (8870 8173, www.taschen.com). S5, S7, 75 Savignyplatz. **Open** 10am-7pm Mon-Sat. **Map** p109 B2 ㉘
This wildly successful publishing house has made a name for itself producing books of alternative arts and erotica, and table-sized gift books. The Berlin flagship store has moved to these spacious – and recently renovated – premises.

Veronica Pohle

Kurfürstendamm 64 (883 3731, www.veronicapohle.de). U7 Adenauerplatz. **Open** 10.30am-7.30pm Mon-Fri; 11am-6.30pm Sat. **Map** p109 C3 ㉙
Womenswear from top international labels such as Missoni, Diane von Fürstenberg, Roberto Cavalli, Vivienne Westwood and Alexander McQueen.

Arts & leisure

A-Trane

Bleibtreustrasse 1 (313 2550, www.a-trane.de). S5, S7, S9, S75 Savignyplatz. **Map** p109 C2 ㉚
A-Trane usually lands at least one top-flight jazz act a month for an extended run. The free late-night Saturday jam sessions are popular with students and tourists. Mondays is free entry too.

Funkturm

Deutsche Oper

*Bismarckstrasse 35 (343 8401, tickets
3438 4343, www.deutscheoperberlin.de).
U2 Deutsche Oper.* **Map** p109 A1 ㉛
With roots dating from 1912, the
Deutsche Oper built its present 1,900-
seat hall in 1961, just in time to carry
the operatic torch for West Berlin during the Wall years. Since reunification,
it has lost out in profile to the grander
Staatsoper, but retains a solid reputation for productions of the classics.
Discounted tickets are available half
an hour before performances.

Schaubühne am
Lehniner Platz

*Kurfürstendamm 153 (890 023, www.
schaubuehne.de). U7 Adenauerplatz,
or S5, S7, S75 Charlottenburg.* **Map**
p109 A3 ㉜
The Schaubühne is most popular
with English audiences and has a
long history of anglophile collabora-
tion. Under artistic director Thomas
Ostermeier, the house style treads a
happy medium between German rad-
icalism and British realism, which,
coupled with the frequent surtitling of
performances in English, makes it an
ideal starting point for anyone looking
for an introduction to German theatre.

Schloss
Charlottenburg & West

The palace that gives Charlottenburg
its name lies a few kilometres north-
west of Bahnhof Zoo. In contrast to
the commercialism and crush of the
latter, this part of the city is wealthy
and serene. Intended as Berlin's
answer to Versailles, **Schloss
Charlottenburg** was built in the
17th century as a summer palace
for Queen Sophie-Charlotte. Nearby
are some impressive museums of
20th-century art. North and west
of the palace are two reminders of
the Nazi era. The **Gedenkstätte
Plötzensee** (Plötzensee Memorial)
preserves the execution shed of the
former Plötzensee prison, where
more than 2,500 people were killed
between 1933 and 1945, while the
Olympiastadion is one of the few
pieces of Fascist-era architecture
still standing in Berlin.

Sights & museums

Bröhan-Museum

*Schlossstrasse 1A (3269 0600,
www.broehan-museum.de). U2
Sophie-Charlotte-Platz, or U7*

Richard-Wagner-Platz. **Open** 10am-6pm Tue-Sun. **Admission** €6; €4 reductions; free under-18s.

Three well-laid-out floors of international art nouveau and art deco pieces that businessman Karl Bröhan began collecting in the 1960s and donated to the city of Berlin on his 60th birthday.

Funkturm

Messedamm (3038 1905, www.funkturm-messeberlin.de). U2 Theodor-Heuss-Platz or Kaiserdamm. **Open** 10am-8pm Mon; 10am-11pm Tue-Sun. **Admission** €5; €2.80 reductions. No credit cards.

The 147m (482ft) high Radio Tower, built in 1926, looks a bit like a smaller version of the Eiffel Tower. There's a zippy lift up to the observation deck, but challenge-seekers can attempt the 610 steps. The tower closes in summer for repairs, so ring ahead.

Gedenkstätte Plötzensee

Hüttigpfad (344 3226, www.gedenkstaette-ploetzensee.de). U9 Turmstrasse then bus 123. **Open** Mar-Oct 9am-5pm daily. Nov-Feb 9am-4pm daily. **Admission** free.

This site was the prison execution chamber where the Nazis murdered nearly 3,000 (largely political) prisoners. It was declared a memorial to the victims of Fascism in 1952, and a commemorative wall was built. There is little to see today, apart from the execution area behind the wall, with its meat hooks from which victims were hanged (many were also guillotined), and a small room with an exhibition.

Georg-Kolbe-Museum

Sensburger Allee 25 (304 2144, www.georg-kolbe-museum.de). S3, S75 Heerstrasse, or bus X34, M49, X49. **Open** 10am-6pm Tue-Sun. **Admission** €5; €3 reductions. No credit cards.

Berlin sculptor Georg Kolbe, regarded as Germany's best in the 1920s, focused on naturalistic human figures. His former studio has examples of his earlier,

graceful pieces, as well as later, more sombre and bombastic works created in accordance with Nazi aesthetic ideals. His famous *Figure for Fountain* is in the sculpture garden, where there's also a great café for coffee and cake.

Museum Berggruen

Westlicher Stülerbau, Schlossstrasse 1 (266 424 242, www.smb.museum/mb). U2 Sophie-Charlotte-Platz, or U7 Richard-Wagner-Platz. **Open** 10am-6pm Tue-Sun. **Admission** €8; €4 reductions.

Heinz Berggruen was one of Picasso's dealers in Paris, and went on to become a major modernist collector. He sold his entire collection to Berlin for a knockdown $100m in 2000. Pablo's astonishingly prolific and diverse output is well represented, but Braque, Giacometti, Cézanne and Matisse also feature, and most of the second floor is given over to the wonderful paintings of Paul Klee.

Olympiastadion

Olympischer Platz 3 (2500 2322, www.olympiastadion-berlin.de). U2 Olympia-Stadion, or S5, S75 Olympiastadion. **Admission** €7; €5 reductions. Guided tours €10; €8 reductions. No credit cards.

Built on the site of Berlin's original 1916 Olympic stadium, the current structure was designed by Werner March and opened in 1936 for the infamous 'Nazi Olympics' (you can see where the swastikas were removed from the old bell). It underwent a major and long-overdue refitting for the 2006 World Cup, including better seats and a roof. Book a guided tour at the visitor centre by the eastern gate.

Sammlung Scharf-Gerstenberg

Schlossstrasse 70 (266 424242, www.smb.museum/ssg). U2 Sophie-Charlotte-Platz. **Open** 10am-6pm Tue-Fri; 11am-6pm Sat, Sun. **Admission** €10; €5 reductions.

Opposite Charlottenburg Palace, this gallery exhibits works by the Surrealists and their forerunners.

Artists run from Piranesi, Goya and Redon to Dali, Magritte and Ernst.

Schloss Charlottenburg

Luisenplatz & Spandauer Damm (320 911, www.spsg.de). U2 Sophie-Charlotte-Platz, or U7 Richard-Wagner-Platz. **Open** Apr-Oct 10am-6pm Tue-Sun. Nov-Mar 10am-5pm Tue-Sun. **Admission** Old Palace €12; €8 reductions. New Wing €4; €3 reductions. Belvedere (Apr-Oct only) €3; €2.50 reductions. Mausoleum (Apr-Oct only) €2; €1. Combined ticket €15; €11 reductions. Gardens free.

Friedrich III (later King Friedrich I) built this sprawling palace and gardens in 1695-99 as a summer home for his queen, Sophie-Charlotte. Severely damaged in World War II, it has been restored and is now the largest surviving Hohenzollern palace.

The easiest option is to buy the combination ticket, which allows entrance to all parts of the palace – with the exception of the state and private apartments of King Friedrich I and Queen Sophie-Charlotte in the Altes Schloss (Old Palace), which are only accessible on a guided tour.

The one must-see is the Neue Flügel (New Wing). The upper floor contains the state apartments of Frederick the Great and the winter chambers of his successor, King Friedrich Wilhelm II. The contrast between the two sections is fascinating: Frederick's rooms are all excessive rococo exuberance, while Friedrich Wilhelm's far more modestly proportioned rooms reflect the more restrained classicism of his time.

The Neue Pavillon (New Pavilion) was built by Karl Friedrich Schinkel in 1824 for Friedrich Wilhelm III – the king liked it so much that he chose to live here in preference to the main palace. Inside is an excellent exhibition on the architect's legacy.

The huge, impeccably kept gardens are a major draw. Laid out in 1697 in formal French style, they were reshaped in a more relaxed English style in the 19th century. Here you'll find the Belvedere (built in 1788 as a teahouse, now containing a collection of Berlin porcelain) and the sombre Mausoleum (containing the tombs of Friedrich Wilhelm III, his wife Queen Luise, Kaiser Wilhelm I and his wife).

Eating & drinking

Alt Luxemburg

Windscheidstrasse 31 (323 8730, www.alt-luxemburg.de). U2 Sophie-Charlotte-Platz. **Open** 5-10.30pm Mon-Sat. **€€€**. **German**

Chef Karl Wannemacher combines classic German flavours with French techniques in his wonderfully romantic dining room. Expect generous helpings of the freshest sweetbreads on lentils and braised balsamic onions, or sea bass with a tapenade crust.

Gasthaus Lentz

Stuttgarter Platz 20 (8871 5871, www.gasthaus-lentz-berlin.de). S5, S7, S75 Charlottenburg. **Open** 9am-1.30am daily. **€€**. No credit cards. **Café**

Bespectacled Charlottenburgers take their time with a newspaper and coffee here. Daily specials of German classics usually involve something porky with potato and salad.

Shopping

Go Asia

Kantstrasse 101 (3151 8606, www.goasia.net). S5, S7, S75 Charlottenburg. **Open** 9am-9pm Mon-Sat.

There are lots of small Asian supermarkets in Berlin, but the vast GoAsia has Sichuan chilli pastes, imported Japanese rice, kimchi varieties and plenty more.

Königsberger Marzipan

Pestalozzistrasse 54A, (323 8254). U7 Wilmersdorfer Strasse. **Open** 11am-6pm Mon-Fri; 10am-1pm Sat. No credit cards.

Irmgard Wald and her late husband arrived in Berlin after the war, when the

Soviets changed Prussian Königsberg to Kaliningrad, to begin their confectionery business anew. The company still produces fresh, soft, melt-in-your-mouth marzipan.

Schöneberg

Geographically and atmospherically, the largely residential district of Schöneberg lies between Kreuzberg and Charlottenburg. The area around Winterfeldtplatz, with its twice-weekly market, is lively with cafés and shops. Further north, Nollendorfplatz is the hub of the area's nightlife. Outside the U-Bahn station, the small memorial to homosexuals killed in concentration camps is a reminder of the area's history: Christopher Isherwood chronicled Berlin from his rooming house at Nollendorfstrasse 17, and Motzstrasse has been a major artery of Berlin's gay life since the 1920s.

Wittenbergplatz, at Schöneberg's north-west corner, is home to **KaDeWe**, Berlin's answer to Harrods. Founded in 1907, it's still the largest department store in continental Europe. From here, Tauentzienstrasse runs west into the Ku'damm at Bahnhof Zoo.

Eating & drinking

Café Aroma

Hochkirchstrasse 8 (782 5821, www. cafe-aroma.de). U7, S1, S2 Yorckstrasse. **Open** 6pm-midnight Mon-Fri; 2pm-midnight Sat; 11am-midnight Sun. €€.
Italian
In a brunch-mad city, this lovely Italian trattoria is a Berlin foodie's favourite for its multi-course marathon of cold cuts, poached salmon, fried risotto balls and roast vegetables. One of the first restaurants to sign up to Germany's Slow Food association in the early 1990s, it takes pains to source sustainable and authentic produce.

Double Eye

Akazienstrasse 22 (0179 456 6960 mobile, www.doubleeye.de). U7 Eisenacher Strasse. **Open** 9.30am-6.30pm Mon-Fri; 10am-6.30pm Sat. €. No credit cards. **Café Map** p119 B4 ❸❸
There's a lot of competition among Berlin's third-wave coffee shops; Double Eye was one of the first, and still draws queues for its potent espressos and creamy custard tarts.

Green Door

Winterfeldtstrasse 50 (215 2515, www.greendoor.de). U1, U2, U3, U4 Nollendorfplatz. **Open** 6pm-3am Mon-Thur, Sun; 6pm-4am Fri, Sat. No credit cards. **Bar Map** p119 B2 ❸❹
Behind an actual green door (ring the doorbell) lies this popular cocktail bar. The heavily kitsch decor – oversized gingham wallpaper, curvy white walls and framed 1970s pictures – may grow on you after a few strong drinks.

Habibi

Goltzstrasse 24 (215 3332). U1, U2, U3, U4 Nollendorfplatz. **Open** 11am-3am Mon-Thur, Sun; 11am-5am Fri, Sat. €. No credit cards. **Middle Eastern Map** p119 B2 ❸❺
Come here to enjoy falafel, kibbeh, tabbouleh and various combination plates. Accompany with freshly squeezed orange or carrot juice, and finish with a complimentary tea and one of the wonderful pastries. It's deservedly busy and can get very full.

Renger-Patzsch

Wartburgstrasse 54 (784 2059, www. renger-patzsch.com). U7 Eisenacher Strasse. **Open** 6pm-1am daily. €€.
German Map p119 B4 ❸❻
The pan-German food – soup and salad starters, a sausage and sauerkraut platter, plus meat and fish dishes that vary daily – is finely prepared by versatile chef Hannes Behrmann, formerly of Le Cochon Bourgeois. House speciality is Alsatian *tarte flambée*: a crisp pastry base with toppings in

BERLIN BY AREA

KaDeWe

seven variations. Communal seating is at long wooden tables, and in summer there's a garden.

Stagger Lee

Nollendorfstrasse 27 (2903 6158, www.staggerlee.de). U1, U2, U3, U4 Nollendorfplatz. **Open** 8pm-late daily. No credit cards. **Bar Map** p119 B2 ③

Low-hanging saloon lamps, Victorian wallpaper and an enormous mechanical till add to the faux-Americana charm of this vaudeville bar. They serve excellent, if unusual, cocktails: the Robert Mitchum is simply a full glass of tequila, a box of matches and a Lucky Strike.

Witty's

Wittenbergplatz 5 (211 9496, www.wittys-berlin.de). U1, U2, U3 Wittenbergplatz. **Open** 11am-8pm daily. **€.** No credit cards. **Imbiss Map** p119 A1 ③

An alternative to your average *imbiss*, Witty's offers a fully organic menu of Berlin staples, including Currywurst and fries.

Shopping

Garage

Ahornstrasse 2 (211 2760, www. kleidermarkt.de). U1, U2, U3, U4 Nollendorfplatz. **Open** 11am-7pm Mon-Fri; 11am-6pm Sat. **Map** p119 B1 ③

The barn-like Garage sells bargain second-hand clothing, priced by the kilo. It's all very well organised, making it easy to root out last-minute party gear.

KaDeWe

Tauentzienstrasse 21-24 (21210, www.kadewe.com). U1, U2, U3 Wittenbergplatz. **Open** 10am-8pm Mon-Fri; 10am-9pm Sat. **Map** p119 A1 ④

Berlin's famous department store has quite an impressive range of high-end designers and some upbeat, younger labels. Its most famous feature is the luxury food hall on the sixth floor; up yet another level is a cavernous glass-roofed restaurant with a fine view of pedestrianised Wittenbergplatz spread out below.

BERLIN BY AREA

Schöneberg

TIERGARTEN
pp96-106

1 Sights & museums
1 Eating & drinking
1 Shopping
1 Nightlife
1 Arts & leisure

0   400 m
0   400 yds

© Copyright Time Out Group 2015

Rogacki p122

Winterfeldtplatz Market

Winterfeldtplatz (0175 437 4303 mobile). U1, U2, U3, U4 Nollendorfplatz. **Open** 8am-2pm Wed; 8am-4pm Sat. **Map** p119 B2 ㉑

In the leafy square surrounding St-Matthias-Kirche, this farmers' market teems with life twice a week. There are more than 250 stalls, most offering high-end gastronomic produce. The emphasis is on the local and seasonal, such as wild herbs, foraged mushrooms and local salami. Many vendors serve cooked food too.

Arts & leisure

Kleine Nachtrevue

Kurfürstenstrasse 116 (218 8950, www. kleine-nachtrevue.de). U1, U2, U3 Wittenbergplatz. **Map** p119 A1 ㉒

Often used as a film location, this is as close as it gets to real nostalgic German cabaret – intimate, dark, decadent, but very friendly. Shows feature short song or dance numbers sprinkled with playful nudity and whimsical costumes.

Odeon

Hauptstrasse 116 (7870 4019, www. yorck.de). U4, S42, S46 Innsbrucker Platz, or S1, S41, S42, S46 Schöneberg. **Map** p119 B5 ㊸

A last hold-out of the big, old, single-screen neighbourhood cinema. It's exclusively English-language, providing a reasonably intelligent, though increasingly mainstream, selection of Hollywood and UK fare.

Wilmersdorf

The middle-class residential area of Wilmersdorf is a great place to get a feel for how the other half of Berlin lives, away from the street art and piercings of the east. The area was farmland until the mid 19th century, when a property boom created the *Millionenbauern* (peasant millionaires), farmers handsomely paid off by developers. It became an affluent neighbourhood and was home to a large Jewish population during the Weimar years.

Preussenpark, an ordinary local park, is transformed in summer by numerous Thai street-food stalls beneath colourful parasols – you can even get an open-air Thai massage.

Eating & drinking

Rum Trader

Fasanenstrasse 40 (881 1428). U3, U9 Spichernstrasse. No credit cards. **Bar**
This tiny bar is a Berlin classic, thanks to its eccentric owner, Gregor Scholl, who is ever present, smartly dressed in bow tie and waistcoat. There is no menu: Scholl will ask which spirit you like, and whether you want something *süss oder sauer* (sweet or sour).

Tian Fu

Berliner Strasse 15 (8639 7780, www. tianfu.de). U7, U9 Berliner Strasse. **Open** 9am-1.30am daily. €€. No credit cards. **Chinese**
Tian Fu provides some real Sichuan fire, of both the hot and numbing type. Kick things off with traditional cold starters such as seaweed salad in black vinegar dressing, then dive into a fiery fish stew swimming in red chillies.

Shopping

Erich Hamann Bittere Schokoladen

Brandenburgische Strasse 17 (873 2085, www.hamann-schokolade.de). U7 Konstanzer Strasse. **Open** 9am-6pm Mon-Fri; 9am-1pm Sat.
This lovely Bauhaus building houses Berlin's oldest functioning chocolate factory. Chocolate thins are boxed by hand in old-fashioned packaging, while the signature chocolate 'bark' is still made in the original machine purpose-built by Erich Hamann's son Gerhard, now in his late seventies.

Galerie Daniel Buchholz

Fasanenstrasse 30 (8862 4056, www. galerie buchholz.de). U1 Uhlandstrasse. **Open** 11am-6pm Tue-Sat.

Boat trips

While Berlin's claims to be the 'Prussian Venice' may meet with deserved scepticism, the German capital is still an engagingly watery place. The Spree meanders through on its journey from the Czech Republic to the Elbe. Beyond the Spree, the entire city and its environs is a maze of interlocking rivers, lakes and canals.

The regular BVG local transport tickets include ferry services across various lakes. An AB zone ticket is enough to get you on the hourly year-round ferry link from Wannsee to Kladow. There's even a decent pub by the pier in a quasi-rural setting on the other side.

A fine range of city-centre tours is offered by Stern und Kreisschiffahrt (www.sternund kreis.de), Reederei Winkler (www.reedereiwinkler.de) and Reederei Riedel (www.reederei-riedel.de). Most operators offer circular tours (about €19 per adult), usually lasting three to four hours, which take in the Spree and the Landwehrkanal. Many operate only from mid March to late November.

A 30-minute train journey to Wannsee offers more options. Stern & Kreis's Seven Lakes Trip (7-Seen-Rundfahrt) gives a chance to ogle some of Berlin's poshest backyards as the boat slides gently past the handsome mansions surrounding the Kleiner Wannsee. A longer trip from Wannsee runs via Potsdam to quaint Werder, one of the most beautiful of Brandenburg villages, with a cluster of fish restaurants around the quay.

BERLIN BY AREA

A hushed repository of elegance and refinement, this gallery left Cologne in 2008 after 20 years and moved to Berlin. It represents a raft of well-known names, such as 2006 Turner Prize winner Tomma Abts, Wolfgang Tillmans and Richard Hawkins.

Rogacki

Wilmersdorfer Strasse 145-146 (343 8250, www.rogacki.de). U7 Bismarck Strasse. **Open** 9am-6pm Mon-Wed; 9am-7pm Thur; 8am-7pm Fri; 8am-4pm Sat.

Attendants in green monogrammed uniforms stand to attention behind sparkling vitrines stuffed with all manner of prepared produce at this splendid delicatessen. Smoked and pickled fish is the mainstay; specialities include *Bratherings* (fried and brined herring) and *Senfgurken* (white gherkins from Spreewald).

V Kloeden

Wielandstrasse 24 (8871 2512, www. vonkloeden.de). U7 Adenauerplatz. **Open** 10am-7pm Mon-Fri; 10am-4pm Sat.

This charming shop proves that educational toys don't need to be boring.

There are shelves of picture books (some in both German and English), and even Asterix comics in Latin. Toys include Brio wooden train sets, eerily life-like Käthe Kruse dolls and Kersa puppets, and rocking horses.

Weichardt Brot

Mehlitzstrasse 7 (873 8099, www.weichardt.de). U7, U9 Berliner Strasse. **Open** 7.30am-6.30pm Mon-Fri; 7.30am-2pm Sat. No credit cards.

Perhaps the best bakery in town, Weichardt Brot grew out of a 1970s Berlin collective. Demeter-certified (biodynamic) flour is stone-ground daily on their three mills. They also produce traditional German sweets.

Arts & leisure

Bar jeder Vernunft

Spiegelzelt, Schaperstrasse 24 (883 1582, www.bar-jeder-vernunft.de). U3, U9 Spichernstrasse.

Some of Berlin's most celebrated entertainers perform in this snazzy circus tent of many mirrors, which takes in a range of shows and performances, including comedy, cabaret, literature and theatre. Dinner is an extra €29.

V Kloeden

Oranienstrasse, Kreuzberg

Kreuzberg & Treptow

Kreuzberg is divided firmly into halves, according to its old postcodes – Kreuzberg 36, the eastern part, is scruffy and hip, great for a night out; Kreuzberg 61, in the west, is quieter, prettier, duller after dark but lovely during the day. Further east, **Treptow** is a quiet residential area concealing leafy Treptower Park, a huge war memorial and an abandoned amusement park.

East Kreuzberg

Kreuzberg is an earthy kind of place, full of cafés, bars and clubs, dotted with indie cinemas, and an important nexus for the gay community.

Sights & museums

FHXB Friedrichshain-Kreuzberg Museum
Adalbertstrasse 95A (5058 5233, www.fhxb-museum.de). U1, U8 Kottbusser Tor. **Open** noon-6pm Wed-Sun. **Admission** free. **Map** p125 A1 ❶
A council-run museum about the area's turbulent history. The permanent exhibition catalogues both the area's Turkish immigrant heritage and its radical political legacy.

Museum der Dinge
Oranienstrasse 25 (9210 6311, www.museum derdinge.de). U1, U8 Kottbusser Tor. **Open** noon-7pm Mon, Thur-Sun. **Admission** €5; €3 reductions. No credit cards. **Map** p125 A1 ❷
The 'Museum of Things' contains every kind of small object you could imagine in modern design from the 19th century onwards – from hairbrushes and fondue sets to beach souvenirs and Nazi memorabilia. It's not a musty collection, but a sleek, minimalist room organised by themes such as 'yellow and black' or 'functional vs kitsch', rather than by era or type. There's a great shop too.

Eating & drinking

5 Elephant

Reichenberger Strasse 101 (9608 1527, www.fiveelephant.com). U1 Görlitzer Bahnhof. **Open** 8.30am-7pm Mon-Fri; 10am-7pm Sat, Sun. No credit cards. **€. Café Map** p125 D3 ❸

You can feel the love at this café run by a charming Austro-American couple – she bakes the cakes, he roasts the beans. There's a selection of cakes and tarts, but the Philadelphia cheesecake is transcendental.

Barbie Deinhoff's

Schlesische Strasse 16 (6107 3616, www.barbie deinhoff.de). U1 Schlesisches Tor. **Open** 7pm-6am daily. No credit cards. **Bar Map** p125 D2 ❹

One of performance artist Lena Braun's many spaces, pitched somewhere between John Waters hyper-kitsch and retro-futuristic, with pink walls and shabby furnishings. It draws a mixed LGBT crowd.

Baretto

Wrangelstrasse 41 (6162 7319). U1 Schlesisches Tor. **Open** 8am-7.30pm Mon-Sat; 9am-7.30pm Sun. **€.** No credit cards. **Café Map** p125 D2 ❺

This lovely little place was serving Italian espresso and fresh panini years before any of the hip third-wave cafés moved into town. A proper locals' breakfast spot.

Bar Raval

Lübbener Strasse 1 (5316 7954, www.barraval.de). U1 Görlitzer Bahnhof. **Open** 6-11pm Mon-Thur; 6pm-midnight Fri; 1pm-midnight Sat; 1-11pm Sun. **€€.** **Spanish Map** p125 C2 ❻

At the helm of Berlin's Spanish tapas wave is Bar Raval, owned by actor Daniel Brühl and restaurateur Atilano González. There's a weekly paella night, and the regional monthly specials feature the likes of Valencian monkfish in paprika sauce or Basque veal cheeks in red wine.

Bei Schlawinchen

Schönleinstrasse 34 (no phone). U8 Schönleinstrasse. **Open** 24hrs daily. No credit cards. **Bar Map** p125 B3 ❼

This dive situated just off Kottbusser Damm is a great example of a Berlin *Kneipe* (pub), with its bizarre decorations of toy dolls, old bicycles and instruments. Naturally, the beer is both cheap and plentiful.

Burgermeister

Oberbaumstrasse 8 (0176 2153 0440 mobile, www.burger-meister.de). U1 Schlesisches Tor. **Open** 11am-3am Mon-Thur,Sun; 11am-4am Fri, Sat. **€.** No credit cards. **Burgers Map** p125 D1 ❽

The hollowed-out remains of an old public toilet under the tracks of the U1 serve as the kitchen for this popular burger joint. A small glasshouse is erected in winter for people to fuel up on a cheeseburger and their famous chilli fries before going clubbing. You might have to queue to get in.

Cocolo

Paul-Lincke Ufer 39-40 (0172 304 7584 mobile, www.oliverprestele.de). U1, U8 Kottbusser Tor. **Open** 6pm-midnight daily. **€€.** No credit cards. **Japanese Map** p125 B2 ❾

The best ramen in Berlin. Originally just a tiny bar in Mitte, it opened this spacious branch by the canal in Kreuzberg. All the classic ramen styles are served, but the cognoscenti always pick tonkotsu.

Doyum Grillhaus

Admiralstrasse 36 (6165 6127). U1, U8 Kottbusser Tor. **Open** noon-1am daily. **€€.** No credit cards. **Turkish Map** p125 A2 ❿

One of the best *ocakbasi* (Turkish grill house) around, Kotti is somehow hidden in plain sight. Turkish locals come to this beautifully tiled dining room for a plate of iskender kebab smothered in yoghurt sauce, or succulent minced lamb adana. No alcohol.

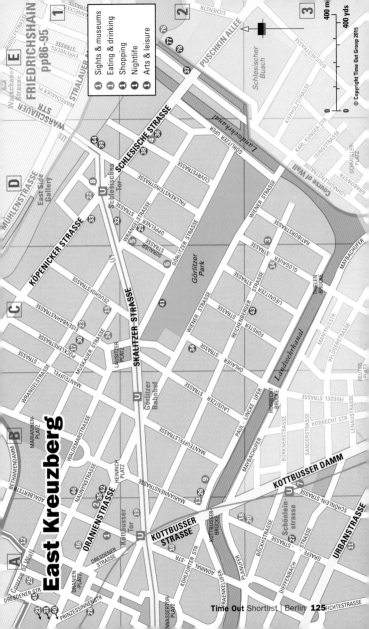

Figl

Urbanstrasse 47 (7229 0850,
www.gasthaus-figl.de). U6, U8
Hermannplatz. **Open** 6pm-midnight
Tue-Sun. €€. No credit cards. **Tarte**
flambée Map p125 A3 ⑪

Figl occupies a former *Kneipe* (pub),
and has kept the beautiful original
fittings: the dark wood bar, a giant
ceramic coal heater and, best of all, a
two-lane skittles alley in the basement.
The menu is based around beefed-up
Flammkuchen: Alsatian flatbread usually topped with crème fraiche, smoked
bacon and red onion.

Henne

Leuschnerdamm 25 (614 7730,
www.henne-berlin.de). U1, U8
Kottbusser Tor. **Open** 6pm-midnight
Tue-Sat; 5-10pm Sun. €€. No credit cards.
German Map p125 A1 ⑫

There's just one thing to order at
Henne: half a crispy fried chicken. The
only decisions you need to make after
that are whether you want cabbage or
potato salad, and which beer to go for
(try the Franconian Landbier).

Horvath

Paul-Lincke-Ufer 44A (6128 9992,
www.restaurant-horvath.de). U1, U8
Kottbusser Tor. **Open** 6-11pm Wed-Sun.
€€€€. **Haute cuisine Map** p125 A2 ⑬

Austrian chef Sebastian Frank gained
a Michelin star in 2011 outside of the
usual Berlin luxury hotel system at this
canalside restaurant. Enjoy a tasting
menu of typical rustic German ingredients transformed through novel techniques: onion, pigeon and kohlrabi, or
sturgeon, rib and celery, are charred,
abstracted and perfectly plated.

Das Hotel

Reichenberger Strasse 86 (6128 0334,
www.das hoteldassic.blogspot.de). U1
Görlitzer Bahnhof. **Open** 6pm-late daily.
No credit cards. **Bar Map** p125 C3 ⑭

Das Hotel occupies some attractive old
altbau buildings, with an ice-cream
parlour, brasserie, bar and dive club
– pretty much everything except for
actual hotel rooms. The bar is all candles and old pianos, and a Spanish DJ
gets the downstairs dancefloor going
on weekends.

Jolesch

Jolesch

Muskauer Strasse 1 (612 3581,
www.jolesch.de). U1 Görlitzer Bahnhof.
Open 11.30am-midnight Mon-Fri;
10am-midnight Sat, Sun. **€€€**. **Austrian**
Map p125 C1 ⑮

All a proper *Wiener Schnitzel* (made
with veal) requires is a slice of lemon
and a side of potato and cucumber
salad to cut through the fat. The classics here are undisputed, but are also
accompanied by a chef's menu of seasonal and often adventurous dishes,
such as venison with quince, or hay-
smoked lamb's tongue.

Luzia

Oranienstrasse 34 (8179 9958, www.
luzia.tc). U1, U8 Kottbusser Tor. **Open**
10am-3am daily. No credit cards. **Bar**
Map p125 A1 ⑯

A club kid favourite, this spot gets
pretty rowdy on weekends. It's decorated with bric-a-brac, with murals
by local artist Chin Chin pitched somewhere between gothic and twee. The
small smoking room in the back doubles up as a club on weekends.

Markthalle

Pücklerstrasse 34 (617 5502, www.
weltrestaurant-markthalle.de). U1
Görlitzer Bahnhof. **Open** 10am-midnight
daily. **€€**. **German Map** p125 C1 ⑰

This unpretentious *Schnitzel* restaurant and bar, with chunky tables and
wood-panelled walls, is popular with
locals and groups. Breakfast is served
until 4pm, lunch specials from noon,
while dinner brings hearty dishes such
as wild boar and red snapper.

Marques Bar

Graefestrasse 92 (6162 5906). U8
Schönleinstrasse. **Open** 6pm-late daily.
No credit cards. **Bar Map** p125 A2 ⑱

Below a rather average Spanish restaurant is this 1920s time-capsule of
a cocktail bar. A host takes you to an
available table – the decor is suitably
solid and mahogany – and asks your
preferred 'flavour profile' or what kind

of drink you usually like. Then the bar
staff do their magic.

Monarch

Skalitzer Strasse 134 (6165 6003, www.
kottimonarch.de). U1, U8 Kottbusser
Tor. **Open** 6pm-late Tue-Sun. No credit
cards. **Bar Map** p125 A2 ⑲

Finding this bar is part of the fun. It's
directly above the Kaisers supermar-
ket in an ugly prefab; you can see it
from the overground platform of the
U1 at Kottbusser Tor. To reach it, take
the stairs to the right of Kaisers and
follow the sound of the bass. It's an
unpretentious place with regular rock
concerts and cheap drinks, and dancing as the night wears on.

Mo's King of Falafel

Graefestrasse 99 (7407 3666). U1, U8
Kottbusser Tor. **Open** 1-11pm daily. **€**.
No credit cards. **Imbiss Map** p125 A3 ⑳

It's actually Mo's wife who forms the
little chickpea balls at this hole-in-the-
wall joint. Enormous wraps stuffed
with freshly fried falafel and salad cost
just a few euros. Expect to queue in
summer months.

Parker Bowles

Prinzenstrasse 85D (5527 9099, www.
parker-bowles.com). U8 Moritzplatz.
Open 9am-8pm Mon-Wed; 9am-late
Thur-Sat. **€€€**. **Modern European**
Map p125 A1 ㉑

Cheekily named by the team behind
the Prince Charles club next door, this
low-key yet elegant supper club serves
eclectic menu of vegetarian, paleo
and meat and fish specialities, many
sourced from local producers.

Schlesisch Blau

Köpenicker Strasse 1A (6981 4538).
U1 Schlesisches Tor. **Open** noon-3pm,
7pm-midnight Mon-Fri; 7pm-midnight
Sat. **€€**. No credit cards. **German**
Map p125 D1 ㉒

Another Kreuzberg curio, this homely
restaurant offers a set menu that
always features a salad, a soup, a few

mains and a dessert. It's not fancy, but you can expect well-braised meats, tasty salads and warming root-based soups. Booking advised.

Schwarze Traube

Wrangelstrasse 24 (2313 5569). U1 Görlitzer Bahnhof. **Open** 7pm-late daily. No credit cards. **Bar** Map p125 C1

This bar on a quiet backstreet shot to fame when the slight but magnificently bearded owner, Atalay Aktasm, represented Germany at the 2013 World Class Bartender of the Year final. Aktas describes his ideal ambience as 'noble trash'. Ask for a custom-made cocktail or request a classic.

Tante Lisbeth

Muskauer Strasse 49 (6290 8742, www.pyonen.de/tantelisbeth). U1 Görlitzer Bahnhof. **Open** 4pm-late Mon-Fri; 6pm-late Sat, Sun. No credit cards. **Bar** Map p125 C1

This spacious bar has a separate smoking room, as well as a folksy granny-flat aesthetic, but hidden downstairs is the real reason to come: a 1970s bowling alley. You can book it online and then bring a group down to enjoy the wood-panelled clubhouse with original fittings.

Zur Kleinen Markthalle

Legiendamm 32 (614 2356, www.zur-kleinen-markthalle.de). U8 Moritzplatz. **Open** 4pm-1am Mon-Sat; noon-1am Sun. No credit cards. **Bar** Map p125 A1

Just across from Henne, this is the less touristy choice, but it's no less of an old-school tavern with its dark wood interior. It's a great place to enjoy draught beers and a silky potato salad.

Shopping

Hard Wax

Paul-Lincke-Ufer 44A (6113 0111, www.hardwax.de). U1, U8 Kottbusser Tor. **Open** noon-8pm Mon-Sat. Map p125 B2

Up a staircase at the back of a Kreuzberg courtyard lies this vinyl mecca, famous for its flawless selection of dub, techno and reggae. It was opened by dub techno pioneers Basic Channel, and many of the city's biggest DJs (Marcel Dettmann, DJ Hell) started out by working here. Beware – it's infamous for its haughty service.

Markthalle IX

Kado

Graefestrasse 75 (6904 1638, www. kado.de). U8 Schönleinstrasse. **Open** 9.30am-6.30pm Tue-Fri; 9.30am-3.30pm Sat. No credit cards. **Map** p125 A3 ㉗

A mind-boggling selection of liquorice from all over the world is beautifully presented in row upon row of glass jars at Kado. All shapes, sizes and varieties are available.

Klemms

Prinzessinnenstrasse 29 (4050 4953, www.klemms-berlin.com). U8 Moritzplatz. **Open** 11am-6pm Tue-Sat. No credit cards. **Map** p125 A1 ㉘

This gallery, run by Sebastian Klemm and Silvia Bonsiepe, promotes offbeat and idiosyncratic shows from a range of photographers, painters and installation artists.

Kumru Kuruyemis

Wrangelstrasse 46 (3013 0216). U1 Schlesisches Tor. **Open** 9am-8.30pm Mon-Sat. No credit cards. **Map** p125 D2 ㉙

There are plenty of shops to feed the Turkish community's deep love of nuts. But Kumru Kuruyemis is a step

up, stocking unshelled salty almonds and churchkhela, a string of nuts dipped in grape must then dried.

Markthalle IX

Eisenbahnstrasse 42-43 (577 094 661, www.markthalleneun.de). U1 Görlitzer Bahnhof. **Open** Café noon-4pm daily. Market 10am-6pm Fri, Sat. Street food 5-10pm Thur. No credit cards. **Map** p125 C1 ㉚

Aligned with the Slow Food movement, this market hosts regular themed events including street food on Thursday evenings, and Cheese Berlin, where'll you find a multitude of artisanal European cheeses.

Modulor

Prinzenstrasse 85 (690 360, www. modulor.de). U8 Moritzplatz. **Open** 9am-8pm Mon-Fri; 10am-6pm Sat. **Map** p125 A1 ㉛

A paradise for the crafty, with everything laid out over several floors. There are rolls of synthetic materials for product designers or fashion students, but also more traditional art supplies – pencils, chalks, charcoals, oils and acrylics.

Motto

Skalitzer Strasse 68 (4881 6407, www.motto distribution.com). U1 Schlesisches Tor. **Open** noon-8pm Mon-Sat. **Map** p125 D1 ㉜

This place is tucked away in a disused frame factory. Fanzines, back issues, artists' books, posters, rare print-runs and cult classics are spread in a comehither way across a long central table.

Overkill

Köpenicker Strasse 195A (6950 6126, www.overkillshop.com). U1 Schlesisches Tor. **Open** 11am-8pm Mon-Sat. **Map** p125 D1 ㉝

At this urban culture hotspot, you'll find limited runs of Adidas, Asics and Nike shoes in unusual colourways, as well as sprays, markers and caps for the budding street artist.

Tabac & Whisky Center

Ohlauer Strasse 4 (612 5168, www. whiskyundwhiskey.de). U1 Görlitzer Bahnhof. **Open** *10am-7pm Mon-Sat.* **Map** p125 C2 ③④

Any lover of fine sipping spirits will get sucked into this great little shop, which stocks an excellent selection of single-malt whisky, bourbon and rare rums. Staff are extremely helpful.

Voo

Oranienstrasse 24 (6165 1119, www.vooberlin.com). U1, U8 Kottbusser Tor. **Open** *11am-8pm Mon-Sat.* **Map** p125 B1 ③⑤

The Voo concept store brings sleek fashions to an area usually associated with punkier looks. Expect well-crafted outerwear from minimal Swedish favourite Acne, classic New Balance sneakers, colourful Kenzo print sweaters, and accessories.

Nightlife

Barbie Deinhoff's

Schlesische Strasse 16 (no phone, www.barbie deinhoff.de). U1 Schlesisches Tor or bus N29. **Map** p125 D2 ③⑥

Sure, this is a queer performance space, but most people come to its bright casual rooms for the young, pan-sexual crowd, the top-notch local DJs and the hilarious art on the walls.

Chalet

Vor dem Schlesischen Tor 3 (6953 6290, www.chalet-berlin.de). U1 Schlesisches Tor. **Map** p125 E2 ③⑦

Chalet is located in a grand, 150-year-old townhouse. It has multiple levels and rooms to explore, as well as a large luscious garden in which to shoot the breeze. A stylish and sultry club with a party most nights; more local on weekdays, more touristy at weekends.

Lido

Cuvrystrasse 7 (6956 6840, www. lido-berlin.de). U1 Schlesisches Tor. No credit cards. **Map** p125 D2 ③⑧

This is the HQ of famed Berlin indie-rockers Karrera Klub, who have been champions of new music in the city for almost 20 years, and it's got one of the best sound systems in Berlin. Friendly Fires, MGMT, Shitdisco and the Horrors have all graced its stage.

Magnet

Falckensteinstrasse 48 (4400 8140, www.magnet-club.de). U1 Schlesisches Tor. No credit cards. **Map** p125 D1 ③⑨

This venue is one of the biggest bookers for the kind of up-and-coming indie bands featured in the NME. Catch them here before they hit the stadium circuit.

Prince Charles

Prinzenstrasse 85F (no phone, www.prince charlesberlin.com). U8 Moritzplatz. No credit cards. **Map** p125 A1 ④⓪

Walking down the concrete underpass to the entrance, it feels more like the approach to a car park than a trendy little club. It's situated in a former swimming pool, and the tiled walls and soft lighting create an intimate atmosphere. Artfully dishevelled young things bop to a house-heavy soundtrack.

Schwarzlicht Minigolf

Görlitzer Strasse 1 (6162 1960, www. indoor-minigolf-berlin.de). U1 Görlitzer Bahnhof. **Map** p125 C2 ④①

Five rooms of neon mini-golf situated beneath the Görlitzer Park café. The UV psychedelic extravaganza element is a little cheesy, but it's good fun for groups. Don't be put off by the zealous drug dealers: the park is perfectly safe after dark.

SO36

Oranienstrasse 190 (tickets 6110 1313, 6140 1306, www.so36.de). U1, U8 Kottbusser Tor. No credit cards. **Map** p125 B1 ④②

A key venue for gays and lesbians. SO36 even makes bingo fun with its brash Super Sexy Bingo night (every second Tuesday, from 7pm).

Soul Cat Music Club

Reichenberger Strasse 73, Kreuzberg (no phone, www.soulcat-berlin.de). U1 Görlitzer Bahnhof. No credit cards. **Map** p125 C3 ⓧ

This two-room bar in Kreuzberg has nightly gigs of soul, blues, folk and jazz, plus a small record shop selling tapes and vinyl.

Watergate

Falckensteinstrasse 49 (no phone, www.water-gate.de). U1 Schlesisches Tor. No credit cards. **Map** p125 D1 ⓧ

This slick two-level club was a driving force behind the rise of minimal techno in mid 2000s Berlin, as well as the first with a ceiling-mounted responsive LED lighting system, now copied all around the world. The downstairs Water Floor is particularly impressive with its panorama windows looking directly on to the Spree, and a floating deck terrace for watching the sunrise over Kreuzberg.

Arts & leisure

Babylon Kreuzberg

Dresdener Strasse 126 (6160 9693, www.yorck.de). U1, U8 Kottbusser Tor. No credit cards. **Map** p125 A1 ⓧ

Another Berlin perennial, this twin-screen theatre runs a varied programme featuring indie crossover and UK films. Once a local Turkish cinema, its films are almost all English-language and it offers a homely respite from the multiplex experience.

Ballhaus Naunynstrasse

Naunynstrasse 27 (7545 3725, www. ballhausnaunynstrasse.de). U1, U8 Kottbusser Tor. No credit cards. **Map** p125 B1 ⓧ

Thanks to artistic director Nurkan Erpulat's play *Theatertreffen*, Ballhaus Naunynstrasse is the fringe theatre to visit. The company is gaining a strong reputation for investigating issues surrounding the immigrant experience and identity in Germany.

West Kreuzberg

The more sedate western part of Kreuzberg contains some of the most picturesque corners of West Berlin, while the north-western portion of Kreuzberg, bordering Mitte, is not the prettiest, but it's where you'll find most of the area's museums and tourist sights.

Sights & museums

Berlin Hi-Flyer

Corner of Wilhelmstrasse & Zimmerstrasse (226 678 811, www. air-service-berlin.de). U6 Kochstrasse. **Open** Apr-Oct 10am-10pm daily. Nov-Mar 11am-6pm daily. **Admission** €19.90; €4.90-€14.90 reductions. **Map** p133 B1 ⓧ

This helium balloon has hovered 150m (490ft) above Berlin since 1999 and, somewhat bewilderingly, is now one of the city's leading tourist attractions – as well as one of its most expensive. You do get a lovely view, but given that the panorama from the dome of the (free) Reichstag is almost as good, you might wish to give this one a miss.

Berlinische Galerie

Alte Jakobstrasse 124-128 (7890 2600, www.berlinischegalerie.de). U6 Kochstrasse. **Open** 10am-6pm Mon, Wed-Sun. **Admission** €8; €5 reductions; free under-18s. **Map** p133 C1 ⓧ

The Berlinische Galerie specialises in art created in Berlin, dating from 1870 to the present, including painting, sculpture, photography and architecture. Its collections cover Dada Berlin, the Neue Sachlichkeit and the Eastern European avant-garde.

Deutsches Technikmuseum Berlin

Trebbiner Strasse 9 (902 540, www. sdtb.de). U1, U7 Möckernbrücke. **Open** 9am-5.30pm Tue-Fri; 10am-6pm Sat, Sun. **Admission** €6; €3.50 reductions. **Map** p133 A2 ⓧ

The German Museum of Technology is an eclectic, eccentric collection of new and antique industrial artefacts. The rail exhibits have pride of place, with the station sheds providing an ideal setting for locomotives and rolling stock from 1835 to the present. Other displays focus on the industrial revolution; street, rail, water and air traffic; computer technology; and printing technology.

Gruselkabinett

Schöneberger Strasse 23A (2655 5546, www.gruselkabinett.com). S1, S2, S25 Anhalter Bahnhof. **Open** 10am-7pm Mon-Fri; noon-8pm Sat, Sun. **Admission** €9.50; €7 reductions. No credit cards. **Map** p133 A2 ㉚

This is the city's only visitable World War II air-raid shelter. Built in 1943, the five-level bunker was part of an underground network connecting various similar structures throughout Berlin. Today, it houses both the 'Chamber of Horrors' and an exhibit on the bunker itself. The 'horrors' include a patented coffin designed to demonstrate the effects of being buried alive and a simulated cemetery. Kids love it, but it's not for those under ten.

Haus am Checkpoint Charlie

Friedrichstrasse 43-45 (253 7250, www. mauermuseum.de). U6 Kochstrasse. **Open** 9am-10pm daily. **Admission** €12.50; €9.50 reductions. **Map** p133 B1 ㉛

This private museum opened not long after the GDR erected the Berlin Wall in 1961, with the purpose of documenting the events that were taking place. The exhibition charts the history of the Wall, and details the ingenious and hair-raising ways people escaped from the GDR – as well as exhibiting some of the actual contraptions that were used, such as a home-made hot-air balloon.

Jüdisches Museum

Lindenstrasse 9-14 (2599 3300, guided tours 2599 3305, www.juedisches-

museum-berlin.de). U1, U6 Hallesches Tor. **Open** (last entry 1hr before closing) 10am-10pm Mon; 10am-8pm Tue-Sun. **Admission** €5; €2.50 reductions. **Map** p133 C2 ㉜

The ground plan of Daniel Libeskind's remarkable building is in part based on an exploded Star of David, in part on lines drawn between the site and former addresses of figures in Berlin's Jewish history, such as Mies van der Rohe, Arnold Schönberg and Walter Benjamin. The permanent exhibition focuses on the personal: it tells the stories of prominent Jews and what they contributed to their community, and to the cultural and economic life of Berlin and Germany. After centuries of prejudice and pogroms, the outlook for German Jews seemed to be brightening. Then came the Holocaust. The museum is undoubtedly a must-see, but expect long queues and big crowds.

Martin-Gropius-Bau

Niederkirchnerstrasse 7 (3025 4860, www.gropiusbau.de). S1, S2, S25 Anhalter Bahnhof. **Open** 10am-8pm Mon, Wed-Sun. **Admission** varies. **Map** p133 A1 ㉝

Cosying up to where the Wall once stood (a short, pitted stretch still runs nearby along the south side of Niederkirchnerstrasse), the Martin-Gropius-Bau is named after its architect, uncle of the more famous Walter. Built in 1881, it is now used for large-scale art exhibitions.

Schwules Museum

Mehringdamm 61 (6959 9050, www.schwulesmuseum.de). U6, U7 Mehringdamm. **Open** 2-6pm Mon, Wed-Fri, Sun; 2-7pm Sat. **Admission** €6; €4 reductions. No credit cards. **Map** p133 B4 ㉞

The Gay Museum, opened in 1985, is still the only one in the world dedicated to homosexual life. The museum, its library and archives are staffed by volunteers, and it functions mostly thanks to private donations and bequests.

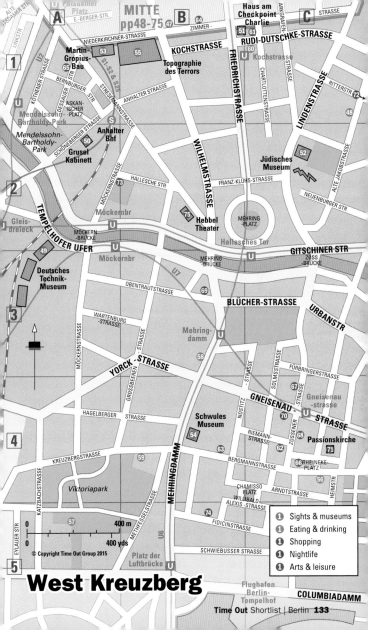

West Kreuzberg

A **B** **C**

1
2
3
4
5

Haus am Checkpoint Charlie

RUDI-DUTSCHKE-STRASSE

NIEDERKIRCHNER-STRASSE

53

55

KOCHSTRASSE

Martin-Gropius-Bau

65

Topographie des Terrors

Kochstrasse

51 61

60

FRIEDRICHSTRASSE

LINDENSTRASSE

RITTERSTR

12

48

Mendelssohn-Bartholdy-Park

Mendelssohn-Bartholdy-Park

50

Anhalter Bhf

Grusel Kabinett

Jüdisches Museum

52

HALLESCHE STR

FRANZ-KLÜHS-STRASSE

NEUENBURGER STR

Gleisdreieck

73

Möckernbr

75

Hebbel Theater

MEHRING-PLATZ

Hallesches Tor

GITSCHINER STR

49

Möckernbr

MEHRING-BRÜCKE

ZOSS-BRÜCKE

Deutsches Technik-Museum

OBENTRAUTSTRASSE

BLÜCHER-STRASSE

URBANSTR

WARTENBURG-STRASSE

69

Mehring-damm

YORCK-STRASSE

58

FÜRBRINGERSTRASSE

67

Gneisenau-strasse

GNEISENAU-

STRASSE

70

Schwules Museum

54

63

62

68

Passionskirche

71

KREUZBERGSTRASSE

59

BERGMANNSTRASSE

RHEINEKE-PLATZ

66

56

Viktoriapark

CHAMISSO PLATZ

WILIBALD ALEXIS-STRASSE

ARNDTSTRASSE

HEIMSTR

400 m

57

74

FIDICINSTRASSE

© Copyright Time Out Group 2015

SCHWIEBUSSER STRASSE

Platz der Luftbrücke

Flughafen Berlin-Tempelhof

COLUMBIADAMM

1 Sights & museums
1 Eating & drinking
1 Shopping
1 Nightlife
1 Arts & leisure

Haus am Checkpoint Charlie p132

Topographie des Terrors

Niederkirchnerstrasse 8 (2545 0950, www.topographie.de). S1, S2, S25 Anhalter Bahnhof, or U6 Kochstrasse. **Open** Outdoor exhibition 10am-dusk daily. Indoor exhibition 10am-8pm daily. **Admission** free. **Map** p133 B1 ⑤⑤

Essentially a piece of waste ground that was once the site of the Prinz Albrecht Palais, headquarters of the Gestapo, and the Hotel Prinz Albrecht, which housed offices of the Reich SS leadership. This was the centre of the Nazi police-state apparatus. There's an outdoor exhibition that gives a pretty comprehensive chronology of Hitler's rise to power, as well as an indoor documentation centre. A segment of the Berlin Wall runs along the site's northern boundary.

Eating & drinking

Austria

Bergmannstrasse 30 (694 4440, www. austria-berlin.de). U7 Gneisenaustrasse. **Open** 6pm- midnight daily. **€€.** **Austrian Map** p133 C4 ⑤⑥

With a collection of antlers, this place does its best to look like a hunting lodge. The Schnitzel famously spills over the edge of the plate. Book at weekends and in summer – when the outdoor seating on a tree-lined square comes into its own.

Golgatha

Viktoria Park, entrance via Katzbachstrasse or Dudenstrasse (785 2453, www.golgatha-berlin.de). U6 Platz der Luftbrücke. **Open** Apr-Sept 10am-late daily. **Bar Map** p133 A5 ⑤⑦

This legendary beer garden can do it all – breakfasts under dappled sunlight, hearty lunches, and drinking and dancing until the wee hours.

Mustafa's Gemüse Kebap

Mehringdamm 32 (no phone, www. mustafas.de). U6, U7 Mehringdamm. **Open** 10am-2am daily. No credit cards. **€. Imbiss Map** p133 B3 ⑤⑧

Easily the most popular kebab stall in town – don't be surprised by half-hour waits, especially for their chicken kebabs. But it's the vegetarian option that's really worth the wait: grilled peppers, aubergines and fried potatoes, finished with crumbled feta and a squirt of lemon juice.

Osteria No.1

*Kreuzbergstrasse 71 (786 9162,
www.osteria-uno.de). U6, U7
Mehringdamm.* **Open** noon-2am
daily. **€€. Italian Map** p133 B4 ⑤⑨
Most of Berlin's best Italian chefs paid
their dues at this 1977-founded establishment, learning their lessons from
a family of restaurateurs from Lecce.
There's an excellent lunch menu and,
in summer, one of Berlin's loveliest
garden courtyards. Kids eat free on
Sundays. Booking recommended.

Sale e Tabacchi

*Rudi-Dutschke-Strasse 25 (252 1155,
www.sale-e-tabacchi.de). U6 Kochstrasse.*
Open from 10am daily. **€€€. Italian
Map** p133 C1 ⑥⓪
An old-school Italian restaurant, ideal
for larger groups looking for some
southern decadence. Food is simple
and delicious rather than spectacular,
but it's the ambience – a comfortable
fug of cosiness and quiet affluence –
that's the big draw.

Shopping

Alexander Levy

*Rudi-Dutschke-Strasse 26 (2529 2276,
www.alexanderlevy.net). U6 Kochstrasse.*
Open 11am-6pm Tue-Sat. **Map** p133
C1 ⑥①
Scion of legendary Hamburg and
Berlin dealers, Alex Levy took over this
boxy space from his father in 2011, continuing the family trait of showcasing
quality art with an experimental edge.

Another Country

*Riemannstrasse 7 (6940 1160,
www.another country.de). U7
Gneisenaustrasse.* **Open** 11am-8pm
Mon-Fri; 11am-4pm Sat. **Map** p133 C4 ⑥②
This second-hand bookshop is a window into a Kreuzberg of the past. The
rooms have the feel of a private study,
with homely blue paintwork, piles of
books laid out on tables, and a fridge
for beers. Events include film nights,
quizzes and dinners.

Colours

*Bergmannstrasse 102 (694 3348, www.
kleidermarkt.de). U7 Gneisenaustrasse.*
Open 11am-7pm Mon-Fri; noon-6pm
Sat. **Map** p133 B4 ⑥③
Part of the Made in Berlin chain, this
shop is mostly known for its gimmick
of selling clothes by the 'kilo'. Up for
grabs are jeans, leather jackets and
dresses, including party stunners and
fetching Bavarian dirndls, plus the odd
gem from the 1950s.

DAAD Galerie

*Zimmerstrasse 90-91 (261 3640, www.
daadgalerie.de). U6 Kochstrasse.* **Open**
noon-6pm Tue-Sat. **Map** p133 B1 ⑥④
Something of a local institution,
DAAD is steeped in postwar Berlin history. The Berliner Künstlerprogramm
sees 20 artists participate in a year-
long residence, the fruits of which are
exhibited in this space.

Johann König

*Dessauerstrasse 6-7 (2610 3080, www.
johann koenig.de). U2, S1, S2, S25
Potsdamer Platz.* **Open** 11am-6pm Tue-
Sat. **Map** p133 A1 ⑥⑤
Johann König is one of Berlin's bona
fide iconoclasts. When he opened this
gallery in 2002, he invited his friend,
artist Jeppe Hein, to install a wrecking
ball, which swung about, knocking
chunks out of the walls whenever anyone entered the room. Nowadays, he's
regarded as a leading light in a scene
that's not short of characters.

Marheineke Markthalle

*Marheinekestrasse 15 (6128 6146,
meine-markthalle.de). U7
Gneisenaustrasse.* **Open** 8am-8pm Mon-
Fri; 8am-6pm Sat. **Map** p133 C4 ⑥⑥
A lovely covered market with French
butchers, Italian charcuterie, flowers
and organic produce, as well as plenty
of prepared foods to take away.

Paul Knopf

*Zossener Strasse 10 (692 1212, www.
paulknopf.de). U7 Gneisenaustrasse.*

BERLIN BY AREA

Badeschiff

Open 9am-6pm Tue, Fri; 2-6pm Wed, Thur. No credit cards. **Map** p133 C4 ⑤⑦ A Kreuzberg institution stocking buttons in every shape, colour and style you can think of. Paul Knopf's patient and untiring service is remarkable considering most of the transactions here are for tiny sums.

Space Hall

Zossener Strasse 33 (694 7664, www. space-hall.de). U7 Gneisenaustrasse. **Open** 11am-8pm Mon-Sat. **Map** p133 C4 ⑥⑧ A favourite of Berlin's resident DJs and producers, Space Hall has a huge selection of new and second-hand CDs and vinyl. Techno, house and electronica are the mainstay, but there's also hip hop, indie and rock.

Nightlife

Gretchen

Obentrautstrasse 19-21 (2592 2701, www.gretchen-club.de). U1, U6 Hallesches Tor, or U6, U7 Mehringdamm. No credit cards. **Map** p133 B3 ⑥⑨ Gretchen is not afraid of forgoing Berlin's ubiquitous tech-house loops in favour of some trap, dubstep, drum 'n' bass or hip hop. The picturesque

nd intricate columns
ssian stable create
gruous setting for
sounds.

...on Bar

...eisenaustrasse 18 (694 6602, café 6981 7421, www.junction-bar.de). U6 Gneisenaustrasse. No credit cards. **Map** p133 C4 🅰

A Kreuzberg landmark that arranges 365 concerts a year of everything from jazz and swing to rock, with DJs keeping the party going into the early hours.

Passionskirche

Marheinekeplatz 1-2 (tickets 6959 3624, 6940 1241, www.akanthus.de). U7 Gneisenaustrasse. No credit cards. **Map** p133 C4 🅰

Folk and world music acts mainly play here, but Beck, Ryan Adams and Marc Almond have also graced the stage of this deconsecrated church.

Ritter Butzke

Ritterstrasse 24 (no phone, www. ritterbutzke.de). U8 Moritzplatz. No credit cards. **Map** p133 C1 🅰

This enormous old factory is a current party hotspot thanks to its reliable booking policy, imaginative decor and amiable bouncers (who are occasionally dressed as knights – Ritter means 'knight'). Brace yourself for a massive queue between 1am and 3.30am.

Tempodrom

Möckernstrasse 10 (747 370, tickets 0180 555 4111 premium, www. tempodrom.de). U7 Möckernbrücke, or S1, S2, S25 Anhalter Bahnhof. **Map** p133 A/B2 🅰

Descendant of the legendary circus tent venue that was pitched in various West Berlin locations, this permanent space in tented form provides a beautiful setting for more upmarket/middle-of-the-road acts such as Chris Rea and the Pet Shop Boys. Plus, there are sports events, comedy, musicals, classical concerts and the Liquidrom spa.

Arts & leisure

English Theatre Berlin

Fidicinstrasse 40 (691 1211, www. etberlin.de). U6 Platz der Luftbrücke. No credit cards. **Map** p133 B5 🅰

Directors Günther Grosser and Bernd Hoffmeister, present a high-quality programme. Expect house productions, international guest shows and co-productions with performers from Berlin's lively international theatre scene, all in English.

HAU

Main office: HAU2, Hallesches Ufer 32 (259 0040, tickets 2590 0427, www.hebbel-am-ufer.de). U1, U7 Möckernbrücke, or U1, U6 Hallesches Tor. **Map** p133 B2 🅰

Since opening in 2003, HAU – the amalgamation of the century-old former Hebbel Theater (HAU1), Theater am Hallesches Ufer (HAU2) and Theater am Ufer (HAU3) – has gained a reputation for hosting Berlin's most innovative and radical theatre programming.

Treptow

The canal and lack of U-Bahn keeps this large district just east of Kreuzberg relatively isolated. It has one of only three remaining GDR watchtowers, overlooking a former 'death strip' of the Wall that ran down the canal, and the abandoned **Spreepark** (www.berliner-spreepark.de). A massively popular amusement park in GDR days, it sank into debt after the Wall fell. Now the rides are all overgrown and the ferris wheel creaks eerily in the wind. Security is tight, but guided tours are available from the main gate (check the website).

Sights & museums

Badeschiff

Eichenstrasse 4 (533 2030, www.arena-berlin.de). S8, S9, S41, S42 Treptower

Park. **Open** 8.30am-midnight daily.
Admission €4; €3 reductions. No credit cards. **Map** p125 E2 ⑦⑥
A former barge docked on the banks of the Spree has been converted into a heated swimming pool. It belongs to the Arena Berlin cultural centre, and has regular open-air parties. In winter, it becomes a covered sauna.

Insel der Jugend

Treptower Park (8096 1850, www. inselberlin.de). S8, S9, S41, S42 Treptower Park. **Open** 24hrs daily.
Admission free.
Connected to the mainland by German's first composite steel bridge, built in 1915, this wooded island is now a lovely small park, with a bar/café that hosts puppet-theatre workshops and other events, and open-air raves in summer.

Sowjetisches Ehrenmal

Treptower Park (901 393 000, www. stadtentwicklung.berlin.de). S8, S9, S41, S42 Treptower Park. **Open** 24hrs daily.
Admission free.

This Soviet war memorial (one of t__ in Berlin) and military cemetery __ quietly in beautiful Treptower Park Architect Yakov Belopolsky's design was unveiled just four years after World War II ended, on 8 May 1949. On entering, you're greeted by statues of two kneeling soldiers, and the view unfolds across a geometrical expanse flanked by 16 stone sarcophagi, which mark the burial site of the 5,000 Soviet soldiers who died in the final Battle of Berlin in spring 1945.

Eating & drinking

Eierschale Zenner

Alt-Treptow 14-17 (533 7370, www.eierschale-zenner.com). S8, S9 Plänterwald. **Open** 10am-11pm Mon-Thur; 10am-4am Fri, Sat; 10am-10pm Sun. **Bar**
On sunny weekends the terrace at this old-fashioned tavern turns into a greying disco, as elderly couples come to waltz and slow-dance the evening away. It has a great view over the River Spree. Steer clear of the grim food.

Club der Visionaere

Nightlife

Arena Berlin

Eichenstrasse 4 (5332 0340, www.arena-berlin.de). U1 Schlesisches Tor, or S8, S9, S41, S42 Treptower Park. No credit cards. **Map** p125 E2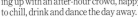

Inside a converted bus garage, Arena Berlin presents A-list artists such as Bob Dylan and Björk, and smaller acts. The riverside complex also includes the Badeschiff swimming pool and the MS *Hoppetosse* party boat.

Club der Visionaere

Am Flutgraben (6951 8942, www. clubdervisionaere.com). U1 Schlesisches Tor, or S8, S9, S41, S42 Treptower Park. No credit cards. **Map** p125 E2 78

This summer-only canalside club is a great way to find out what makes Berlin so special. There's a small indoor dancefloor and a rickety open-air area of wooden decking with a large jetty stretching out across the water. The place comes to life at the weekend, filling up with an after-hour crowd, happy to chill, drink and dance the day away.

Clubbing lore

Party tips and tricks.

It's not unusual to head off to a party on Friday night and stumble into bed at some point on Sunday afternoon. The real party animals go out during the week too. While this approach is hardcore, the general attitude to clubbing is laid-back; no dressing up, no planning. People don't head to clubs until 2am at the earliest. Admission prices are reasonable, around €10-€12 for big clubs and half that for smaller DJ bars. Wear what you like, but bear in mind that Berliners tend not to dress up in a British sense – short frocks or high heels might be better left at home.

More and more clubs operate some sort of door policy. At peak times outside Berghain on a Saturday night, at least a third of the people in the queue won't get past the scary bouncer with a tattoo on his face – you'll know you're in if he nods; if he points to his left, hard luck. Argue the toss if you're feeling brave. If you want to increase your chances of getting in, there are a few simple rules. Don't be too loud. Don't be obviously off your face. Don't take pictures of one another in the queue. Don't have this guide in your hand. Use English sparingly.

To find out what's on where, pick up a copy of *Zitty* or *Tip*, Berlin's two fortnightly listings magazines, or their English-language monthly equivalent *Exberliner*. Discerning websites include www.iheartberlin.de, www.unlike.net/berlin and www.sugarhigh.de.

Rathaus Neukölln,
Karl-Marx-Strasse

Neukölln

Neukölln has gone from making headlines for rampant crime to being the city's hippest district. A vibrant ethnic mix, dominated by the Turkish community, draws the city's bohemians and artists, leading to an abundance of gritty bars and pubs as well as discreet but definite signs of gentrification.

Kreuzkölln

The small strip bordering the canal just across from Kreuzberg was, until about ten years ago, a quiet, mainly working-class area with a large Turkish population. But now, other languages are heard on the streets – English, French, Spanish, Swedish, Italian, Japanese – and it's full of charming cafés and restaurants. The canalside Maybachufer, home to the lively **Turkischer Markt** and **Nowkoelln Flowmarkt**, makes for a jolly stroll. From here, head south for espresso bars, and vintage

fashion and wooden-toy shops. Quiet by day, Weserstrasse comes alive at night and is adjacent to the Levantine food paradise that is Sonnenallee.

Eating & drinking

Azzam

Sonnenallee 54 (3013 1541). U7, U8 Hermannplatz. **Open** 7am-midnight daily. €. No credit cards. **Middle Eastern Map** p143 C2 ❶

People flock from all over the city to sample Azzam's houmous, made fresh throughout the day. The grilled minced lamb is perfectly seasoned, and the falafel a crunchy, sesame-speckled delight. You get a lot for your money too: each dish comes with raw veg, olives, garlicky mayo or tahini sauce, and a basket of stacked pitta.

Berlin Burger International

Pannierstrasse 5 (0160 482 6505 mobile, www.berlinburgerinternational.com). U7, U8 Hermannplatz. **Open** noon-midnight Mon-Thur; noon-1am Fri, Sat; noon-10pm Sun. €. No credit cards. **Imbiss Map** p143 C2 ❷

A proper hole-in-the-wall. The pavement tables are constantly packed, whatever the season: BBI has punters hooked on stacked hamburgers, served with three types of salad, and with a small amount of lamb mince in the patty for extra succulence.

Black Lodge

Sanderstrasse 6 (no phone). U8 Schönleinstrasse. **Open** 9pm-late Tue-Sat. No credit cards. **Bar Map** p143 B1 ❸

Hidden behind the façade of a crusty old *Kneipe* (pub) lies this moody watering hole. The back room is a replica of the dream sequence room from *Twin Peaks*; the cocktails are sharp.

Bullys Bakery

Friedelstrasse 7 (2532 5500, www.bullys bakery.com). U7, U8 Hermannplatz. **Open** 7am-6pm Mon-Fri; 9am-6pm Sat; 10am-6pm Sun. €. No credit cards. **Café Map** p143 B2 ❹

Daniel, the half-Spanish, half-German proprietor, bakes the best croissants in town. After breakfast, there are also various *Flammkuchen* – crisp pastries from Alsace topped with cheese and pear or ham – as well as fruity crumble cakes, tarts and a selection of muffins.

Burrito Baby

Pflügerstrasse 11 (3385 1520, www. burritobaby.de). U8 Schönleinstrasse. **Open** 1-10pm Wed-Fri; 4-10pm Sat; 4-9pm Sun. €. No credit cards. **Mexican/ Vegan Map** p143 D2 ❺

In a nod to neighbourhood trends, this cutesy Mexican canteen is fully vegan. They even make their own lemonade.

California Breakfast Slam

Innstrasse 47 (686 9624, www.cabslam. com). U7 Karl-Marx-Strasse. **Open** 10am-midnight daily. €€. **North American Map** p143 B1 ❻

Cabslam has done much to popularise US-style brunch culture among the

Berlin hip set, offering potent bloody marys alongside eggs benedict and Tex-Mex breakfast dishes. It started out as a pop-up, but has now opened this permanent space.

Chez Dang

Friedelstrasse 31 (5305 1205, www.chez-dang.com). U8 Schönleinstrasse. **Open** 11.30am-11.30pm Mon, Tue, Thur, Fri; 4-11.30pm Sat, Sun. €€. No credit cards. **Vietnamese Map** p143 B1 ❼

Head to Chez Dang for a fresh and healthy Vietnamese fix. This family-run restaurant is far more inventive than the usual fast-food noodle joints.

City Chicken

Sonnenallee 59 (624 8600). U7 Rathaus Neukölln. **Open** 9am-1am daily. €. No credit cards. **Rotisserie Map** p143 C2 ❽

Kreuzberg's Hühnerhaus gets a run for its money at City Chicken, the scene of frenzied rotisserie action. There's only really one option: a silver platter with half a roast chicken, a pile of fries, garlicky mayonnaise, assorted pickles and some pitta to mop up the juices.

Espera

Sonnenallee 35 (no phone). U7, U8 Hermannplatz. **Open** 7am-7pm Mon-Fri; 8.30am-7pm Sat, Sun. €. No credit cards. **Café Map** p143 B2 ❾

Sitting among the Syrian and Lebanese snack joints of Sonnenallee, this modern café offers filled focaccia and cakes. Enjoy an excellent cortado at an outdoor table made from an old wine crate.

Fräulein Frost

Friedelstrasse 39 (9559 5521). U8 Schönleinstrasse. **Open** 2-8pm daily. No credit cards. **Ice-cream Map** p143 B1 ❿

Fräulein Frost is one of the city's best seasonal ice-cream parlours. Yummy mummies flock here, and sleds provide outside seating (and fun) for kids. Refresh yourself with their signature GuZiMi (cucumber, lemon, mint) or go all out with a velvety pistachio.

Geist im Glas

Lenaustrasse 27 (0176 5533 0450 mobile). U7, U8 Hermannplatz. **Open** 7pm-late daily. No credit cards. **Bar Map** p143 B1 ⑪

The space here is built up with wooden platforms and great attention to detail, such as the Victorian curios laid into the bar or the esoteric toilet. They specialise in infused alcohols, shots of which are poured out of a giant bottle at the bar or mixed into their house cocktails, such as the Geist Russian, a rich blend of vodka infused with vanilla, cinnamon, Kahlúa and cream.

Das Gift

Donaustrasse 119 (no phone, www. dasgift.de). U7, U8 Hermannplatz. **Open** 5pm-late daily. No credit cards. **Bar Map** p143 B2 ⑫

Famously owned by Mogwai's Barry Burns, Das Gift is his attempt at mashing a Glaswegian pub into a Berlin *Kneipe*. Lots of ales and single malts behind the bar, regular pie nights and a rowdy pub quiz go somewhat towards comforting the homesick Anglo expats that frequent the place.

Hamburger Heaven

Sanderstrasse 17 (6298 6070, www.hamburgerheaven.de). U8 Schönleinstrasse. **Open** noon-10pm Mon-Thur, Sun; noon-11pm Fri, Sat. **€**. No credit cards. **Burgers Map** p143 B1 ⑬

For a long time it was just a hole-in-the-wall near the Kottbusser Brücke, but Hamburger Heaven moved into its own digs in early 2014. Their recipe for success is clear: organic beef patties, excellent steaks cut to order and crisp fries – even if their home-made ketchup is a source of contention.

Herz

Weichselstrasse 15 (0176 6476 0499 mobile). U7, U8 Hermannplatz. **Open** 8pm-late Tue-Sat. No credit cards. **Bar Map** p143 C2 ⑭

An experimental dance bar put together by a left-field French crew,

Herz makes a welcome change from the usual Weserstrasse living-room bar. DJs play everything from glam rock to no wave, and there's a secret record/fashion shop in the back called Uni+Form.

Imren Grill

Karl-Marx-Strasse 75 (no phone, www. imren-grill.de). U8 Schönleinstrasse. **Open** 9am-3am daily. **€**. No credit cards. **Imbiss Map** p143 C2 ⑮

Part of a small chain, Imren Grill provides some of the best Turkish snacks in town. Order the classic *Döner im Brot* (kebab in toasted bread), with its stuffing of lamb grilled in neck fat, salad, tahini and chilli flakes. Then join the suited elderly gents at the park in front, who put the world to rights over cups of sweet black tea.

Kokolores

Weichselstrasse 3 (2574 4568, www. kokolores-neukoelln.de). U7 Rathaus Neukölln. **Open** 6-11pm Tue-Thur, Sun; 6pm-midnight Fri, Sat. **€€**. No credit cards. **Polish Map** p143 C2 ⑯

This cosy place is packed every evening with the hip local youth who come for the massive plates of Polish food at dirt-cheap prices. Wednesday is *pierogi* (steamed dumplings) night.

Mama

Hobrechtstrasse 61 (0157 7386 4042 mobile). U7, U8 Hermannplatz. **Open** 7pm-late daily. No credit cards. **Bar Map** p143 B1 ⑰

Nearer to a grandmother in Neukölln years, Mama was one of the area's first bars to nail down the look with its GDR living-room furniture, intricate murals and sound system veering towards Balkan beats. The unpasteurised Svijany beer on tap is excellent.

Melbourne Canteen

Pannierstrasse 57 (6273 1602, www. melbournecanteen.com). U7, U8 Hermannplatz. **Open** 9am-late daily. **€**. No credit cards. **Café Map** p143 B2 ⑱

This Aussie café is most beloved for its bloody mary, which will sledgehammer its way through even the most demonic of hangovers. They serve brunch classics, such as eggs benedict, and a tidy cocktail menu in the evenings.

Nansen

Maybachufer 39 (6630 1438, www. restaurant-nansen.de). U8 Schönleinstrasse. **Open** 6-11pm daily. €€€. No credit cards. **German Map** p143 C1 ⑲

This long-time neighbourhood favourite is one of the city's best restaurants. Ingredients are locally sourced and quality is superb: braised and smoked meats, seasonal greens and pickled roots are some of the elements at play in the modern German dishes. The low-lit dining room is made for romance.

Pizza a Pezzi

Weserstrasse 208 (no phone). U7, U8 Hermannplatz. **Open** 11am-midnight daily. €. No credit cards. **Pizza Map** p143 B2 ⑳

This blue-tiled pizzeria has plenty of seating in its large corner location. They offer excellent *al taglio*-style pizzas – pre-made small squares finished to order in the oven – as well as standard whole pizzas, missable baked pastas and a fabulous tiramisu.

Silver Future

Weserstrasse 206 (7563 4987, www. silverfuture.net). U7, U8 Hermannplatz. **Open** 5pm-2am Mon-Thur, Sun; 5pm-3am Fri, Sat. **Bar Map** p143 B2 ㉑

Neukölln's longstanding queer destination. 'You are now leaving the heteronormative zone' announces a playful sign above the bar – and it's not kidding. Fun for groups of any sexual or gender definition, SF is welcoming, witty and charmingly rough around the edges.

Sing Blackbird

Sanderstrasse 11 (no phone, www. singblackbird.com). U8 Schönleinstrasse. **Open** 10.30am-8pm daily. €. No credit cards. **Café Map** p143 B1 ㉒

An instant hit on opening, this charming vegetarian café doubles up as an excellent vintage clothes shop, where you can bring in your clothes for trade or credit. It's also home to the Daily Dose cold-pressed juice company.

Tier

Weserstrasse 42 (no phone). U7 Rathaus Neukölln. **Open** 7pm-late daily. No credit cards. **Bar Map** p143 C2 ㉓

Seen through the frosted windows, Tier's long bar could be a facsimile of Hopper's iconic *Nighthawks*. The vinyl collection sticks to the trusted classics, as does the cocktail menu, though there's a rotating experimental special.

Shopping

Azafran

Lenaustrasse 5 (6583 4970, www. azafrangourmet.com). U7, U8 Hermannplatz. **Open** 2-8pm Tue-Sat. No credit cards. **Map** p143 B2 ㉔

This fantastic Spanish deli carries produce sourced directly from small farms, including potent matured manchego and acorn-fed Domecq Ibérico ham. Prices reflect the quality.

Heil Quelle

Pannierstrasse 58 (6272 7822, www.heil-quelle-berlin.de). U7, U8 Hermannplatz. **Open** 8am-8pm Mon-Fri; 9am-8pm Sat; 10am-4pm Sun. No credit cards. **Map** p143 B2 ㉕

This *super-Späti* (convenience store) amalgamated with a local DIY shop and now offers not only foreign ales, English-language press and obscure tobacco brands but also screws, paint and rope.

Let Them Eat Cake

Weserstrasse 164 (6096 5095, www. letthemeatcake-berlin.tumblr.com). U7 Rathaus Neukölln. **Open** 1-7pm Tue-Sat. **Map** p143 C2 ㉖

A Swedish vintage shop (plus gallery space) specialising in chunky 1990s clothing and designer jewellery.

Oye Kreuzkölln

Nowkoelln Flowmarkt

*Maybachufer (no phone, www.nowkoelln.
de). U8 Schönleinstrasse.* **Open** Mar-Nov
10am-6pm 2nd Sun of mth. Closed Dec-
Feb. No credit cards. **Map** p143 B1 ㉗
This massively popular canalside flea-
market has grown considerably. Local
hipsters hawk vintage apparel, and
there's plenty of food, with smoked fish
sandwiches, *Käsespätzle* and hot apple
pie on offer.

Oye Kreuzkölln

*Friedelstrasse 49 (8937 2815, www.oye-
records.com). U7, U8 Hermannplatz.*
Open 1-8pm Mon-Sat. **Map** p143 B2 ㉘
The southern branch of Oye Records
(the other is in Prenzlauer Berg), this
small shop packs in a quality pick of
house, techno and bass vinyl. Big-name
DJs often do in-store events.

Peppikäse

*Weichselstrasse 65 (0176 5030 7656
mobile, www.peppikaese.de). U7 Rathaus
Neukölln.* **Open** 2-9pm Tue, Wed; 10am-
9pm Thur-Sat. No credit cards. **Map**
p143 C2 ㉙
Owner Georg, a local Slow Food
champion, stocks Austrian and Swiss
cheeses with a particular emphasis on
raw-milk varieties.

Rag & Bone Man

*Brieselstrasse 9 (no phone). U7 Karl-
Marx-Strasse.* **Open** 1-7pm Mon, Wed-
Fri; 1-6pm Sat. **Map** p143 C3 ㉚

An excellent vintage clothes shop that
also stocks a selection of young designers. Its racks are strong on velour, fake
animal prints and silky things.

Turkischer Markt

*Maybachufer (no phone, www.
tuerkenmarkt.de). U8 Schönleinstrasse.*
Open 11am-6.30pm Tue, Fri. No credit
cards. **Map** p143 B1 ㉛
A lively market by the canal catering
for the local Turkish community: fresh
veg piled high, wonderful spices and,
near closing time, whole crates of fruit
sold off at bargain prices.

Vintage Galore

*Sanderstrasse 12 (6396 3338, www.
vintagegalore.de). U8 Schönleinstrasse.*
Open 2-8pm Tue-Fri; noon-6pm Sat.
Map p143 B1 ㉜
One of the best places for mid-century
Danish furniture: it stocks everything
from floor lamps to snack plates in the
distinctive rounded teak style.

Nightlife

Sameheads

*Richardstrasse 10 (7012 1060, www.
sameheads.com). U7 Karl-Marx-Strasse.*
No credit cards. **Map** p143 C3 ㉝
A friendly hipster enclave – it began
as an offbeat fashion boutique and
quickly evolved into a bar and late-
night party space. Vintage threads
are sold in the day, while all manner of

antics kick off as the sun goes down. You might stumble upon any or all of the following: comedy open mics, art shows, pub quizzes, film screenings and sweaty raves. It's all masterminded by three British brothers – Nathan, Leo and Harry – aka the Sameheads.

SchwuZ

Rollbergstrasse 26 (5770 2270, www. schwuz.de). U7 Rathaus Neukölln. No credit cards. **Map** p143 C3 ③④

One of Berlin's longest-running dance institutions got a shot in the arm when it moved into the old Neukölln Kindl brewery in 2013. Saturday is the main disco night at the Schwulen Zentrum ('gay centre'), attracting a mixed and ready-to-mingle crowd. Assorted one-nighters include the wildly popular London Calling, on the first Friday of the month, with indie and pop music. L-Tunes (for lesbians) is on the last Friday. For a grittier vibe, Thursdays is reserved for a more experimental, techno soundtrack.

Schillerkiez & Rixdorf

Schillerkiez is the newest area to feel the effects of gentrification, as Spanish restaurateurs, Swedish fashion designers and English bar-owners throw in their lot with the Turkish kebab shops and betting parlours. With leafy Herrfurthplatz at its heart, it ends at Hermannstrasse in the east and the **Tempelhofer Feld** in the west. The city solved the problem of this enormous former airport (built by the Nazis) by turning it into a public park.

Across the busy shopping street of Karl-Marx-Strasse is the picturesque 18th-century 'village' of **Rixdorf**. There's a blacksmith and farmhouse dating from the original settlement, as well as the older 15th-century Bethlehemskirche. A horse-and-carriage business is still in operation, and the square holds traditional events including a Christmas craft market.

Tempelhofer Feld

Sights & museums

Hufeisensiedlung

Lowise-Reuter-Ring (no phone). U7 Parchimer Allee. **Open** 24hrs daily. **Admission** free.

Heading far south into Britz, you'll find this vast housing estate, one of Berlin's six modernist estates listed as a UNESCO World Heritage Site. Built in the late 1920s by Bruno Taut and Martin Wagner, with some of the Garden City movement's ideals, the large horseshoe-shaped building contains 1,200 flats overlooking a large green space. Many of the flats retain their original Bauhaus fittings and distinctive brightly coloured doors.

Eating & drinking

Bierbaroness

Braunschweigerstrasse 46 (8669 1699). U7, S41, S42, S45, S46, S47 Neukölln. **Open** 9pm-3am daily. No credit cards. **Bar** This Canadian-owned dive bar attracts regulars heavy on the facial hair and even heavier on the bonhomie. There's free pool and a no-cocktails policy, and the indie DJs double up as masseurs.

Café Rix

Karl-Marx-Strasse 141 (686 9020, www. caferix.de). U7 Karl-Marx-Strasse. **Open** 9am-midnight Mon-Thur; 9am-1am Fri, Sat; 10am-midnight Sun. €. No credit cards. **Café Map** p143 C3 ㉟ Hidden behind noisy Karl-Marx-Strasse is this grand café housed in a former 19th-century ballroom. There's a lovely courtyard for coffee and cake or breakfast (served until 5pm).

Café Vux

Wipperstrasse 14 (no phone, www.vux-berlin.org). U7, S41, S42, S45, S46, S47 Neukölln. **Open** noon-7pm Wed-Sat; noon-6pm Sun. €. No credit cards. **Café** This Brazilian-run café brings to mind a twee tea parlour. Enjoy incredible vegan versions of black forest gateau and coconut cheesecake.

Circus Lemke

Selchower Strasse 31 (no phone). U8 Boddinstrasse. **Open** noon-10pm Mon-Fri; 10am-10pm Sat, Sun. No credit cards. **Bar Map** p143 B3 ㊱ Doing double service as a café serving brunches by day and a cocktail bar come the evening, Circus Lemke's wooden furniture accommodates a crowd of welcoming regulars.

Lava

Flughafenstrasse 46 (2234 6908, www.lava-berlin.de). U8 Boddinstrasse. **Open** 1-11pm daily. €€. **Bistro Map** p143 B3 ㊲ Originally the deli of Lavanderia Vecchia, this emerald-green offshoot has matured into a fine restaurant of its own under head chef Mathias Bartelmes.

Lavanderia Vecchia

Flughafenstrasse 46 (6272 2152, www.lavanderiavecchia.de). U8 Boddinstrasse. **Open** noon-2.30pm, 7pm-midnight Tue-Fri; 7pm-midnight Sat. €€. **Italian Map** p143 B3 ㊳ Tricky to locate from the street, this cute Italian joint is in a courtyard behind its newer sibling, trattoria Lava. There's just one set menu for dinner (booking essential), costing a very reasonable €40 a head. Wines come from the Sabina region of Italy.

La Pecora Nera

Herrfurthplatz 6 (6883 2676, www.pecoraberlin.de). U8 Boddinstrasse. **Open** 6pm-late Tue-Sun. €€. No credit cards. **Italian Map** p143 B3 ㊳ Schillerkiez really upped its restaurant game with the arrival of this charming Venetian place with extremely reasonable prices. They make their own *bigoli*, a buckwheat pasta particular to the Veneto region, and Aperol spritz costs just €2.50 from 6pm to 7pm daily.

Rundstück Warm

Okerstrasse 40 (5485 6849). U8 Leinestrasse. **Open** 4-11pm Tue-Sun. €. No credit cards. **Burgers Map** p143 B3 ㊵

Headed by an excellent Guatemalan chef, this little burger place adjoins a larger bar next door. Spanish tiles line the wall, and charred padrón peppers are available as a side to the juicy burgers, as are home-made chilli sauces.

Zsa Zsa & Louis

Richardstrasse 103 (0157 7153 1002 mobile). U7 Karl-Marx-Strasse. **Open** noon-late daily. €. No credit cards. **Sandwiches Map** p143 C3 ④

Yummy doorstop sandwiches, including their spin on *vitello tonnato* – sliced veal, tuna mayo and cress – and Time for Fiesta, with chorizo, manchego, a fried egg and aïoli.

Shopping

Blutwurst Manufaktur

Karl-Marx-Platz 9-11 (687 2004, www.blutwurstmanufaktur.de). U7 Karl-Marx-Strasse. **Open** 8am-6pm Mon-Fri; 8am-1pm Sat. **Map** p143 C3 ④

Rixdorf's award-winning butcher Markus Benser sells all sorts of pork products, both fresh and cured, and his shop also a great place to source game, but it's the creamy blood sausage that draws the crowds.

Fantasiakulisse

Flughafenstrasse 32 (0178 335 7354 mobile, www.fantasiakulisse.de). U8 Boddinstrasse. **Open** 10am-6pm Mon-Fri; or by appointment. No credit cards. **Map** p143 B2 ④

Flughafenstrasse is junk-shop central, and Fantasiakulisse is a particular gem, rammed full of the eccentric owner's film memorabilia, theatre props and mannequin collection.

Nightlife

Columbiahalle

Columbiadamm 13-21, Tempelhof (tickets 6110 1313, www.c-halle.com). U6 Platz der Luftbrücke. No credit cards. A roomy venue with a reputation for the best sound in town, Columbiahalle

Hufeisensiedlung p147

promotes larger acts that haven't made it to blockbuster status, such as Bon Iver or Manu Chao, or hip hop superstars such as Snoop Dogg. Next door, C-Club (tickets 8099 8715, www.c-club-berlin.de) showcases mid-size acts of every genre, from Cannibal Corpse to the Horrors.

Huxley's Neue Welt

Hasenheide 107-112 (780 9980, www.huxleysneuewelt.com). U7, U8 Hermannplatz. **Map** p143 B2 ④

This early 20th-century ballroom on the corner of Hasenheide Park is now situated, incongruously, inside a modern retail park. It has a bit of a Wild West atmosphere and aesthetic, hosting poker championships and tattoo expos when not hosting gigs by the likes of Elbow and Kasabian.

Fischerhütte p155

Other Districts

As it consists of two cities – once divided and now fused back together – it's not surprising that Berlin sprawls for miles in every direction. Although most of the fun stuff is in the gentrified east and the key sites are in the centre, exploring the outlying boroughs – especially perennial upcomer Wedding and the bucolic Grünewald – is well worth the effort. If the distances look daunting on a map, remember that the capital's late 19th-century expansion into a hinterland of lakes and forests coincided with the age of railways, which means that public transport will whisk you to most of the far-flung districts.

Wedding

The working-class industrial district of Wedding, formerly on the western side of the Wall, is now politically part of Mitte. Few visitors venture far into its largely grim vastness. The area is continually being hailed as the next for gentrification, and the low rents have encouraged artists to move their studios here, but it hasn't developed a real restaurant or bar scene, as in Neukölln. It's refreshingly multicultural in feel, with a large African community and also Turkish, Chinese and Arabic residents.

The main sight is one of the few remaining stretches of the Wall, at the **Gedenkstätte Berliner Mauer** (Berlin Wall Memorial).

Sights & museums

Anti-Kriegs-Museum

Brüsseler Strasse 21 (4549 0110, tours 402 8691, www.anti-kriegs-museum.de). U9 Amrumer Strasse. **Open** 4-8pm daily. **Admission** free.

The original Anti-War Museum was founded in 1925 by Ernst Friedrich, author of *War Against War*, but it was destroyed by the Nazis in 1933. In 1982, a group of teachers including Tommy Spree, Friedrich's grandson, re-established the museum here. It hosts films, discussions, lectures and exhibitions, as well as a permanent display that takes in World War I photos and artefacts from the original museum, children's war toys, information on German colonialism in Africa and anti-Semitic material from the Nazi era.

Gedenkstätte Berliner Mauer

Bernauer Strasse 111 (467 986 666, www.berliner-mauer-gedenkstaette.de). U8 Bernauer Strasse, or S1, S2 Nordbahnhof. **Open** Documentation centre Apr-Oct 9.30am-7pm Tue-Sun. Nov-Mar 9.30am-6pm Tue-Sun. **Admission** free.

Immediately upon reunification, the city bought this stretch of the Wall on Bernauer Strasse to keep as a memorial. Impeccably restored, including death strip, watch tower and border fortifications, it's the best place to get a sense of just how brutally Berlin was severed in two. Start off at the visitor centre by Nordbahnhof, but don't miss the excellent documentation centre across the street from the Wall, which includes a very good aerial video following the route of the Wall in 1990: it's the best chance you have of really getting your head around it. From the centre's tower, you can look down over the Wall – or the 'Anti-Fascist Protection Wall', as the East Germans called it – and the Kapelle der Versöhnung (Chapel of Reconciliation). The Gedenkstätte is a work in progress; eventually, the trustees hope to extend along 1.4 kilometres (nearly a mile) of the former border strip.

Further down the road in the old Nordbahnhof station is an excellent exhibition, 'Border Stations and Ghost Stations in Divided Berlin', which tells the story of how East Germany closed down and then fiercely guarded stations through which West German trains travelled during the Cold War.

Eating & drinking

Asia Deli

Seestrasse 41 (4508 4219). U6 Seestrasse. **Open** noon-11pm daily. €. No credit cards. **Chinese**

Asia Deli keeps unwary tongues away from its scorching dishes by having two menus – so chilli lovers should ask for the 'real' menu. Then you can feast on the Hunanese and Sichuan dishes – steamed fish, pig offal, stir-fried greens – piled high with shredded red chilli and numbing Sichuan peppercorns.

L'Escargot

Brüsseler Strasse 39 (453 1563, www.l-escargot.net). U6 Seestrasse. **Open** 5pm-midnight Tue-Sat. €€. No credit cards. **French/Italian**

Chef-patron Martino frequently welcomes guests, and will discuss requirements and tastes before bustling into the kitchen. The cooking is a vague mix of French and Sicilian – the house speciality is a vast plate of garlicky snails – but the menu gallops cheerily across western Europe. Allow up to an hour for mains, as he cooks from scratch.

Moritz Bar

Adolfstrasse 17 (680 7670, http://moritzbar.com). U6, S41, S42 Wedding. **Open** 7pm-late daily. No credit cards. **Bar**

Wedding's very own living-room bar, complete with upcycled wooden counter, bottled Augustiner and vintage furniture. The south German brothers who run the place offer a weekly vegan food night, gay student Mondays and communal viewings of cult German TV detective series *Tatort*.

Vagabund Brauerei

Antwerpener Strasse 3 (5266 7668, www.vagabundbrauerei.com). U6 Seestrasse. **Open** 5pm-late daily. No credit cards. **Bar**

Three old friends from Maryland, USA, started a craft brewery after a wildly successful crowdfunding initiative.

They run a homely taproom at the microbrewery, with a rotating menu of beers that includes their own Imperial IPA and Coffee Stout, as well as local guests from the likes of Heiden Peter.

Volta

Brunnenstrasse 73 (0176 7755 6422 mobile, www.dasvolta.com). U8 Voltastrasse. **Open** 6pm-late Mon-Sat. **€€.** No credit cards. **Gastropub**
The space ticks all the hipster boxes: exposed industrial walls, low-hanging industrial lamps and a long, makeshift wooden bar. Everyone raves about the Volta burger, a wodge of rare mince doused in spicy barbecue sauce, with a local Spreewald gherkin, a sesame brioche bun and hand-cut fries on the side.

Shopping

Du Bonheur

Brunnenstrasse 39 (5659 1955, www.dubonheur.de). U6 Französische Strasse. **Open** 8am-7pm Mon-Fri; 9am-7pm Sat, Sun.
Anna Plagens trained under Pierre Hermé himself, the man credited with fetishising the macaroon at Fauchon, Ladurée and now under his own brand name. So the macaroons here are pretty spectacular, with fillings such as orange, salted caramel and liquorice. Croissants are made daily, and they also do classics such as paris-brest, and elegant birthday cakes with raspberry, chocolate cream and meringue.

Nightlife

Stattbad

Gerichtstrasse 65 (4679 7350, www.stattbad.net). U6, S41, S42 Wedding, or S1, S2, S25 Humboldthain. No credit cards.
Spearheading the forever-touted rise of Wedding, this imposing old bathhouse is now a cultural centre. It's primarily used as a club and – with all the original fittings intact – is a particularly impressive place to party. You enter through underground tunnels lined with giant pipes, emerging into the large, empty swimming pool: the DJ is at the deep end, with the floor being the dancefloor. By day, it doubles as an urban art gallery.

Spandau

Berlin's western neighbour and eternal rival, Spandau is a little Baroque town that seems to contradict everything about the city of which it is now, reluctantly, a part. Spandauers still talk about 'going into Berlin'; Berliners, meanwhile, basically consider Spandau to be part of west Germany. Travelling there is easy on the U7, alighting at either Zitadelle or Altstadt Spandau. There's nothing thrilling to see, but it makes for a low-key escape from the city. The old town centre is mostly pedestrianised, with 18th-century townhouses interspersed with chain burger joints and department stores. One of the most pleasant times to visit is Christmas, when the market square houses a life-size Nativity scene with real sheep and the famous Christmas market is in full swing.

Sights & museums

Luftwaffenmuseum der Bundeswehr Berlin-Gatow

Kladower Damm 182, Gatow (3687 2601, www.luftwaffenmuseum.de). U7 Rathaus Spandau then bus 135, then 20mins walk. **Open** 10am-6pm Tue-Sun. **Admission** free.
For propeller-heads only, this museum is on the city's far western fringes at what was formerly the RAF base in divided Berlin; it's a long journey by public transport followed by a 20-minute walk (or you can get a cab from the U-bahn station). There are more than 100 aircraft scattered around the airfield, plus exhibits in two hangars and the former control tower. The emphasis is on the history of military aviation

in Germany since 1945, although there's also a World War I triplane and a restored Handley Page Hastings (as used during the Berlin Airlift).

Zitadelle

Am Juliusturm 64 (354 9440, tours 334 6270, www.zitadelle-spandau.net). U7 Zitadelle. **Open** 10am-5pm daily. **Admission** €4.50; €2.50 reductions. No credit cards.

Most of the Zitadelle was constructed between 1560 and 1594, in the style of an Italian fort, to dominate the confluence of the Spree and Havel rivers. Since then, it's been used as everything from a garrison to a prison to a poison-gas laboratory. The oldest structure here (and the oldest secular building in Berlin) is the Juliusturm, probably dating back to an Ascanian fortress from about 1160. The present tower was home until 1919 to 120 million goldmarks, a small part of the five billion paid as French reparations to Germany in 1874 after the Franco-Prussian War. There are two museums within the Zitadelle: one tells the story of the building with models and maps; the other covers local history.

Eating & drinking

Brauhaus Spandau

Neuendorferstrasse 1 (353 9070, www.brauhaus-spandau.de). U7 Altstadt Spandau. **Open** 4pm-midnight Mon; 11am-midnight Tue-Thur; 11am-1am Fri, Sat; 10am-midnight Sun. €€.
German
This large beer hall is about as German as they come: a large dining room with gallery, big hunks of pork and potato on the plate and mugfuls of frothy home-brewed beer. The food is stodgy but hits the spot.

Satt & Selig

Carl-Schurz-Strasse 47 (3675 3877, www.sattundselig.de). U7 Altstadt Spandau. **Open** 9am-11pm daily. €€. **German**

Brauhaus Spandau

Housed in an 18th-century inn, this restaurant with an outdoor terrace is a useful spot for a reviving coffee after a turn around Spandau's old town. The food is serviceable, with many meat, sauce and carb combos, as well as snacks such as nachos.

Zehlendorf & the Dahlem

South-west Berlin contains some of the city's wealthiest suburbs, and in the days of division was the American sector, from which various landmarks survive. A major draw are the museums at Dahlem, including the world-class **Ethnologisches Museum** (Ethnological Museum). The **Domäne Dahlem** working farm is a great place to take kids, while nature lovers will enjoy the **Botanischer Garten & Botanisches Museum** (Botanical Garden & Museum).

Sights & museums

Botanischer Garten & Botanisches Museum

Königin-Luise-Strasse 6-8 (8385 0100, www.botanischergartenberlin.de). S1 Botanischer Garten then 15mins walk. **Open** Garden *May-July* 9am-9pm daily. *Apr, Aug* 9am-8pm daily. *Sept* 9am-7pm daily. *Mar, Oct* 9am-6pm daily. *Feb* 9am-5pm daily. *Nov-Jan* 9am-4pm daily. Museum 10am-6pm daily. **Admission** Garden & Museum €6; €3 reductions. Museum only €2.50; €1.50 reductions. No credit cards.

The Botanical Garden was landscaped at the beginning of the 20th century. Today, it's home to 18,000 plant species, 16 greenhouses and a museum. The gardens make for a pleasant stroll, but the museum is a bit dilapidated and there's no information in English. Every Monday, they run a wild mushroom advice workshop.

Domäne Dahlem

Königin-Luise-Strasse 49 (666 3000, www.domaene-dahlem.de). U3 Dahlem-Dorf. **Open** Museum 10am-6pm Sat, Sun. **Admission** Museum €3; €1.50 reductions. No credit cards.

On this organic working farm, children can see how life was lived in the 17th century. Craftspeople preserve and teach their skills. There are several annual festivals, when kids can ride ponies, tractors and hay wagons.

Ethnologisches Museum

Lansstrasse 8 (266 424242, www.smb. museum/em). U3 Dahlem-Dorf. **Open** 10am-5pm Tue-Fri; 11am-6pm Sat, Sun. **Admission** €6; €3 reductions. This museum is a stunner: extensive, authoritative, and beautifully laid out and lit. It encompasses cultures from Oceania, Central America and Africa to the Far East. Only the true ethno-fan should attempt to see it all, but no one should miss the Südsee (South Sea) room. Here, you'll find New Guinean masks and effigies, and a remarkable collection of canoes and boats. The African rooms are also impressive; look out for the superb carvings from Benin and the Congo, and beaded artefacts from Cameroon. An enlightening display explores the influence of African art on the German Expressionists.

Two other institutions are housed in the same building. The Museum of Asian Art has archaeological objects and fine art from India, Japan, China and Korea, from the early Stone Age to the present; while the Museum of European Cultures covers everyday culture from the 18th century to now. One highlight is a mechanical model of the Nativity, displayed during Advent.

Eating & drinking

Krasselts

Steglitzer Damm 22 (796 9147, www. krasselts-berlin.de). U9, S1 Rathaus Steglitz. **Open** 9am-midnight Mon-Sat; 10am-midnight Sun. **€. Imbiss**

Family-run Krasselts has been knocking out the Berlin street-food classic of Currywurst for over half a century. They closely guard their secret sauce recipe and grind and stuff all their own sausages. Enjoy at a standing table with fries or a crusty white roll.

Luise

Königin-Luise-Strasse 40-42 (841 8880, www.luise-dahlem.de). U3 Dahlem-Dorf. **Open** 10am-1am daily. **€€. Brasserie**
This traditional Berlin brasserie does all sorts, with a pizza menu (the buffalo mozzarella is made locally in Brandenburg), German snacks such as Currywurst, and breakfast too. It's near the Freie Universität, so the large beer garden gets packed with students.

Xochimilco Café

Steglitzer Damm 19 (6431 8770, www.xochimilco-cafe.de). U9, S1 Rathaus Steglitz. **Open** 8.30am-6.30pm Mon-Fri; 9am-2pm Sat. **€. Café**
Opened in 2013 by a German-Mexican couple, and named after an area of Mexico City, Xochimilco has planted the third-wave coffee flag firmly in Steglitz. Colourful Aztec masks adorn the walls, and you can snack on sandwiches, soup or fiery chilli con carne.

Grunewald

The western edge of Zehlendorf is formed by the Havel river and the extensive **Grunewald**, the largest of Berlin's many forests. Due to its easy accessibility by S-Bahn, its lanes and pathways fill with walkers, runners, cyclists and horse riders at weekends. One popular destination is the **Teufelsee**, a tiny lake packed with nudist bathers (and mosquitoes) in summer, reached by heading west from the station for 15 minutes. Close by is the legendary **Teufelsberg**, a by-product of wartime devastation – 25 million cubic metres of rubble eventually became Berlin's highest point. There are great views from

the summit and the eerie abandoned spy structure atop it.

Further south, **Krumme Lanke** and **Schlachtensee** are pleasantly clear urban lakes along the south-eastern edge of the Grunewald, perfect for picnicking, swimming or rowing – and each with its own train station. There's a particularly lovely beer garden and restaurant at Schlachtensee. On the west side of the Grunewald, halfway up Havelchaussee, is the **Grunewaldturm**, a tower built in 1897 in memory of Wilhelm I. It has an observation platform 105 metres (344 feet) above the lake, with expansive views as far as Spandau and Potsdam.

Sights & museums

Alliierten Museum

Clayallee 135, at Huttenweg (818 1990, www.alliiertenmuseum.de). U3 Oskar-Helene-Heim then 10mins walk, or bus 115. **Open** 10am-6pm Tue-Sun. **Admission** free.
The Allies arrived as conquerors, kept West Berlin alive during the 1948 Airlift and finally went home in 1994. In what used to be a US Forces cinema, the Allied Museum is mostly about the period of the Blockade and Airlift, documented with photos, tanks, jeeps, planes, weapons and uniforms. Outside is the former guardhouse from Checkpoint Charlie and an RAF Hastings TG 503 plane. Guided tours in English can be booked in advance.

Berliner Teufelsberg

Teufelsseechaussee 10 (0163 858 5096 mobile, http://berliner-teufelsberg.com). **Open** Tours noon-4pm daily. **Tickets** €7-€15; €8 reductions; free under-14s. Under-18s must be accompanied by an adult. No credit cards.
During the Cold War, the Allies built this listening station on the top of one of Berlin's highest hills to eavesdrop on what the East Germans were up to

Berliner Teufelsberg

on the other side of the Wall. The site was abandoned when the Iron Curtain fell, and soon became a favourite spot for urban explorers and ravers looking for a trippy place to throw an open-air party. The days of illegally exploring the site are now over, with city-sanctioned guided tours taking you through the decrepit structure, its varied history, the stunning view over the city and the unnerving acoustics of the giant radar dome.

Brücke-Museum

Bussardsteig 9 (831 2029, www.bruecke-museum.de). U3 Oskar-Helene-Heim then bus 115. **Open** 11am-5pm Mon, Wed-Sun. **Admission** €5; €3 reductions. No credit cards.

This small but satisfying museum is dedicated to Die Brücke, a group of expressionist painters that was founded in Dresden in 1905 before moving to Berlin. A large collection of oils, watercolours, drawings and sculptures by the main members of the group – Schmidt-Rottluff, Heckel, Kirchner, Mueller and Pechstein – is rotated in temporary exhibitions.

Eating & drinking

Fischerhütte am Schlachtensee

Fischerhuttenstrasse 136 (8049 8310, www.fischerhuette-berlin.de). U1 Krumme Lanke or S1 Mexikoplatz. **Open** 10am-midnight daily. **€€€.**
German

Overlooking the lake is the Fischerhütte, with a large beer garden and a more formal restaurant inside. It was built in the mid 18th century as a rest house on the road between Berlin and Potsdam. Its heyday was the 1920s, when these lakes were Berlin's answer to the French Riviera.

Wannsee & Pfaueninsel

At the south-west edge of the Grunewald, you'll find boats and beaches in summer, and castles and forests all through the year. **Strandbad Wannsee** is the largest inland beach in Europe. Between May and September, there are boats,

Strandbad Wannsee p155

pedalos and two-person hooded wicker sunchairs called *Strandkorb* for hire, a playground and a separate section for nudists. Service buildings house showers, toilets, cafés, shops and kiosks. The water is warm enough for comfortable swimming; there's a strong current, though, so don't stray beyond the floating markers. The town of Wannsee is clustered around the bay of the Grosser Wannsee and is dominated by a long promenade scattered with hotels and fish restaurants.

The island of **Pfaueninsel** was inhabited in prehistoric times, but it was only at the start of the Romantic era that its windswept charms began to attract more serious interest. Friedrich Wilhelm II purchased it in 1793 and built a castle for his mistress, but he died before they had a chance to move in. Later, a royal menagerie was developed; peacocks, pheasants, parrots, goats and sheep remain. A walk around the island – with its monumental trees, rough meadows and views over the Havel – provides one of the most complete sensations of escape to be had within the borders of Berlin.

Sights & museums

Gedenkstätte Haus der Wannsee-Konferenz

Am Grossen Wannsee 56-58 (805 0010, www.ghwk.de). S1, S7 Wannsee then bus 114. **Open** 10am-6pm daily. **Admission** free.

On 20 January 1942, a group of leading Nazis, chaired by Heydrich, gathered at this elegant Gründerzeit mansion to draw up plans for the Final Solution, for the extermination of the Jewish race. It's now a place of remembrance, with a photo exhibit on the conference and its genocidal consequences. Call in advance if you want an English-language tour, though the information is in both English and German.

Museumsdorf Düppel

Clauertstrasse 11 (802 6671, www. dueppel.de). S1 Mexikoplatz then bus 118, 622. **Open** Apr-Oct 10am-5pm Sat, Sun. **Admission** €3; free-€1.50 reductions. No credit cards.

At this reconstructed 14th-century village, built around archaeological excavations, workers demonstrate medieval handicrafts, technology and farming techniques.

Zwinger, Dresden p159

Day Trips

Potsdam

Potsdam, a beautiful neighbour just south-west of Berlin's city limits, is the capital of the state of Brandenburg. Its 18th-century Baroque architecture makes it a magnet for tourists but be warned: the crowds on summer weekends can be overwhelming. Neglected during the DDR years, it was given UNESCO World Heritage status in 1990 and some 80 per cent of the historic buildings have since been restored.

One of the dominant buildings in the old centre is the 19th-century **Nikolaikirche** – it's hard to miss the huge dome. Rather more graceful is the mid-18th-century **Altes Rathaus** (Old Town Hall), diagonally opposite – nowadays it houses the **Potsdam Museum**. Both the Nikolaikirche and Altes Rathaus were badly damaged in World War II and rebuilt in the 1960s.

The old **Stadtschloss** (City Palace), by the Nikolaikirche, was also war-damaged then demolished in 1960 – all that remains are its former stables, home to **Filmmuseum Potsdam**. The Stadtschloss itself was rebuilt between 2010 and 2013 and is the meeting place for Brandenburg's state parliament.

A short walk north is Potsdam's impressive **Baroque Quarter**. Some of the best houses can be found in Gutenbergstrasse and Brandenburger Strasse, the city's pedestrianised shopping drag. Around the corner is **Gedenkstätte Lindenstrasse**, once the house of a Prussian officer and later a Stasi detention centre; you can now tour the cells. Three town gates (**Nauener Tor**, **Jägertor** and **Brandenburger Tor**) stand sentinel on the quarter's northern and western edges.

East of the Baroque Quarter, two churches bear witness to Potsdam's cosmopolitan past. **Französische Kirche** on Hebbelstrasse was built for the town's Huguenots, while **St Peter & Paul's** in Bassinplatz was built for Catholic immigrants who came to this Protestant area in response to a drive calling for skilled workers and soldiers. The **Holländisches Viertel** (Dutch Quarter) was also created as a lure: Friedrich Wilhelm I had Dutch builders construct 134 gable-fronted houses to make workers from Holland feel at home. **Jan Bouman Haus** on Mittelstrasse has an original interior.

Another curiosity is the Russian colony of **Alexandrowka**, 15 minutes' walk north from the town centre: it has wooden-clad, two-storey dwellings with steeply pitched roofs laid out in the form of a St Andrew's Cross. There's even a Russian Orthodox church with an onion dome where services are held: **Alexander-Newski-Kapelle**.

Back towards the town centre is Potsdam's biggest tourist magnet, the quite lovely **Park Sanssouci**. It's a legacy of Frederick the Great, who was drawn to the area by its fine views. His nearby **Bildergalerie** was the first purpose-built museum in Germany. After victory in the Seven Years' War, Frederick commissioned the huge **Neues Palais** on the park's western edge – some of the rooms are astonishing. Other attractions include the **Orangery**; the **Spielfestung**, or toy fortress, built for Wilhelm II's sons; the **Chinesisches Teehaus** (Chinese Teahouse), with its collection of Chinese and Meissen porcelain; and the **Drachenhaus** (Dragonhouse), a pagoda-style café. In the park's south-west corner lies **Schloss Charlottenhof**, with its copper-plate engraving room, built in the 1830s on the orders of the crown prince, Friedrich Wilhelm IV.

North-east of the town centre is another large park, the **Neuer Garten**, designed on the orders of Friedrich Wilhelm II of Prussia. He died a premature death in the neo-classical **Marmorpalais**, allegedly as a result of his dissolute lifestyle. At the park's most northern corner is **Schloss Cecilienhof**, the last Hohenzollern royal palace to be built in Germany, between 1914 and 1917. This incongruous, mock-Tudor mansion was created for Kaiser Wilhelm II's son and his wife. Spared damage during World War II, in summer 1945 it hosted the Potsdam Conference, where Stalin, Truman and Churchill (later replaced by Attlee) met to carve up the world.

On the east side of the River Havel is the **Telegrafenberg** – once the site of a telegraph station. In 1921, it became home to Erich Mendelsohn's expressionist **Einsteinturm** (Einstein Tower), built to house an observatory that could confirm the General Theory of Relativity. Wonderfully whimsical, it was one of the first products of the inter-war avant-garde.

Babelsberg

The unique selling point of Potsdam's very near neighbour, **Babelsberg**, is its studio complex and **Filmpark Babelsberg**. In the 1920s, this was the world's largest studio outside Hollywood; it was here that Fritz Lang's *Metropolis*, Josef von Sternberg's *The Blue Angel* and other masterpieces were produced. During the Nazi period, it churned out thrillers, light entertainment and propaganda like Leni Riefenstahl's *Triumph of the Will*. More than 700 features were made during the Communist era and they still function as a working film and TV production facility but with the populist theme park tacked on.

Dresden

On the night of 13 February 1945, **Dresden** – 180 kilometres (112 miles) south of Berlin – was the target of one of World War II's largest Allied bombing raids. The attack caused huge firestorms that killed 25,000 people or more – even the death toll is controversial. During the DDR years, reconstruction was erratic, but cranes sprang up in the 1990s and the capital of Saxony has been making up for lost time since.

Its major attractions are buildings that date from the reign of Augustus the Strong (1670-1733). The **Hofkirche** and **Zwinger** complex are fine examples of the city's Baroque legacy while the main draw for art fans is the **Gemäldegalerie Alte Meister** in the Zwinger, with its superb collection of Old Masters.

The royal tendency to build was continued by Augustus's successor, Augustus III, who then lost the Seven Years' War to Prussia (1756-63). Frederick the Great destroyed much of the city during the war, though not the lovely **Brühlsche Terrasse** riverside promenade. The **Semperoper** opera house (1838-41) is impressive while there's more art at the **Albertinum**, with paintings and sculpture from the Romantic period to the present day.

The industrialisation of Dresden heralded a new phase that produced the **Rathaus** (Town Hall, 1905-10) at Dr-Külz-Ring; the **Hauptbahnhof** (1892-95) at the end of Prager Strasse; and the mosque-like **Yenidze cigarette factory** (1912) on Könneritzstrasse. The finest example of inter-war architecture is the **Deutsches Hygiene-Museum** (1929) at Lingner Platz 1.

The **Neue Synagoge** in Rathenauplatz was dedicated in November 2001, 63 years after its

Thomaskirche, Leipzig p160

predecessor was destroyed in the Nazi pogroms. Reconstruction of the domed **Frauenkirche** at Neumarkt was completed and the restored cathedral was reconsecrated in October 2005. The communists left it as rubble throughout the Cold War as a reminder of Allied aggression.

Architecture and culture aside, if you're visiting in December, head for Altmarkt where you'll find the oldest Christmas market in Germany, the **Striezelmarkt**, founded in 1434. Try the mulled wine and the stollen, said to be Germany's finest.

Neustadt, on the north bank of the Elbe, means 'new town', though it's more than 300 years old. Having escaped major damage during the war, much of its original architecture is intact. The 18th-century townhouses in Hauptstrasse and Königstrasse are charming.

Leipzig

Leipzig is a centre of trade, education and culture, and where East Germany's mass movement for political change began. Its restored old centre has Renaissance and Baroque churches, narrow lanes, old street markets and the ancient university; it's hard to believe that it was bombed to bits during the war.

The city is around 150 kilometres (93 miles) south-west of Berlin; most visitors arrive at **Hauptbahnhof**, the central railway station. The first place to visit is the **tourist office** at Katharinenstrasse 8. Pick up a guide to the city in English and head for **Markt** nearby, the old market square. The eastern side is occupied by the lovely Renaissance **Altes Rathaus** (Old Town Hall), built in 1556-57. It now houses the **Stadtgeschichtliches Museum** (Town Museum). On the square's south side are the huge bay windows of the **Könighaus**, home to Saxony's rulers when visiting the city.

The church off the south-west corner of Markt is **Thomaskirche**, where **Johann Sebastian Bach** spent 27 years as choirmaster of **St Thomas's Boys' Choir**; he's buried in the chancel and his statue is outside. Opposite the church, in the Bosehaus, is the **Bach Museum**.

Behind the Altes Rathaus is the delightful **Alte Börse** (Old Stock Exchange). Built in 1687, it's fronted by a statue of **Goethe**. Follow his gaze to **Mädlerpassage**, Leipzig's finest shopping arcade, home to **Auerbachs Keller**, one of Germany's most famous restaurants.

North of the Alte Börse is **Sachsenplatz**, site of the city's main outdoor market, and home of the **Museum der Bildenden Künste** (Museum of Arts Picture Gallery). Its 2,200-strong collection stretches from 15th- and 16th-century Dutch, Flemish and German paintings to DDR art.

Just south-east of here is the medieval **Nikolaikirche** where regular protest meetings started in 1982. These evolved into the Swords to Ploughshares peace movement that led to the first anti-DDR demonstration on 4 September 1989 in the **Nikolaikirchhof**.

To the south is the DDR-era **City-Hochhaus**, rising to 142 metres (466 feet). Originally part of **Leipzig University**, and meant to resemble an open book, it was sold into the private sector post-reunification, then refurbished. The achingly modern buildings at neighbouring **Augustusplatz** now form the university's main site.

For more recent history, ten minutes' walk north-west you'll find the **Museum in der 'Runden Ecke'** (Museum in the 'Round Corner'). The building once housed the local Stasi headquarters and now has an exhibition detailing its methods. For a cuddlier alternative, head for **Leipzig Zoo**.

Essentials

Das Stue p171

Hotels

With an average room price hovering at just over €100 per night, Berlin ranks among the least expensive western cities in which to stay – in stark comparison to New York's average of a whopping €217. There's so much choice that hoteliers are going the extra mile to stand out: **Amano** near Hackescher Markt has its own iPhone app with themed walking tours and city guide, while **Nhow** by the river in Friedrichshain touts itself as a 'music and lifestyle hotel', complete with two recording studios and a spa – and Gibson guitars available on room service. Meanwhile, in trendy Neukölln, you can sleep in vintage caravans parked in an old vacuum cleaner factory at the **Hüttenpalast**.

Prices and information

We've divided the hotels by area, then marked them in four price categories, according to the standard prices (not including seasonal offers or discounts) for one night in a double room with en suite shower/bath. As a rule of thumb: **€€€€** starts from €190 and goes up and away; **€€€** means €120 to €190; **€€** is the €60 to €120 range; while rooms marked as **€** cost less than €60.

Check if breakfast is included in the room price. Most hotels offer it as a buffet, which can be as simple as coffee and bread rolls (called *schrippen* in Berlin) with cheese and salami, or the full works, complete with smoked meats, muesli with fruit and yoghurt, and even a glass of sparkling wine.

Note that, since 1 January 2014, visitors have to pay a new city tax, amounting to 5 per cent of the price of their room per night. Business travellers are exempt, but have to prove they're in Berlin on business.

Booking.com

Reservations +44 20 3320 2609,
www.booking.com.

With offices Europe-wide, this English-language booking service has pre-reserved beds in hotels of all categories in the city. Check for special offers too.

VisitBerlin

Reservations & information 2500 2333,
www.visitberlin.de.

This private tourist service can sort out hotel reservations, tickets for shows and travel arrangements to Berlin.

Mitte

The city's historic administrative quarter is thriving, with an ever-growing number of hotels in all price brackets. While many hipper tourists have started to move into less trafficked areas, the faded post-Wall charm of one of the city's oldest quarters is still popular with many.

Adlon Kempinski Berlin

Unter den Linden 77 (226 10, www.hotel-adlon.de). U6 Französische Strasse, or S1, S2 Brandenburger Tor. €€€€.

Not quite the Adlon of yore, which burned down after World War II, this new, more generic luxury version was rebuilt by the Kempinski Group in 1997 on the original site next to the Brandenburg Gate. Apart from a few original features, you're really paying for the prime location and the superlative service: bellboys who pass you a chilled bottle of water when you return from a jog in nearby Tiergarten.

Albrechtshof

Albrechtstrasse 8 (308 860, www.hotel-albrechtshof.de). U6, S1, S2, S5, S7, S25, S75 Friedrichstrasse. €€€.

Located close to the Berliner Ensemble and Friedrichstrasse station, the Albrechtshof is a member of Verband Christlicher Hotels (Christian Hotels Association). They don't make a song and dance about it, but it has its own

ESSENTIALS

chapel, named after former guest Martin Luther King. The rooms are comfortable and clean, if not particularly stylish, and staff are friendly. The restaurant offers pedestrian north German cuisine, and in summer breakfast is served in the courtyard garden.

Amano

Auguststrasse 43 (809 4150, www.hotel-amano.com). U8 Rosenthaler Platz. €€.
The nice thing about Amano is that it doesn't try too hard – and it doesn't need to, given its perfect location right in the centre of Berlin. The rooms and apartments are modern and unpretentious with free Wi-Fi. Other perks are the backyard garden and a roof-terrace lounge where older hotel guests mingle with young preppy professionals. Bikes are also available to rent.

Arte Luise Kunsthotel

Luisenstrasse 19 (284 480, www.arte-luise.com). U6, S1, S2, S5, S7, S25, S75 Friedrichstrasse. €€.
Housed in a neoclassical former residential palace just a short walk from the Reichstag and Brandenburger Tor, this 'artist home' is one of the city's more imaginative small hotels, with each of its 50 rooms decorated by a different renowned artist. There's graffiti artist Thomas Baumgärtel's 'Royal Suite', a golden room spray-painted with bananas; and Guido Seiber's 'Berlin Society', covered in the artist's humorous renditions of Berlin celebrities and streetlife.

Art'otel Berlin Mitte

Wallstrasse 70-73 (240 620, www.artotels.de). U2 Märkisches Museum. €€.
A real gem on the Spree. This delightful hotel is a creative fusion of old and new, combining restored rococo reception rooms with ultra-modern bedrooms designed by Nalbach & Nalbach. As well as highlighting the artwork of George Baselitz – originals hang in the corridors and all 109 rooms – the hotel's decor has been meticulously thought out to the smallest detail, from the Philippe Starck bathrooms to the Breuer chairs in the conference rooms. Staff are pleasant, and the views from the top suites across Mitte are stunning.

Baxpax Downtown Hostel Hotel

Ziegelstrasse 28 (2787 4880, www.baxpax.de). U6, S1, S2, S5, S7, S25, S75 Friedrichstrasse. No credit cards. €.
This new, third addition to the Baxpax hostel empire is an excellent place to stay, in a brilliant location. Clean, contemporary and well designed, it has all the usual amenities, from a luggage room to darts, with the additional luxury of a fireplace lounge, courtyard and rooftop terrace. There's a dorm just for women, 24-hour reception and key-card access for security, and a friendly, relaxed atmosphere.

Casa Camper

Weinmeisterstrasse 1 (2000 3411, www.casacamper.com/berlin). U8 Weinmeisterstrasse. €€€€.
In 2011, the Spanish shoe company opened this luxury boutique hotel right in the heart of the Scheunenviertel. Tired shoppers and partygoers alike can take a break and grab some refreshments any time at the hotel's free 24-hour snack bar, which is included in the price of the room in lieu of room service. Full meals are served at the restaurant, Dos Paillos, which specialises in fusion Asian-style cuisine served as a tapas-sized tasting menu with delicacies such as toro sushi (the fatty neck of tuna) on offer.

Circus

Weinbergsweg 1A (2839 1433, www.circus-berlin.de). U8 Rosenthaler Platz. €.
Almost the standard by which other hostels should be measured, the Circus is a rarity – simple but stylish, warm and comfortable. And the upper-floor apartments have balconies and lovely views. The laid-back staff can help get discount tickets to almost anything,

or give directions to the best bars and clubs, of which there are plenty nearby. The place is deservedly popular and is always full, so be sure to book ahead.

CityStay

Rosenstrasse 16 (2362 4031, www. citystay.de). S5, S7, S75 Hackescher Markt. No credit cards. €.

On a small, quiet street – but as central as you can get – this is a great modern hostel for the price. The rooms are clean and simple, and there are showers on every floor. Security is top-notch, with access cards for the video-monitored entrance and floors. The breakfast buffet features fresh organic bread, and eggs any way you like them.

Dude

Köpenicker Strasse 92 (411 988 177, www.thedudeberlin.com). U8 Heinrich-Heine-Strasse. €€€.

Housed in an elegant 19th-century townhouse, this 30-room boutique hotel was created by an advertising executive to provide an antidote to identikit design and a sense of humour befitting Berlin. There are a number of house rules – no photography, ringing a doorbell for access, no large groups – to help foster an atmosphere of discretion. The rooms are quite stark, with brass-knobbed beds offset by block-coloured walls, and Molton Brown goodies in the bathroom.

Generator Mitte

Oranienburger Strasse 65 (921 037 680, www.generatorhostels.com). S1, S2, S25 Oranienburger Strasse. €.

The Generator hostel empire continues its spread across Europe, with two locations in Berlin: this funky flagship on Oranienburger Strasse, and a larger but blander site in Prenzlauer Berg. It positions itself somewhere between a traditional backpackers' hostel and a boutique hotel. There are plenty of useful services, such as a 24-hour laundry, luggage storage and an affordable daily menu dished out in the evenings. It's definitely geared towards a younger crowd, with urban art on the walls and a late-night bar with DJs at weekends. As well as the usual bunk dorms, there are a number of private rooms (sleeping up to four), as well as female-only dormitories.

Gendarm

Charlottenstrasse 61 (206 0660, www.hotel-gendarm-berlin.de). U2, U6 Stadtmitte. €€€.

If you fancy a five-star location but don't want to spend a fortune, this place is just the ticket. Aside from a few pink frills, it doesn't have a lot of extras, but the 21 rooms and six suites are smart and comfortable, and it's close to the restaurants of Gendarmenmarkt, shopping on Friedrichstrasse and the State Opera. At rates around half those of the nearby Sofitel or Hilton, you can't really go wrong.

Hackescher Markt

Grosse Präsidentenstrasse 8 (280 030, www.dassik-hotel-collection.de). S5, S7, S75 Hackescher Markt. €€€.

This elegant hotel in a nicely renovated townhouse avoids the noise of its central Hackescher Markt location by cleverly having many rooms face inwards on to a tranquil green courtyard. Some have balconies, all have their own bath with heated floor, and the suites are spacious and comfortable. The pleasant, helpful staff speak good English. While you don't necessarily get the most atmosphere for the money, you can't beat the address.

Heart of Gold Hostel Berlin

Johannisstrasse 11 (2900 3300, www.heartofgold-hostel.de). S1, S2, S25 Oranienburger Strasse. €.

The prime location aside (it's only 50m from Oranienburger Strasse), this member of the Backpacker Germany Network (www.backpacker-network. de) is loosely themed on Douglas Adams' *The Hitchhiker's Guide to the Galaxy*. Rooms are bright and cheerful, with parquet floors. Lockers are free; individual bathrooms and showers, and a keycard system guarantee security. The laundry is cheap, as are the shots in the bar; what more could a backpacker (or hitchhiker) need? Towels, of course, which are available for free at reception.

Honigmond Garden Hotel

Invalidenstrasse 122 (2844 5577, www. honigmond.de). U6 Oranienburger Tor. €€€.

This is one of the most charming hotels in Berlin, and it doesn't cost an arm and a leg. Choose between large bedrooms facing the street, smaller ones overlooking the fish pond and Tuscan-style garden, or spacious apartments on the upper floor. As with all great places, the secret is in the finer detail. The rooms are impeccably styled with polished pine floors, paintings in massive gilt frames, antiques and iron bedsteads. There's also a charming sitting room overlooking the garden. Highly recommended.

Honigmond Restaurant-Hotel

Tieckstrasse 12 (284 4550, www. honigmond.de). U6 Oranienburger Tor. €€.

The 40 rooms in this beautiful 1899 building are spacious and lovely, and although some of the less expensive ones lack their own shower and toilet, don't let that put you off: this is probably the best and prettiest mid-price hotel east of the Zoo. The reception area has comfy chairs around a gas fireplace, and breakfast is served in the Honigmond restaurant, open since 1920. The friendly staff speak English, and the hotel is perfectly sited, within walking distance of the Scheunenviertel and Hackescher Markt. More affordable luxury would be hard to find.

Hotel Pension Kastanienhof

Kastanienallee 65 (443 050, www. kastanienhof.biz). U8 Rosenthaler Platz. €€.

Nicely located, this is a warm, cosy, old-fashioned hotel. The pastel-coloured rooms are generously proportioned and well equipped, and there are three breakfast rooms and a bar. The English-speaking staff are friendly. It's especially popular at weekends, so book ahead.

Lux 11

Rosa-Luxemburg-Strasse 9-13 (936 2800, www.lux-eleven.com). U2 Rosa-Luxemburg-Platz. €€€.

A member of the Design Hotels group, this former apartment house for the DDR secret police is a stylish, no-nonsense apartment-hotel. The cool, modern, white-walled apartments are elegant and nicely appointed, with everything from intercom for visiting guests to microwave and dishwasher in the kitchen, and queen-sized beds in between. Rates drop dramatically the longer the stay.

Meliá Berlin

Friedrichstrasse 103 (2060 7900, www.meliaberlin.com). U6, S1, S2, S5, S7, S25, S75 Friedrichstrasse. €€€.

Casa Camper p164

Just across from Friedrichstrasse station, this shiny corner building on the banks of the Spree is a huge link in the Spanish Sol Meliá chain. All 364 rooms are similarly and tastefully appointed, many with fine views of the river and the Reichstag beyond, but the rich wood units and headboards seem a little incongruous. The helpful staff are pleasant, making this an ideal and convenient stop-over for the harried business traveller; but for simple folk in search of atmosphere, there's better value for money elsewhere.

Miniloftmitte
Hessische Strasse 5 (847 1090, www. miniloft.com). U6 Naturkundemuseum. €€.
A brilliant alternative to the hotel hustle, these 14 flats – housed in a combined renovated apartment building and award-winning steel/concrete construction – are modern, airy and elegant. Each comes with a queen-sized bed, couch and dining area (the frosted-glass panels separating bath and kitchen are an interesting touch), with warm-coloured fabrics, organic

basics in the kitchen, and lots of space and light. The owners/designers/architects are a young, friendly couple who live and work on the premises. Rates are greatly reduced the longer the stay.

Platte Mitte
Rochstrasse 9 (0177 283 2602 mobile, www.plattemitte.de). S5, S7, S75 Hackescher Markt. €€.
Proudly calling itself a 'No Hotel', these three apartments on the 21st floor of a 1967-built Plattenbau are airy and well designed, each with spectacular views of the city around Alexanderplatz. Colourfully decorated and eclectic to say the least, the furnishings mix original pieces of the period with artfully fanciful touches such as poster-plastered walls and mannequins by the bed. As most of the neighbours are original tenants, this is a wonderfully unique way to experience Berlin. Rates are greatly reduced for longer stays.

Radisson Blu Hotel Berlin
Karl-Liebknecht-Strasse 3 (238 280, www.radisson blu.com/hotel-berlin). S5, S7, S75 Hackescher Markt. €€€.

With interiors by German designer Yasmine Mahmoudieh (responsible for the cabins of the Airbus A380), the 427 rooms here are fresh, uncluttered and free of the normal blandness typical of big hotel chains. The Radisson's claim to fame, however, is 'the tank' – a 25m (82ft) high aquarium with a million litres of saltwater housing 2,500 varieties of fish. Many of the bedrooms even have a view of it.

Sofitel Berlin Gendarmenmarkt

Charlottenstrasse 50-52 (203 750, www.sofitel.com). U2, U6 Stadtmitte. €€€€.

This is a truly lovely hotel. From the lobby, with its soothing colour scheme and wonderful lighting, onwards the atmosphere is intimate and elegant; the rooms are beautifully styled and have perhaps the best bathrooms in the city. In summer, you can wind down on the sun deck, which perches high above the surrounding rooftops overlooking the splendid domed cathedrals of Gendarmenmarkt.

Soho House

Torstrasse 1 (405 0440, www.sohohouse berlin.com). U2 Rosa-Luxemburg-Platz. €€€.

The average Berliner has a healthy scepticism towards anything 'private' or 'exclusive', so eyebrows were raised when Soho House opened its branch in the German capital in 2010. But even the toughest critic would have to admit that the building and its history are too unique to be dismissed out of hand. The imposing Bauhaus structure has history: it initially housed a Jewish-owned department store before it was taken over first by the Nazis, then by the communist regime. These days, Soho House occupies eight floors, and has installed one of their excellent Cowshed spas, a library and its own cinema. In the rooms, beautiful old wooden floors and 1920s furniture mix with raw concrete walls.

Westin Grand

Friedrichstrasse 158-164 (202 70, www. westingrandberlin.com). U6 Französische Strasse. €€€.

Despite its East German prefabricated exterior, the Westin Grand is pure five-star international posh (the Stones stay here when they're in town). The decor is gratifyingly elegant, with lots of polished crystal and brass and a grandiose foyer and staircase. The rooms are tastefully traditional, and the 35 suites are individually furnished with period decor themed after their names. There's also a garden, bar and restaurant, and the haunts of the Gendarmenmarkt are just outside the door.

Wombat's City Hostel Berlin

Alte Schönhauserstrasse 2 (8471 0820, www.wombats-hostels.com/berlin). U2 Rosa-Luxemburg-Platz. €

Situated virtually on Berlin's hipster heaven of Torstrasse, Wombat's City Hostel Berlin is minutes from Alexanderplatz and the scuzzier surroundings of Mitte's bar drag, leading up to Rosenthalerplatz. A colourful, cosy spot, it's well equipped with a laundry, coffee shop, computers and free Wi-Fi; best of all is the seventh-floor bar with its outdoor terrace. Next door is a Cajun restaurant.

Prenzlauer Berg

From the cool of Kastanienallee to the funky chic of Helmholtzplatz, this neighbourhood just north of Mitte may be charming, but it has a dearth of decent hotels – surprising, considering the number of visitors the area attracts.

Ackselhaus & Bluehome

Belforter Strasse 21 & 24 (4433 7633, www.ackselhaus.de). U2 Senefelderplatz. €€€.

Just doors apart, what ties these two establishments together – aside from their shared reception desk – is a wonderfully realised, luxurious 'modern colonial' style. Each room is lovingly decorated, with much attention to detail; themes range from China to Maritime to Movie, so there should be a room for every taste. Bluehome (at no.24), with its blue façade, and balconies overlooking Belforter Strasse, houses the Club del Mar restaurant, which offers a breakfast buffet. There's also a lovely back garden, complete with lawn chairs in summer.

Lette'm Sleep Hostel
Lettestrasse 7 (4473 3623, www.backpackers.de). U2 Eberswalder Strasse. €.
Just off Helmholtzplatz, this small hostel has new floors and bathrooms, and a beer garden in the back for summer barbecues. Free tea and coffee are provided, but not breakfast – so you can either make it yourself in the kitchen or visit one of the many decent cafés around the corner. All rooms have hand basins, and hot showers are always available. Each of the three large apartments sleeps up to ten people, and there are reduced rates for longer stays.

Myer's Hotel
Metzer Strasse 26 (440 140, www.myershotel.de). U2 Senefelderplatz, or tram M2. €€.
This renovated 19th-century townhouse sits on a tranquil street. There's a garden and a glass-ceilinged gallery, and the big leather furniture seems to beg you to light up a cigar. In addition, the beautiful Kollwitzplatz is just around the corner, as are a bunch of decent bars and restaurants. Although the tram stop is just down the street, it's a lovely walk from here into Mitte.

Transit Loft
Immanuelkirchstrasse 14A (4849 3773, www.transit-loft.de). Tram M2, M4. €.
This loft hotel in a renovated factory is ideal for backpackers and young travellers. All the rooms have en suite bathrooms, and there's a private sauna,

gym and billiard room with special rates for hotel guests. Staff are friendly and well informed, and there's good wheelchair access too.

Friedrichshain

Friedrichshain hasn't quite panned out as the city's new bohemia, but with decent transport connections, a still somewhat 'Eastie' alternative feel, good cafés and lots of nightlife, it continues to be a great area to stay in, especially on a tight budget.

Almodovar Hotel
Boxhagener Strasse 83 (692 097 080, www.almodovarhotel.com). U5 Samariterstrasse. €€.
This new boutique hotel is 'Berlin' through and through: fully vegetarian, with organic products in the rooms and even a complimentary yoga mat. Rooms are bright and spacious, and the penthouse suite has its own sauna – but there's also a spa with ayurvedic treatments available to all guests. The lovely rosewood furniture was sustainably made specifically for the hotel.

Eastern Comfort
Mühlenstrasse 73-77 (6676 3806, www.eastern-comfort.com). U1, S5, S7, S75 Warschauer Strasse. €.
Berlin's first 'hostel boat' is moored on the Spree by the East Side Hotel, across the river from Kreuzberg. The rooms – or, rather, cabins – are clean and fairly spacious (considering it's a boat), and all have their own shower and toilet. The four-person room can feel a little cramped, but if you need to get up and stretch there are two common rooms, a lounge and three terraces offering lovely river views.

Industriepalast Hostel
Warschauer Strasse 43 (7407 8290, www.ip-hostel.com). U1, S5, S7, S75 Warschauer Strasse. No credit cards. €.
This vast red-brick hostel on bleak Warschauer Strasse was once an

Michelberger

industrial works. Renovated in a pleasingly functional and colourful way, it's a popular spot. With 400 beds over 90 rooms, accommodation options are manifold, from dorms to an entire apartment, plus a disabled-access room. A good choice if you're after a clean, warm bed and a cheerful atmosphere.

Michelberger
Warschauer Strasse 39-40 (2977 8590, www.michelbergerhotel.com). U1, S5, S7, S75 Warschauer Strasse.€€.
With its purposefully unfinished look and effortlessly creative vibe, Michelberger might seem like Berlin in a nutshell to some. While the cheaper rooms are characterised by a stylish simplicity reminiscent of a school gym, the pricier rooms have an air of tongue-in-cheek decadence – decked out in gold from floor to ceiling or in the style of a mountain resort – complete with sunken bathtubs and movie projectors. Michelberger might not be as spotlessly clean as other hotels (though it's far from being dirty), but it's much more fun.

Nhow
Stralauer Allee 3 (290 2990, www.nhow-hotels.com). U1, S5, S7, S75 Warschauer Strasse. €€.
If you're allergic to pink, you'd be well advised to check in elsewhere. In a huge modern building right by the River Spree, New York designer Karim Rashid has implemented his eye-popping vision of a music and lifestyle hotel. Even the elevators are illuminated by different coloured lights, and some are decorated with photos of Rashid and his wife. As you'd expect from a music hotel, all rooms are equipped with iPod docking stations, and if you're in the mood for a spontaneous jam, you can order a Gibson guitar or an electric piano up to your room.

Ostel Das DDR Design Hostel
Wriezener Karree 5 (2576 8660, www.ostel.eu). S5, S7, S75 Ostbahnhof. €.
The four clocks on the wall read: Berlin, Moscow, Peking and Havana. There's a stern-looking poster of Erich Honecker on the wall. But there's no political message at this

budget East German-themed hostel: just a cheap bed for the night. For an additional €3.50, guests are given a Lebensmittelmarke (food-ration coupon) for breakfast at the Ossi Hof pub out front. And for those who just can't get enough of Ostalgie (nostalgia for the East), there's a hotel Konsum (state-run market), which sells everything from plaster egg cups to chocolate DDR coins.

Tiergarten

Tiergarten is now officially part of Mitte, but don't tell the locals. There are a few notable establishments dotting the edges of the park that gives the district its name, as well as big modern embassies and a complex of cultural institutions located by the New National Gallery.

Mandala

Potsdamer Strasse 3 (590 050 000, www.the mandala.de). U2, S1, S2, S25 Potsdamer Platz. **€€€€**.
This privately owned addition to the Design Hotels portfolio is, given the address, an oasis of calm, luxury and taste. The 144 rooms and suites, most of which face their glass walls upon an inner courtyard, are perfectly designed for space and light, decorated in warm whites and beiges, with comfortable minimalist furnishings and TVs. The rooftop spa, windowed from end to end, offers spectacular city views. Reduced rates are available for longer stays.

Ritz-Carlton

Potsdamer Platz 3 (337 777, www. ritzcarlton.com). U2, S1, S2, S25 Potsdamer Platz. **€€€€**.
It's flashy, it's trashy, it's Vegas-meets-Versailles. The Ritz-Carlton is so chock-a-block with black marble, gold taps and taffeta curtains that the rooms seem somewhat stuffy, small and cramped. It's supposedly art deco in style, but feels more like a Dubai shopping mall. Still, the oyster and lobster restaurant is deliciously decadent, and the service is fantastic: the technology butler will sort out the bugs in your computer connection, and the bath butler will run your tub.

Sheraton Berlin Grand Hotel Esplanade

Lützowufer 15 (254 780, www. esplanade.de). U1, U2, U3, U4 Nollendorfplatz. **€€€**.
With an entry wall of gushing water lit overhead by glittering lights, this is one of Berlin's better luxury hotels, overlooking the Landwehr Canal and close to the Tiergarten. The lobby is equally grand, spacious and beautifully decorated, while the rooms are tasteful and gratifyingly free of frilly decor. There's also a fitness centre and a triangular swimming pool, plus three restaurants to choose from.

Das Stue

Drakestrasse 1 (311 7220, www.das-stue.com). S5, S7, S75 Tiergarten. **€€€€**.
The newest (and hippest) member of Berlin's luxury hotel family, Das Stue has restored the 1930s Royal Danish Embassy to its former splendour with the help of Spanish designer Patricia Urquiola. There's a long list of reasons to stay at this Design Hotel, including a pearl-white spa, rooms overlooking the Tiergarten, the original three-storey library, and the Michelin-starred Cinco restaurant. The central location means it's a short walk to most major sights.

Charlottenburg

This is the smart end of town, with fine dining and elegant shopping, and where five-star luxury hotels sit happily alongside the traditional charms of pensions housed in grand 19th-century Gründerzeit townhouses.

25hours Hotel Bikini Berlin

Budapester Strasse 40 (120 2210, www.25hours-hotels.com). U2, U9, S5, S7, S75 Zoologischer Garten. **€€€**.

25hours Hotel Bikini Berlin p171

Breathing new life into the iconic 1950s Bikini-Haus office block that adjoins the Tiergarten, the revamped shopping mall also features a 149-room branch of Design Hotels' funky 25hours brand. The design is a blend of exposed brick and industrial lighting, plenty of greenery and brightly coloured furnishings. There's great attention to detail, such as rooms that come with window-side hammocks, free Mini rental and the fab Middle Eastern restaurant Neni. The West is finally getting hip.

Art Nouveau Berlin

Leibnitzstrasse 59 (327 7440, www. hotelart nouveau.de). U7 Adenauerplatz, or S5, S7, S75 Savignyplatz.€€€.
This is one of the most charming small hotels in Berlin. The rooms are decorated with flair, in a mix of Conran-modern and antique furniture, each with an enormous black and white photo hung by the bed. The en suite

bathrooms are cleverly integrated into the rooms without disrupting the elegant townhouse architecture. Even the TVs are stylish.

Berlin Plaza

Knesebeckstrasse 62 (884 130, www. plazahotel.de). U1 Uhlandstrasse.€€.
Despite a rather plain minimalist decor and colour scheme in the rooms, there's an understated poshness about the Plaza. All double rooms, and even some singles, have both a shower and bath. The restaurant and bar serve regional German specialities, and the breakfast buffet is excellent. A further plus – under-13s can stay with parents for free.

Bleibtreu

Bleibtreustrasse 31 (884 740, www. bleibtreu.com). U1 Uhlandstrasse, or S5, S7, S75 Savignyplatz.€€€.
The Bleibtreu is a friendly, smart and cosy establishment popular with the

media and fashion crowds. Although on the smaller side, the rooms are all very modern, and decorated with environmentally sound materials. Private yoga classes are offered, as well as reflexology. A wonderful choice for the health-conscious, certainly, but good service with lots of pampering and attention means it should appeal to anyone.

Ellington
Nürnberger Strasse 50-55 (683 150, www.ellington-hotel.com). U1, U2, U3 Wittenbergplatz, or U3 Augsburger Strasse. €€€.
This is one of the classiest, most sophisticated joints in Berlin. Hidden within the shell of a landmark art deco dance hall, it combines cool contemporary elegance with warmth and ease. The rooms, mostly white with polished wood accents, are brilliantly simple, with modern free-standing fixtures and half-walls, and absolute calm

behind the original double windows. The staff are helpful and remarkably cheerful given the daft flat caps they're made to wear.

Hotel-Pension Dittberner
Wielandstrasse 26 (884 6950, www. hotel-dittberner.de). U7 Adenauerplatz, or S5, S7, S75 Savignyplatz. €€.
From the ride up the 1911 elevator and into the sitting room, this is a grand place, stylish and eclectic, and an obvious labour of love. It's filled with fine original artworks, enormous chandeliers and handsome furnishings. Everywhere, including the beautiful breakfast room, is airy and elegant, and some of the rooms and suites are truly palatial (one has a winter garden around the courtyard, for example). But the main draw here is comfort. Frau Lange, the owner, is friendly and helpful, and goes out of her way to make her guests feel at home. Truly one of the best pensions in the city.

Hotel Pension Funk
Fasanenstrasse 69 (882 7193, www.hotel-pensionfunk.de). U1 Uhlandstrasse. €.
This wonderful pension, hidden away on a quiet side street, is a real gem. The house, built in 1895, used to be home to the Danish silent movie star Asta Nielsen and has been lovingly restored. The 14 rooms have elegant dark wood furniture and art deco detailing, and everything is spotless. The owner has done his best to make the bathrooms match modern standards without destroying the overall feel – in one room, the bathroom is hidden inside a replica of an antique wardrobe but some fall slightly short of the standards you would expect from a newer hotel. However, the very reasonable prices make up for this.

JETpak Flashpacker
Pariserstrasse 58 (784 4360, www. jetpakberlin.com). U1, U2, U3, U9 Spichernstrasse. €.

A great choice for those wishing to strike camp in the heart of West Berlin. This clean, well-equipped 'upmarket' edition of Berlin's three JETpak hostels is definitely the best of the bunch and especially recommended for couples on a budget. Staff are known for their friendly, helpful attitude (not always a given in Berlin).

Kempinski Hotel Bristol Berlin

Kurfürstendamm 27 (884 340, www.kempinskiberlin.de). U1, U9 Kurfürstendamm. **€€€**.

This famous Berlin hotel was first a celebrated restaurant before being rebuilt in its present form in 1951. While the rooms aren't as plush as you might expect, the grand atmosphere, nice staff, original Berlin artwork, wonderful pool and saunas make up for it.

Midi Inn City West

Wielandstrasse 26 (885 7010, http://kudamm.midi-inn.de). U7 Adenauerplatz, or S5, S7, S75 Savignyplatz. **€€**.

This thoroughly unassuming 19-room pension is charming, sweet and nicely priced. The mainly white rooms, with stripped floorboards or parquet, are calm, and the atmosphere is relaxed. Staff are very friendly and accommodating, and speak English. A top choice if you're travelling as part of a group and want to be in the West End.

Savoy Hotel Berlin

Fasanenstrasse 9-10 (311 030, www.hotel-savoy.com). U2, U9, S5, S7, S75 Zoologischer Garten. **€€€**.

Erected in 1929, and a favourite of author Thomas Mann, this is a smart, stylish hotel with lots of low-key flair. The rooms are elegant and

Ku'Damm 101

HOTEL

understated, but the suites jazz it up a bit, such as the white Greta Garbo suite and black marble Henry Miller suite. A further bonus is the location, set back just far enough from the hustle and bustle of Zoologischer Garten to be quiet and convenient.

Sofitel Berlin Kurfürstendamm

Augsburger Strasse 41 (800 9990, www. sofitel.com). U1, U9 Kurfürstendamm. **€€€**.

Designed by Berlin architect Jan Kleihues, this grandly proportioned, five-star establishment resembles the bow of an ocean liner. The 311 rooms (including 44 huge suites) are decorated in warm woods and colour tones, with intimate lighting and modern art, to elegant and understated effect. For those staying in the suites, there's an 'Executive' Club Sofitel on the top floors offering a wonderful panorama of the city.

Wilmersdorf

Wilmersdorf may not be the most interesting of areas, but it does play host to Berlin's most decadent luxury hotel (Schlosshotel im Grunewald Berlin), its most discreet hotel (Brandenburger Hof Hotel), its coolest designer hotel (Ku'Damm 101) and its wackiest hotel (Propeller Island).

Brandenburger Hof Hotel

Eislebener Strasse 14 (214 050, www. brandenburger-hof.com). U1, U9 Kurfürstendamm, or U3 Augsburger Strasse. **€€€€**.

This discreet, privately owned gem, tucked down a quiet street behind KaDeWe, is the epitome of modern luxury without the stuffiness. Staff are friendly, and the 72 rooms, all done out in a contemporary-elegant style, are warm and relaxing. There's a beautiful Japanese garden in the middle, surrounded by individually decorated salons available for meetings and special occasions. Chef Bobby Bräuer helms the Quadriga restaurant, famous for its extensive German wine cellar. Highly recommended.

Ku'Damm 101

Kurfürstendamm 101 (520 0550, www. kudamm101.com). U7 Adenauerplatz, or S41, S42, S45, S46 Halensee. **€€€**.

This hotel is a huge hit with style-conscious travellers. The lobby, created by Berlin designers Vogt and Weizenegger, is enjoyably more funk than functional, while the 170 rooms, with lino floors and Le Corbusier colour palette, were designed by Franziska Kessler, whose mantra is clarity and calm. There's also a breakfast garden terrace, and the Lounge 101 is good for daytime snacks or a late-night cocktail.

ESSENTIALS

Propeller Island City Lodge

Albrecht Achilles Strasse 58 (891 9016, www.propeller-island.com). U7 Adenauerplatz. €€

More than just a hotel, Propeller Island City Lodge is a work of art. Artist-owner Lars Stroschen has created 32 incredible rooms, each themed, and decorated like jaw-dropping theatre sets. The Flying Room, for example, has tilted walls and floors, and a large bed seemingly suspended in air. The Therapy Room, all in white with soft, furry walls, has adjustable coloured lights to change with your mood. Reservations can be made via the website, where you can view each room, then choose your favourite three.

Schlosshotel im Grunewald Berlin

Brahmsstrasse 10 (895 840, www.schlosshotel berlin.com). S7 Grunewald. €€€€

Designed down to the dust ruffles by Karl Lagerfeld, this restored 1914 villa on the edge of Grunewald is a luxury that mere mortals can only dream of. There are 12 suites and 54 rooms with elegant marble bathrooms, a limousine and butler service, and well-trained staff to scurry after you. This is a beautiful place, in a beautiful setting, but so exclusive that it might as well be on another planet. It's worth checking the internet for deals, nonetheless.

Schöneberg

This very pleasant leafy area is full of cafés, restaurants and shops, as well as the traditional gay area of Nollendorfplatz, but has a dearth of decent accommodation. You're better off staying further east in Kreuzberg.

Lindemanns

Potsdamer Strasse 171-173 (526 854 909, www.lindemanns-hotel.de). U7 Kleistpark. €€

The strict monochrome palette in rooms here can become monotonous,

Indoor caravan

The Hüttenpalast (literally 'Cabin Palace', see p178) is a large hall that was once the factory floor of an old vacuum cleaner company. Since 2011, it's been home to three vintage caravans and three little cabins, each sleeping two people. It's set out like a mini indoor campsite, with separate male and female shower rooms and a tree in the middle. Each morning, guests emerge from their boltholes to discover the tree has borne fruit – well, little bags containing croissants. There's fresh coffee on hand and the streetfront café does an à la carte menu for those with particularly grumbling stomachs. Each caravan is different – Kleine Schwester (Little Sister) is decked out with white wood panelling and matching linen; the Herzensbrecher (Heartbreaker) has a domed metal ceiling; the Schwalbennest (Swallow's Nest) is big enough to squeeze in a table. If you're at all claustrophobic, the huts, each one unique in design and decoration, are slightly better – but they also have regular rooms of varying sizes. Free Wi-Fi too.

ESSENTIALS

but they are well proportioned, with big windows and some even have circular tubs. The hotel itself is efficiently run and is the perfect base for gallery-hopping in the new art hotspot of Potsdamer Strasse.

Kreuzberg

The former centre of (West) Berlin's alternative scene, Kreuzberg has some of the city's most picturesque streets, liveliest markets, best bars and most interesting alternative venues. The area around Schlesisches Tor is a particular party hotspot.

Die Fabrik

Schlesische Strasse 18 (611 7116, www.diefabrik.com). U1 Schlesisches Tor. No credit cards. €.
Smack bang in the middle of a newly invigorated Schlesische Strasse, this former telephone factory (hence the name) with turn-of-the-century charm intact, has 50 clean and comfortable no-frills rooms. There's no kitchen, no TV and no billiards. Just a bed and a locker. But with a café next door for breakfast, and plenty of restaurants, bars and galleries nearby, you don't need much more.

Grand Hostel

Tempelhofer Ufer 14 (2009 5450, www.grandhostel-berlin.de). U1, U7 Möckernbrücke. €.
This fantastic hostel is located in a suitably grand 19th-century building with high ceilings and plenty of period character. The rooms are spacious and spotless, and there are no bunks, even in the dorms, just comfy real beds with good-quality linen. There are bikes for hire, and the cheerful, well-informed staff know everything from the best kebab shops in Berlin to where to do karaoke on a Wednesday. The only possible downer is that it's situated in one of the less happening parts of Kreuzberg, albeit with great transport links to the hotspots.

Johann

Johanniterstrasse 8 (225 0740, www.hotel-johann-berlin.de). U1, U6 Hallesches Tor. €€.
This spotlessly clean – if slightly utilitarian – hotel is located in the sleepiest bit of Kreuzberg, one block from the canal and the great Brachvogel beer garden. It's a ten-minute stroll to the Jewish Museum and a pleasant 20-minute walk by the water to reach the restaurants and bars of eastern Kreuzberg. The rooms are big and airy; some (such as room 301 – the pick of the crop) retain original arched ceilings that date from the building's first function as an army barracks in the 19th century.

Lekker Urlaub

Graefestrasse 89 (3730 6434, www. lekkerurlaub.de). U8 Schonleinstrasse. No credit cards. €.
This charming and bijoux B&B is in one of the prettiest and buzziest bits of Kreuzberg. Set on the ground floor of a typical Berlin tenement, the rooms are small but clean. Each is a one-off: the bed in one room is only reachable by a ladder, so avoid this option if you're scared of heights. The lovely café attached to Lekker Urlaub serves meals from 9am to 6pm, but there are also dozens of restaurants and bars close by.

Motel One Berlin-Mitte

Prinzenstrasse 40 (7007 9800, www.motel-one.com). U8 Moritzplatz. €.
Who'd have thought that such a seemingly anonymous chain could produce such a smart hotel? The 180 rooms, relatively recently remodelled and refreshed, are basic but done with flair: check out the large dark wood headboards, flat-screen TVs and modern free-standing sinks. Even the appliqué on the curtains and pillows is bearable. Throw in the bargain rates and top location (firmly in Kreuzberg, despite the hotel's name) and you have a winner.

ESSENTIALS

Riehmers Hofgarten

*Yorckstrasse 83 (7809 8800,
www.hotel-riehmers-hofgarten.de).
U6, U7 Mehringdamm.* €€€.

In a historic building with one of
Berlin's prettiest courtyards, this is a
wonderful hotel. The 22 exquisitely
styled rooms are airy and elegant
(the furniture was custom-designed),
the staff are charming, and Thomas
Kurt, the larger-than-life chef at the
hotel restaurant, e.t.a. hoffmann, is
widely praised. Although the location
is somewhat off the beaten track, the
neighbourhood has its charms, with
Victoria Park and Bergmannstrasse's
shops and cafés nearby. Reasonably
priced, and recommended.

Rock 'n' Roll Herberge

*Muskauer Strasse 11 (6162 3600, www.
rnrherberge.de). U1 Görlitzer Bahnhof.
No credit cards.* €.

As the name suggests, this budget
hotel is aimed particularly at bands
on tour and for music lovers to feel
at home. It's a great place, on a quiet
stretch just blocks from the main drags
of Kreuzberg. The downstairs rooms
are small, but some have bathrooms.
Staff are friendly, there's a Currywurst
party every Thursday with vegan
and vegetarian sausages, and the bar-
restaurant is popular with colourful
locals. Free Wi-Fi is included among
the extras.

Transit

*Hagelberger Strasse 53-54 (789
0470, www.hotel-transit.de). U6,
U7 Mehringdamm.* €.

Located in one of the most beautiful
parts of Kreuzberg, this former factory is now a bright and airy hotel
with 49 basic but clean rooms, each
with a shower and toilet. There's also
a 24-hour bar, and the staff speak
good English. With Victoria Park
around the block and a wealth of bars,
cafés and restaurants in the area, it's
often full – so it's wise to book ahead.
Women-only dorms are also available.

Neukölln

For all sorts of hip newcomers,
this is the place to be in today's
Berlin. The influx has been met
with a huge increase in subletting
and Airbnb usage – which has got
residents increasingly irritated.

Cat's Pajamas Hostel

*Urbanstrasse 64 (6162 0534, www.
thecatspajamashostel.com). U7, U8
Hermannplatz.* €.

A brand-new, light and airy hostel,
with new wooden furniture and en
suite bathrooms throughout its dorms
and private rooms. The location is
extremely convenient too, in the middle
of Kreuzkölln and a direct metro ride
from Schönefeld airport.

Hüttenpalast

*Hobrechtstrasse 65-66 (3730 5806,
www.huettenpalast.de). U7, U8
Hermannplatz.* €.

See p176 **Indoor caravan.**

Rixpack Hostel

*Karl-Marx-Strasse 75 (5471 5140, www.
rixpack.de). U7 Rathaus Neukölln.* €.

Located near the lovely medieval village of Rixdorf, this hostel was one of
the first in the area. It's a no-frills affair
with metallic bunk beds and industrial
carpeting, and one room fitted into the
back of an old firetruck. It's about as
cheap as it gets.

Scube Parks

*Columbiadamm 160 (6980 7841, www.
scubepark.berlin). U8 Boddinstrasse.* €.

The irritating attempt to make
'Scubeing' a verb aside, this is an interesting alternative to a hostel, with 30
Scubes laid out over a couple of square
kilometres of greenery behind the
Hasenheide park. Essentially a wooden
hut, each Scube comes with two to four
beds (and bedding), electrical outlets,
windows and not much else. There's a
cosy common room with shower and
also a shared kitchen.

Getting Around

Arriving & leaving

By air

The new Berlin Brandenburg Willy Brandt Airport (BER) should have opened some years ago. But, following years of confusion and controversy, no one seems to know exactly when it will open, with current estimates stretching to 2018 and beyond. Until then, Berlin remains served by two airports: Tegel and Schönefeld. Information in English on all airports (including live departures and arrivals) can be found at www.berlin-airport.de. Both Tegel and Schönefeld are likely to close as soon as BER opens, just south of the Schönefeld site.

Flughafen Tegel (TXL) *Airport information 0180 5000 186, www.berlin-airport.de.* **Open** 4am-midnight daily.
The more upmarket scheduled flights from the likes of BA and Lufthansa use the compact Tegel airport, just 8km (5 miles) north-west of Mitte.

Buses 109 and X9 (the express version) run via Luisenplatz and the Kurfürstendamm to Zoologischer Garten (also known as Zoo Station, Bahnof Zoo or just Zoo) in western Berlin. Buses run every 5-15 minutes, and the journey takes 30-40 minutes. Tickets cost €2.70 and can also be used on U-Bahn and S-Bahn services. At Zoo you can connect to anywhere in the city. From the airport, you can also take bus 109 to Jacob-Kaiser-Platz U-Bahn (U7), or bus 128 to Kurt-Schumacher-Platz U-Bahn (U6), and proceed on the underground from there. One ticket (€2.70) can be used for the combined journey.

The JetExpressBus TXL is the direct link to Berlin Hauptbahnhof and Mitte. It runs from Tegel to Alexanderplatz, with useful stops at Beusselstrasse S-Bahn (connects with the Ringbahn), Berlin Hauptbahnhof (regional and inter-city train services as well as the S-Bahn) and Unter den Linden S-Bahn (north and south trains on the S1 and S2 lines). The service runs every 10-20 minutes, 4.30am-12.30am (5.30am-12.30am at weekends) and takes 30-40 minutes; a ticket is €2.70.

A taxi to anywhere central will cost around €20-€25 and take 20-30 minutes.

Flughafen Schönefeld (SXF) *Airport information 0180 5000 186, www.berlin-airport.de.* **Open** 24hrs daily.
The former airport of East Berlin is 18km (11 miles) south-east of the city centre. It's small, and much of the traffic is to eastern Europe and the Middle East. Budget airlines from the UK and Ireland also use it – EasyJet flies in from Bristol, Gatwick, Glasgow, Liverpool, Luton and Manchester; Ryanair from Dublin, East Midlands, Edinburgh and Stansted.

Train is the best means of reaching the city centre. S-Bahn Flughafen Schönefeld is a five-minute walk from the terminal (a free S-Bahn shuttle bus runs every ten minutes, 6am-10pm, from outside the terminal; at other times, bus 171 also runs to the station). From here, the Airport Express train runs to Mitte (25 minutes to Alexanderplatz), Berlin Hauptbahnhof (30 minutes) and Zoo (35 minutes) every half hour from 5am to 11.30pm. You can also take S-Bahn line S9, which runs into the centre every 20 minutes (40 minutes to Alexanderplatz, 50 minutes to Zoo), stopping at all stations along the way. The S45 line from Schönefeld connects with the Ringbahn, also running every 20 minutes. Bus X7, every 10-20 minutes, 4.30am-8pm, runs non-stop from the airport to Rudow U-Bahn (U7), from where you can connect with the underground. This is a good option if you're staying in Kreuzberg, Neukölln or Schöneberg. When it's not running, bus 171 takes the same route.

Tickets from the airport to the city cost €3.30, and can be used on any combination of bus, U-Bahn, S-Bahn and tram.

A taxi to Zoo or Mitte is quite expensive (€30-€35) and takes around 45 minutes.

Flughafen Berlin Brandenburg Willy Brandt (BER) *www.berlin-airport.de.*

The airport's operators promise a fast train shuttle will transport passengers to the city centre in just 20 minutes.

By rail

Berlin Hauptbahnhof
0180 599 6633, www.bahn.de.
Berlin's central station is the main point of arrival for all long-distance trains, with the exceptions of night trains from Moscow and Kiev, which usually start and end at Berlin Lichtenberg (S5, S7, S75).

Hauptbahnhof is inconveniently located in a no-man's land north of the government quarter, and is linked to the rest of the city by S-Bahn (S5, S7, S9, S75), and by the new U55 underground line that runs to the Bundestag and, in 2016, the Brandenburger Tor only (connecting there with S-Bahn lines S1, S2, S25). Eventually, the line will extend to connect to the U5 at Alexanderplatz, via Museumsinsel and Unter den Linden, but not until at least 2019.

Inter-city trains now also stop at Gesundbrunnen, Südkreuz and Spandau, depending on their destinations.

By bus

Zentraler Omnibus Bahnhof (ZOB)
Masurenallee 4-6, Charlottenburg (301 0380, www.iob-berlin.de).
Open 6am-9pm Mon-Fri; 6am-3pm Sat, Sun.
Buses arrive in western Berlin at the Central Bus Station, opposite the Funkturm and the ICC. From here, U-Bahn line U2 runs into the city centre.

Public transport

Berlin is served by a comprehensive and interlinked network of buses, trains, trams and ferries. It's efficient and punctual, but not that cheap. With the completion of the inner-city-encircling Ringbahn in 2002, the former East and West Berlin transport systems were finally sewn back together, though it can still sometimes be complicated travelling between eastern and western destinations. But services are usually regular and frequent, timetables can be trusted, and one ticket can be used for two hours on all legs of a journey and all forms of transport.

The Berlin transport authority, the BVG, operates bus, U-Bahn (underground) and tram networks, and a few ferry services on the outlying lakes. The S-Bahn (overground railway) is run by its own authority, but services are integrated within the same three-zone tariff system.

Information

The BVG website (www.bvg.de) has a wealth of information (in English) on city transport, and there's usually someone who speaks English at the 24-hour BVG Call Center (194 49). The S-Bahn has its own website at www.s-bahn-berlin.de.

The Liniennetz, a map of U-Bahn, S-Bahn, bus and tram routes for Berlin and Potsdam, is available free from info centres and ticket offices. It includes a city-centre map. A map of the U- and S-Bahn can also be picked up free at ticket offices or from the grey-uniformed *Zugabfertiger* – passenger-assistance personnel.

Fares & tickets

The bus, tram, U-Bahn, S-Bahn and ferry services operate on an integrated three-zone system. Zone A covers central Berlin, zone B extends out to the edge of the suburbs and zone C stretches into Brandenburg.

The basic single ticket is the €2.70 *Normaltarif* (zones A and B). Unless going to Potsdam or Flughafen Schönefeld, few visitors are likely to travel beyond zone B, making this in effect a flat-fare system. Apart from the longer-term *Zeitkarten*, tickets for Berlin's public transport system can be bought from the yellow or orange machines at U- or S-Bahn stations, and by some bus stops. These take coins and sometimes notes, give change and have a limited explanation of the ticket system in English. You can often pay by card, but don't count on it (if you do, don't forget to collect your card – infuriatingly, the machines keep the card until all the tickets are printed, making it very easy to forget). An app, FahrInfo Plus, is also available for iOS and Android, which allows you to purchase and carry tickets on your smartphone; details on www.bvg.de/en/travel-information/mobile.

Once you've purchased your ticket, validate it in the small red or yellow box next to the machine, which stamps it with the time and date. (Tickets bought on trams or buses are usually already validated.)

There are no ticket turnstiles at stations, but if an inspector catches you without a valid ticket, you will be fined €40. Ticket inspections are frequent, and are conducted while vehicles are moving by pairs of plain-clothes personnel.

Single ticket (Normaltarif) Single tickets cost €2.70 (€1.70 6-14s) for travel within zones A and B, €3 (€2) for zones B and C, and €3.30 (€2.40) for all three zones. A ticket allows use of the BVG network for two hours, with as many changes between bus, tram, U-Bahn and S-Bahn as necessary, travelling in one direction.

Short-distance ticket (Kurzstreckentarif)
The *Kurzstreckentarif* (ask for a *Kurzstrecke*) costs €1.60 (€1.20 reductions) and is valid for three U- or S-Bahn stops, or six stops on the tram or bus. No transfers allowed.

Day ticket (Tageskarte)
A *Tageskarte* for zones A and B costs €6.90 (€4.70 reductions), or €7.40 (€5.30) for all three zones. A day ticket lasts until 3am the morning after validating.

Longer-term tickets (Zeitkarten)
If you're in Berlin for a week, it makes sense to buy a *Sieben-Tage-Karte* ('seven-day ticket') at €29.50 for zones A and B, or €36.50 for all three zones (no reductions). A stay of a month or more makes it worth buying a *Monatskarte* ('month ticket'), which costs €79.50 for zones A and B, and €98.50 for all three zones.

Tourist travelcards
There are two excellent-value travelcards aimed at tourists, which pack in unlimited transport within designated zones, with a bundle of other attractive perks – discounts and deals with partnering tourist and cultural attractions, shops, bars and clubs. For zones A and B, the Berlin CityTourCard (www.citytourcard.com) costs €17.40 for a 48-hour pass, €24.50 for 72 hours and €31.90 for five days, while the Berlin WelcomeCard (www.berlin-welcomecard.de) is €19.50 for 48 hours, €26.70 for 72 hours (€40.50 including access to museums at Museum Island) and €34.50 for five days.

U-Bahn

The U-Bahn network consists of ten lines and 170-plus stations. The first trains run shortly after 4am; the last between midnight and 1am, except on Fridays and Saturdays when most trains run all night at 15-minute intervals. The direction of travel is indicated by the name of the last stop on the line.

S-Bahn

Especially useful in eastern Berlin, the S-Bahn covers long distances faster than the U-Bahn and is a more efficient means of getting to outlying areas. The Ringbahn, which circles central Berlin, was the final piece of the S-Bahn system to be renovated, though there are still disruptions here and there.

ESSENTIALS

Buses

Berlin has a dense network of 150 bus routes, of which 54 run in the early hours. The day lines run from 4.30am to about 1am the next morning. Enter at the front of the bus and exit in the middle or at the back. The driver sells only individual tickets, but all tickets from machines on the U- or S-Bahn are valid. Most bus stops have clear timetables and route maps.

Trams

There are 21 tram lines (five of which run all night), mainly in the east, though some have been extended a few kilometres into the western half of the city, mostly in Wedding. Hackescher Markt is the site of the main tram terminus. Tickets are available from machines on the trams, at the termini and in U-Bahn stations.

Other rail services

Berlin is also served by the Regionalbahn ('regional railway'), which once connected East Berlin with Potsdam via the suburbs and small towns left outside the Wall. Run by Deutsche Bahn (www.bahn.de), it still circumnavigates the city. The website has timetable and ticket information in English.

Travelling at night

Berlin has a comprehensive *Nachtliniennetz* ('night-line network') that covers all parts of town, with more than 50 bus and tram routes running every 30 minutes between 12.30am and 4.30am. Maps and timetables are available from BVG kiosks at stations, and large maps of the night services are found next to the normal BVG map on station platforms. Ticket prices are the same as during the day.

Buses and trams that run at night have an 'N' in front of the number. On all buses travelling through zones

B and C after 8pm, the driver will let you off at any point along the route via the front door.

Truncated versions of U-Bahn lines U1, U2, U3, U5, U6, U7, U8 and U9 run all night on Fridays and Saturdays, with trains every 15 minutes. The S-Bahn also runs at 30-minute intervals.

Boat trips

Getting about by water is more of a leisure activity than a practical means of navigating the city, but the BVG network has a handful of boat services on Berlin's lakes. There are also several private companies offering tours of Berlin's waterways.

Reederei Heinz Riedel
Planufer 78, Kreuzberg (693 4646, www.reederei-riedel.de).
U8 Schönleinstrasse. No credit cards.
A tour through the city's network of rivers and canals costs €4.50-€18.

Stern und Kreisschiffahrt
Puschkinallee 15, Treptow (536 3600, www.sternundkreis.de). S8, S9, S41, S42 Treptower Park. **Open** *Apr-early Oct* 9am-6pm Mon-Fri; 9am-2pm Sat.
Around 25 cruises along the Spree and around the lakes. A 3hr 30min tour costs €18.50.

Taxis

Berlin taxis are pricey, efficient and numerous. The starting fee is €3.40 and thereafter the fare is €1.79 per kilometre for the first seven kilometres, and €1.28 per kilometre thereafter. The rate remains the same at night. For short journeys, ask for a *Kurzstrecke* – up to two kilometres for €4, but only available when you've hailed a cab and not from taxi ranks.

Taxi stands are numerous, especially in central areas near stations and at major intersections. You can phone for a cab 24 hours daily on 261 026. Most firms can

ESSENTIALS

transport people with disabilities, but require advance notice. Cabs accept all credit cards except Diners Club, subject to a €1.50 charge.

If you want an estate car (station wagon), request a combi. As well as normal taxis, Funk Taxi Berlin (261 026) operates vans than can carry up to seven people (ask for a *grossraum Taxi*; same rates as for regular taxis) and has two vehicles for people with disabilities.

Driving

Despite some congestion, driving in Berlin presents few problems. Visitors from the UK and US should bear in mind that, in the absence of signals, drivers must yield to traffic from the right, except at crossings marked by a diamond-shaped yellow sign. Trams always have right of way. An *Einbahnstrasse* is a one-way street.

Parking

Parking is usually metered in Berlin side streets (residents get an Anwohnerplakette pass), but spaces are hard to find. Buy a parking ticket from a nearby machine; if you don't have one, or park illegally, you risk getting your car clamped or towed.

There are long-term car parks at Schönefeld and Tegel airports, and many Parkgaragen and Parkhäuser (multi-storey and underground car parks) around the city, open 24 hours, that charge around €2/hr.

Cycling

West Berlin is wonderful for cycling – flat, with lots of cycle paths, parks and canals to cruise beside. East Berlin has fewer cycle paths and more cobblestones and tram lines.

Cycles can be taken on the U-Bahn (except during rush hour, 6-9am and 2-5pm), up to a limit of two at the end

of carriages that have a bicycle sign. More may be taken on S-Bahn carriages, and at any time of day. In each case an extra ticket (€1.80 for zones A and B) must be bought for each bike. A good guide to cycle routes is the ADFC Fahrradstadtplan (€6.90), available in bike shops.

Berlin's bike rental scheme, Call-A-Bike, operates in summer only. The bikes are parked in designated docking stations. You have to register to use the system; you can register at a docking station terminal, via the website (www.callabike-interaktiv.de, in German only) or by calling 0700 0522 5522. There's a one-off registration fee of €12 and a charge of 8c per minute, up to a maximum of €15 per 24 hours. The Pauschal annual subscription (€36) allows unlimited journeys of up to 30 minutes for free, and make sense for those making longer visits.

Bike hire

Fahrradstation

Dorotheenstrasse 30, Mitte (2838 4848, www.fahrradstation.de). U6, S1, S2, S5, S7, S9, S75 Friedrichstrasse. **Open** 10am-7.30pm Mon-Fri; 10am-6pm Sat; 10am-4pm Sun. **Rates** from €15 per day; €35 3 days.

Other locations Auguststrasse 29A, Mitte (2250 8070); Leibzigerstrasse 56, Mitte (6664 9180); Kollwitzstrasse 77, Prenzlauer Berg (9395 8130); Bergmannstrasse 9, Kreuzberg (215 1566); Goethestrasse 46, Charlottenburg (9395 2757).

Pedalpower

Grossbeerenstrasse 53, Kreuzberg (7899 1939, www.pedalpower.de). U1, U7 Möckernbrücke. **Open** 10am-6.30pm Mon-Fri; 11am-2pm Sat. Rates from €10/day. No credit cards.

Other location Pfarrstrasse 115, Lichtenberg (5515 3270).

Resources A-Z

Accident & Emergency

Police 110.
Ambulance/Fire Brigade 112.

If you are too ill to leave your bed, phone the **Ärztlicher Bereitschaftsdienst** (emergency doctor's service, 310 031). This service specialises in dispatching doctors for house calls. Charges vary according to the treatment required. All will be expensive, so be sure to have either your EHIC or your private insurance documents at hand if seeking treatment.

Below are the most central hospitals. All have 24-hour emergency wards.

Charité *Schumannstrasse 20-21, Mitte (45050, www.charite.de). U6 Oranienburger Tor.*
Klinikum Am Urban *Dieffenbachstrasse 1, Kreuzberg (130 210, www.vivantes.de/kau). U7 Südstern, or bus M41.*
St Hedwig Krankenhaus Grosse *Hamburger Strasse 5, Mitte (23110, www.alexius.de). S5, S7, S75 Hackescher Markt, or S1, S2 Oranienburger Strasse.*

Age restrictions

The legal age for drinking in Germany is 16 for beer and wine, 18 for hard liquor; for smoking it's 18; for driving it's 18. The age of consent for both heterosexual and homosexual sex is 16.

Credit card loss

If you've lost a credit card, or had one stolen, phone the relevant 24-hour emergency number:

American Express *069 9797 2000.*
Diners Club *0180 5070 704.*
MasterCard *0800 819 1040.*
Visa *0800 811 8440.*

Customs

EU nationals over 17 years of age can import limitless goods for personal use, if bought with tax paid on them at source. For non-EU citizens and for duty-free goods, the following limits apply: 200 cigarettes or 50 cigars or 250 grams of tobacco; 1 litre of spirits (over 22% by volume) or 2 litres of fortified wine (under 22% by volume); 4 litres of non-sparkling wine; 16 litres of beer; other goods to the value of €300 for non-commercial use, up to €430 for air/sea travellers. The import of meat, meat products, fruit, plants, flowers and protected animals is restricted and/or forbidden.

Disabled

Many but not all U-Bahn and S-Bahn stations have ramps and/or elevators for wheelchair access; the map of the transport network (look for the wheelchair symbol) indicates which ones. These stations are equipped with folding ramps to allow passengers in wheelchairs to board the trains. These passengers are required to wait at the front end of the platform to signal to the driver their need to board. All bus lines and most tram lines are also wheelchair-accessible.

Public buildings and most of the city's hotels have disabled access. However, if you require more specific information about access, try either of the following organisations:

Beschäftigungswerk des BBV
Weydemeyerstrasse 2A, Mitte (5001 9100, www.bbv-tours-berlin.de). U5 Schillingstrasse. **Open** 9am-8pm Mon-Fri; 10am-6pm Sat.
The Berlin Centre for the Disabled provides legal and social advice, together with a transport service and travel information.

Touristik Union International
0511 5678 0105, www.tui.com.
The TUI provides information on
accommodation and travel in Germany
for the disabled.

Electricity

Electricity in Germany runs on 230V,
the same as British appliances. You will
require an adaptor (G to F) to change the
shape of the plug. US appliances (120V)
require a voltage converter.

Embassies & Consulates

Australian Embassy *Wallstrasse
76-79, Mitte (880 0880, www.germany.
embassy.gov.au). U2 Spittelmarkt.*
Open 8.30am-5pm Mon-Thur;
8.30am-4.15pm Fri.
British Embassy *Wilhelmstrasse
70, Mitte (204 570, www.gov.uk/
government/world/germany). S1,
S2 Unter den Linden.* **Open**
9.30am-noon Mon, Tue, Thur, Fri.
Embassy of Ireland *Jägerstrasse 51,
Mitte (220 720, www.embassyof
ireland.de). U2, U6 Stadtmitte.*
Open 9.30am-12.30pm Mon-Fri,
by appointment only.
US Embassy *Clayallee 170, Zehlendorf
(83050, visa enquiries 032 221 093
243, www.germany.usembassy.gov).
U3 Oskar-Helene-Heim.* **Open** *US
citizen services* By phone 2-3pm Mon-
Thur (visits by appointment only).
Visa enquiries By phone 8am-8pm
Mon-Fri.
A new US embassy building opened
in 2008 on Pariser Platz, next to the
Brandenburg Gate, but consular
services still operate out of the
original embassy in Zehlendorf.

ID

By law you are required to carry
some form of ID, which – for UK
and US citizens – means a passport.

If police catch you without one, they may
accompany you to wherever you've left it.

Left luggage

Airports

There is a left luggage office at Tegel
(4101 2315; open 5am-10.30pm daily) and
there are lockers at Schönefeld (in the
Multi Parking Garage P4). *See p183.*

Rail & bus stations

There are left luggage lockers at
Bahnhof Zoo, Friedrichstrasse,
Alexanderplatz, Potsdamer Platz,
Ostbahnhof and Hauptbahnhof.
In addition, Zentraler Omnibus
Bahnhof (ZOB) also provides left
luggage facilities.

Lost/stolen property

If any of your belongings are stolen
while in Germany, you should go
immediately to the police station nearest
to where the incident occurred (listed in
the *Gelbe Seiten/Yellow Pages* under
'Polizei') and report the theft. There you
will be required to fill in report forms for
insurance purposes. If you can't speak
German, don't worry: the police will call
in one of their interpreters, a service that
is provided free of charge.
If you leave something in a taxi, call
the number that's on your receipt and
tell them the time of your journey, the
four-digit *Konzessions-Nummer* that
will be stamped on the receipt, a number
where you can be reached, and what
you've lost. They'll pass this information
to the driver, and he or she will call you
if they have your property.
For information about lost or stolen
credit cards, *see p184.*

BVG Fundbüro
*Potsdamer Strasse 180, Schöneberg
(194 49). U7 Kleistpark.* **Open** 9am-6pm
Mon-Thur; 9am-2pm Fri.

Contact this office if you have any queries about property lost on Berlin's public transport system. If you're robbed on one of their vehicles, you can ask about the surveillance video.

Zentrales Fundbüro *Platz der Luftbrücke 6, Tempelhof (902 773 101). U6 Platz der Luftbrücke.* **Open** 9am-2pm Mon, Tue, Fri; 1-6pm Thur.

The central police lost property office.

Money

One euro (€) is made up of 100 cents. There are seven banknotes and eight coins. The notes are of differing colours and sizes (€5 is the smallest, €500 the largest) and the designs represent different periods of European architecture. They are: €5 (grey-green), €10 (red), €20 (blue), €50 (orange), €100 (green), €200 (yellow-brown), €500 (purple).

The eight denominations of coins vary in colour, size and thickness – but not enough to make them easy to tell apart. They share one common side; the other features a country-specific design (all can be used in any participating state). They are: €2, €1, 50 cents, 20 cents, 10 cents, 5 cents, 2 cents, 1 cent.

Opening hours

Most banks are open 9am to noon Monday to Friday, and 1pm to 3pm or 2pm to 6pm on varied weekdays.

Shops can stay open from 6am to 10pm, except on Sundays and holidays, though few take full advantage of the fact. Big stores tend to open at 9am and close between 8pm and 10pm. Most smaller shops will close around 6pm.

An increasing number of all-purpose neighbourhood shops (*Späti*) stay open until around midnight. Many Turkish shops are open on Saturday afternoons and on Sundays from 1pm to 5pm. Many bakers open to sell cakes on Sundays from 2pm to 4pm. Most 24-hour petrol

stations and many internet cafés also sell basic groceries.

Pharmacies

Prescription and non-prescription drugs (including aspirin) are sold only at pharmacies (*Apotheken*). You can recognise these by a red 'A' outside the front door. A list of the nearest pharmacies open on Sundays and in the evening should be displayed in the window of every pharmacy. A list of emergency pharmacies (*Notdienst-Apotheken*) is available online at www.akberlin.de/notdienst.

Postal services

Most post offices (*Post* in German) are open from 8am to 6pm Monday to Friday, and 8am to 1pm Saturday.

For non-local mail, use the *Andere Richtungen* ('other destinations') slot in postboxes. Letters of up to 20g to anywhere in Germany cost €0.60 in postage. For postcards it's €0.45. For anywhere outside Germany, a 20g airmail letter or postcard costs €0.75.

Postamt Friedrichstrasse *Georgenstrasse 14-18, Mitte (0228 4333 111). U6, S1, S2, S5, S7, S25, S75 Friedrichstrasse.* **Open** 6am-10pm Mon-Fri; 8am-10pm Sat, Sun.

Berlin has no main post office. However, this branch, which is to be found inside Friedrichstrasse station, keeps the longest opening hours of the Berlin offices.

Smoking

Many Berliners smoke, though the habit is in decline. Smoking is banned on public transport, in theatres and many public institutions. Many bars and restaurants have closed-off smoking rooms. Smaller, one-room establishments (under 75sq m/800sq ft) may allow smoking if they want to, but must post a sign outside denoting a *Raucherkneipe* (smoker pub). There's no problem with smoking at outside tables – which means that, even in winter, lots of places have outside tables.

Telephones

All phone numbers in this guide are local Berlin numbers (other than in the Escapes & Excursions chapter). Numbers beginning 0180 have higher tariffs, and numbers beginning 015, 016 or 017 are mobiles.

Dialling & codes

To phone Berlin from abroad, dial the international access code (00 from the UK, 011 from the US, 0011 from Australia), then 49 (for Germany) and 30 (for Berlin), followed by the local number.

To phone another country from Germany, dial 00, then the relevant country code: Australia 61; Canada 1; Ireland 353; New Zealand 64; United Kingdom 44; United States 1. Then, dial the local area code (minus the initial zero) and the local number.

To call Berlin from elsewhere in Germany, dial 030 and then the local number.

Making a call

Numbers prefixed 0180 are service numbers charged at €0.04-€0.14 per minute when calling from a land-line telephone, and up to €0.42 per minute when calling from a mobile, depending on the network's policies.

Operator services

For online directory enquiries, go to www.teleauskunft.de.
International directory enquiries 11834.
Operator assistance/German directory enquiries 11833 (11837 in English).
Phone repairs 080 0330 2000.
Time 0180 4100 100 (automated, in German).

Time

Germany is on Central European Time – one hour ahead of Greenwich Mean Time.

Tipping

A ten per cent service charge will already be part of your restaurant bill, but it's common to leave a small tip too. In a taxi, round up the bill to the nearest euro.

Tourist information

EurAide
DB Reisezentrum, Hauptbahnhof, Tiergarten (www.euraide.de). S5, S7, S75 Hauptbahnhof. **Open** *Mar, Apr* 11am-7pm Mon-Fri. *May-July* 10am-8pm Mon-Fri. *Aug-Oct* 10am-7pm Mon-Fri. Nov 11am-6.30pm Mon-Fri. *Dec* 10am-7.30pm Mon-Fri.
Staff advise on sights, hostels, tours and transport, and sell rail tickets.

VisitBerlin
250 025, www.visitberlin.de.
Berlin's official (if private) tourist organisation has information points at Kurfürstendamm 22, Charlottenburg; Brandenburg Gate; Hauptbahnhof (ground floor, Europaplatz exit); Tegel Airport (next to gate 1); and at the base of the TV Tower at Alexanderplatz. All are open daily.

Visas & immigration

A passport valid for three months beyond the length of stay is all that is required for EU, US, Canadian and Australian citizens for a stay in Germany of up to three months. Citizens of EU countries with valid national ID cards need only show their ID cards.

Citizens of other countries should check with their local German embassy or consulate whether a visa is required. As with any trip, confirm visa requirements well before you plan to travel.

ESSENTIALS

Vocabulary

Pronunciation

z – pronounced 'ts'
w – like English 'v'
v – like English 'f'
s – like English 'z', but softer
r – like a throaty French 'r'
a – as in father
e – sometimes as in bed, sometimes as in day
i – as in seek
o – as in note
u – as in loot
ch – as in Scottish loch
ä – combination of 'a' and 'e', like 'ai' in paid or like 'e' in set
ö – combination of 'o' and 'e', as in French 'eu'
ü – combination of 'u' and 'e', like true
ai – like pie
au – like house
ie – like free
ee – like hey
ei – like fine
eu – like coil

Useful phrases

Greetings

hello/good day *guten Tag;* goodbye *auf Wiedersehen,* (informal) *tschüss;* good morning *guten Morgen;* good evening *guten Abend;* good night *gute Nacht.*

Basic words & requests

yes *ja,* (emphatic) *jawohl;* no *nein, nee;* maybe *vielleicht;* please *bitte;* thank you *danke;* thank you very much *danke schön;* excuse me *entschuldigen Sie mich, bitte;* sorry! *Verzeihung!;* I'm sorry, I don't speak German *Entschuldigung, ich spreche kein Deutsch;* do you speak English? *sprechen Sie Englisch?;* can you please speak more slowly? *können Sie bitte langsamer sprechen?;* my name is… ich *heisse…;* I would like… *ich möchte…;* how much is…? *wieviel kostet…?;* please can I have a receipt? *darf ich bitte eine Quittung haben?;* please can you call me a cab? *können Sie bitte mir ein Taxi rufen?;* open/closed *geöffnet/geschlossen;* with/without *mit/ohne;* cheap/expensive *billig/teuer;* big/small *gross/klein;* entrance/exit *Eingang/Ausgang;* bureau de change *die Wechselstube;* help! *Hilfe!*

Directions

left *links;* right *rechts;* straight ahead *gerade aus;* corner *ecke;* far *weit;* near *nah;* street *die Strasse;* square *der Platz;* city map *der Stadtplan;* how do I get to…? *wie komme ich nach…?;* how far is it to…? *wie weit ist es nach…?;* where is…? *wo ist…?*

Travel

arrival/departure *Ankunft/Abfahrt;* airport *der Flughafen;* railway station *der Bahnhof;* ticket *die Fahrkarte, der Fahrschein;* airline ticket *die Flugkarte, der Flugschein;* passport *der Reisepass;* petrol *das Benzin;* lead-free *bleifrei;* traffic *der Vehrkehr.*

Health

I feel ill *ich bin krank;* doctor *der Arzt;* dentist *der Zahnarzt;* pharmacy *die Apotheke;* hospital *das Krankenhaus;* I need a doctor *ich brauche einen Arzt;* please call an ambulance *rufen Sie bitte ein Krankenwagen;* please call the police *rufen Sie bitte die Polizei.*

ESSENTIALS

Numbers

0 *null*; 1 *eins*; 2 *zwei*; 3 *drei*; 4 *vier*; 5 *fünf*; 6 *sechs*; 7 *sieben*; 8 *acht*; 9 *neun*; 10 *zehn*; 11 *elf*; 12 *zwölf*; 13 *dreizehn*; 14 *vierzehn*; 15 *fünfzehn*; 16 *sechzehn*; 17 *siebzehn*; 18 *achtzehn*; 19 *neunzehn*; 20 *zwanzig*; 21 *einundzwanzig*; 22 *zweiundzwanzig*; 30 *dreissig*; 40 *vierzig*; 50 *fünfzig*; 60 *sechzig*; 70 *siebzig*; 80 *achtzig*; 90 *neunzig*; 100 *hundert*; 101 *hunderteins*; 110 *hundertzehn*; 200 *zweihundert*; 201 *zweihunderteins*; 1,000 *tausend*; 2,000 *zweitausend*.

Days & times of day

Monday *Montag*; Tuesday *Dienstag*; Wednesday *Mittwoch*; Thursday *Donnerstag*; Friday *Freitag*; Saturday *Samstag, Sonnabend*; Sunday *Sonntag*; morning *Morgen*; noon *Mittag*; afternoon *Nachmittag*; evening *Abend*; night *Nacht*; today *Heute*; yesterday *Gestern*; tomorrow *Morgen*

Time

Germany uses a 24-hour system. 8am is *8 Uhr* (usually written 8h), noon is *12 Uhr Mittags* or just *12 Uhr*, 5pm is *17 Uhr* and midnight is *12 Uhr Mitternachts* or just *Mitternacht*. 8.15 is *8 Uhr 15* or *Viertel nach 8*; 8.30 is *8 Uhr 30* or *halb 9*; and 8.45 is *8 Uhr 45* or *Viertel vor 9*.

Food & drink

Basics

breakfast *Frühstück*; lunch *Mittagessen*; dinner *Abendessen*; snack *Imbiss*; appetiser *Vorspeise*; main course *Hauptgericht*; dessert *Nachspeise*; fried, roasted *gebraten*; boiled *gekocht*; breaded, battered *paniert*; egg, eggs *Ei, Eier*; cheese *Käse*; noodles/pasta *Nudeln/ Teigwaren*; sauce *Sosse*.

Phrases

I'd like to reserve a table for… people *Ich möchte einen Tisch für… Personen reservieren*.
I am a vegetarian *Ich bin Vegetarier*.
The menu, please *Die Speisekarte, bitte*.
We'd/I'd like to order *Wir möchten/ Ich möchte bestellen*.
The bill, please *Bezahlen, bitte*.

Meat (Fleisch)

meatball *Boulette*; mince *Hackfleisch*; venison *Hirsch*; chicken *Huhn, Huhnerfleisch*; rabbit *Kaninchen*; chop *Kotelett*; lamb *Lamm*; liver *Leber*; kidneys *Nieren*; turkey *Puten*; beef *Rindfleisch*; ham *Schinken*; pork *Schweinefleisch*; bacon *Speck*; sausage *Wurst*.

Fish (Fisch)

eel *Aal*; trout *Forelle*; prawns *Garnelen*; lobster *Hummer*; cod *Kabeljau*; carp *Karpfen*; crab or shrimp *Krabbe*; salmon *Lachs*; haddock *Schellfisch*; tuna *Thunfisch*; squid *Tintenfisch*; clams *Venusmuscheln*.

Vegetables (Gemüse) & fruit (Obst)

pineapple *Ananas*; apple *Apfel*; pear *Birne*; cauliflower *Blumenkohl*; beans *Bohnen*; green beans *Brechbohnen*; mushrooms *Champignons, Pilze*; green peas *Erbsen*; strawberries *Erdbeeren*; cucumber *Gurke*; raspberries *Himbeeren*; potato *Kartoffel*; cherry *Kirsch*; garlic *Knoblauch*; cabbage *Kohl*; carrots *Möhren*; peppers *Paprika*; chips *Pommes*; lettuce *Salat*; asparagus *Spargel*; onions *Zwiebeln*.

ESSENTIALS

Index

Sights & Areas

ESSENTIALS